W9-DEU-059

FAST FOOD FACTS

FIFTH EDITION

The Original Guide for Fitting Fast
Food Into a Healthy Lifestyle

FAST FOOD FACTS

FIFTH EDITION

The Original Guide for Fitting Fast
Food Into a Healthy Lifestyle

MARION J. FRANZ MS, RD, LD, CDE

IDC Publishing
MINNEAPOLIS

Note: The menu items and nutritional data listed here are current as of publication. However, restaurants often develop new menu items or change product nutrition formulations. If you have questions about menu items and their nutritional information, please contact restaurants directly.

All brand-name products cited in this book are the registered trademark properties of their respective companies.

©1998 International Diabetes Center
Institute for Research and Education HealthSystem Minnesota

IDC Publishing
3800 Park Nicollet Boulevard
Minneapolis, Minnesota 55416-2699
(612) 993-3393
www.idcpublishing.com

Library of Congress Cataloging-in-Publication Data
Franz, Marion J.
Fast food facts: the original guide for fitting fast food into a healthy lifestyle / Marion J. Franz. — 5th ed.
    p.   cm.
    ISBN 1-885115-42-3 (pbk.)
1. Convenience foods—Composition—Tables. 2. Food—Composition—Tables. 3. Diabetes—Nutritional aspects. 4. Fast food restaurants—United States. I. Title.
TX551.F74 1998
613.2—dc21   97-38030
                                                   CIP

Printed in the United States of America

Publisher: Karol Carstensen
Production Manager: Gail Devery
Associate Editor: Sara Frueh
Cover and Text Design: MacLean & Tuminelly

Table of Contents

Acknowledgments

I would like to thank the following for their invaluable assistance in completing this book. A special thanks to the many restaurants that provided us with nutrition information about their menu items. Without their willingness to share their nutritional data this book would be impossible. Thanks also to dietetic students Stephanie Olson and LeAnn Reinhardt for their willing and capable assistance in the early stages of draft development.

I'd also like to acknowledge my colleagues—the skilled dietitians at the International Diabetes Center who are a constant source of encouragement and support as we endeavor to provide people with relevant, up-to-date information about nutrition in general and nutrition and diabetes in particular. A heart-felt thanks to the publishing department, Karol Carstensen, director of IDC Publishing, Gail Devery, and Sara Frueh, for their ideas, editorial suggestions, and careful considerations. Last but not least, I'd like to thank the rest of the International Diabetes Center staff for their continued interest and encouragement in these publishing ventures.

Finally, thank you, readers, for making Fast Food Facts such a success. I hope this new edition is especially helpful to you as you seek to eat wisely and live well.

Marion J. Franz, MS, RD, LD, CDE

Introduction

TRYING TO ESTIMATE the nutrient content of the fast food you eat can be difficult. If you routinely count calories, fat grams, or carbohydrates as you plan and prepare meals, you may think that you can apply the knowledge you've gained from practice and come pretty close when judging the nutritional value of a hamburger. But when you compare your guesses with the numbers in this book, you'll probably discover that you're wrong more often than right. You're not alone.

The knowledge and skills of more than 200 dietitians and nutritionists were put to the test when they were asked to determine the number of fat grams and calories in five restaurant meals. Overall they underestimated by about 20 percent, and their performance on some meals was worse than on others. For example, the group estimated that a hamburger and onion rings contained an average of 44 grams of fat and 863 calories. The actual content was 101 grams of fat and 1550 calories – a miscalculation of about 50 percent!

If nutrition professionals are unable to correctly estimate the fat and calories in fast food, we can assume that the average consumer doesn't have a clue about what's actually in the restaurant food they consume. Does it matter? It does when you consider that a recent survey reported that Americans eat out more than nine times weekly and that three out of four consumers dine regularly at fast-food restaurants.

1

Selection and Serving Size

Because we eat out at such a high rate, the fat and calories in fast foods can cause problems when it comes to our waistlines and our health. But how can we make better choices when the fat and calories are so difficult to decipher? Is the hamburger patty four ounces or six? Is the slice of cheese on the cheeseburger one ounce or two?

Help is not only on the way, it's right here in your hands. The keys to survival are selection and serving size, and you need quick, reliable data to come out on top in both arenas. In short, *Fast Food Facts* can be your guide.

In one recent study, ten fast-food meals were planned using nutrition data similar to the information that appears in this book. Study participants incorporated the ten fast-food meals into their diets over a two-week period. Even after eating frequent fast-food meals, fat intake among participants was reduced by an average of eight percent, and blood cholesterol levels went down. The study proved that thoughtful food choices and planning can result in healthy fast-food meals and that fast food isn't so bad for you after all.

What's Good About Fast Food?

Fast food is a distinctly American part of the food service business; however, it's an aspect of American life that is growing outside of the United States every day. It's unusual today to travel to any country in the world and not find fast-food restaurants. Quickness and convenience are winning over even the harshest critics of the American fast-food phenomenon. And whether you're in Pittsburgh or Paris, your favorite fast-food restaurant is likely to be serving up familiar fare.

Studies of the leading chains show remarkable uniformity in the portion size and the nutritional value of specific menu items. Regardless of the restaurant's location, it's fairly easy to predict the fat and calories in your food choices. Foods at fast-food restaurants also are fresh and safe to consume. Menu items turn over rapidly because of the number of customers served and because most restaurants limit the number of items on their menus. Food safety and cleanliness guidelines are stringent, and each individual restaurant is required to meet them.

Food selection at fast-food restaurants is constantly improving as well. Many now offer salad bars, grilled or baked meat or fish, baked potatoes, and healthy soups. Diet soft drinks and reduced-fat milk also are readily available. However, all of these health-conscious options are only helpful if you choose one of them. The decision is yours.

Smart Choices, Smart Meals

For most people an occasional fast-food meal will not upset an otherwise healthy diet and lifestyle. What you order and how often you order it are the real issues. If you eat at fast-food restaurants every day, you need to be very careful about your food choices. Select only Smart Choices, which are indicated in the food lists in this book by the symbol ☀. (The guidelines we used for designating Smart Choices appear on page 12.) If you only occasionally eat at fast-food restaurants, the individual choices you make are not as crucial. However moderation, as always, is important.

Look for meals that meet the following guidelines. If sodium is a concern, try to keep to a limit of 1000 milligrams or less for any fast-food meal.

Men	Women
700–900 calories	500–700 calories
30–35 fat grams	20–25 fat grams

To give you ideas for choosing menu items that add up to a nutritious and healthful fast-food meal, we've created Smart Meals. These meal menus appear at the end of most restaurant listings in the book. The guidelines we used for creating Smart Meals appear on page 12.

Good nutrition can be assured, even when fast food is part of your lifestyle, by eating a variety of foods every day, including vegetables and fruits, low-fat dairy products, and whole-grain breads and cereals. For added assurance when restaurant choices are limited, you can supplement a fast-food meal with fruit or vegetables from home. To make sure you're getting the nutrients you need every day, whether fast food is part of your diet or not, take the Nutrition Quotient Quiz.

Nutrition Quotient Quiz

Answer the questions based on your food intake for one day, then read the evaluations that follow. Put a check by the evaluation that best describes your responses.

Yes   No

☐   ☐   Did I eat a total of five servings of fruits and/or vegetables?

☐   ☐   Did I eat two or three servings of low-fat dairy foods such as skim or low-fat milk, nonfat or low-fat yogurt, or low-fat cheese?

☐   ☐   For men: Did I eat 7 ounces or less of meat, poultry, and fish?

☐   ☐   For women: Did I eat 5 ounces or less of meat, poultry, and fish?

☐   ☐   Were most of my grain choices whole-grain rather than refined?

☐   ☐   Did I limit my intake of foods that contain added sugars and fats?

☐   ☐   And although not a food choice, did I accumulate 30 minutes of physical activity?

If you answered "yes" to all of the questions, your nutrition quotient is excellent, and you don't need to worry about incorporating fast food into your diet.

If you can answer "yes" to the majority of the questions for most days over a period of one week, your nutrition quotient is very good. You too can be comfortable about fitting fast food into your life, but you should stick to Smart Choices whenever possible.

If you're like many people and answered "no" to most of the questions, you need to become more conscious of the food choices you make – especially the fast-food choices.

Making the Best Fast-food Choices

Whether eating out or at home, all of us should try to eat a variety of foods in moderate portions and to consume no more than one-third of our daily calories from fat. Consider these suggestions when making your own smart choices.

Burgers – Single, no sauce

Set your sights on a single-patty burger, if you want to keep the fat and calories to a minimum. Even two regular, plain hamburgers usually have less fat than a double burger with cheese and special sauces. The ultimate double cheeseburger may sound terrific, but just be sure your Nutrition Quotient can offset nearly 1000 calories and over 60 grams of fat! Cheese adds 100 calories per slice as well as added fat and sodium, and mayonnaise-based sauces add even more of the same. So if you've got a double-decker appetite, skip the usual dressings and pile on the lettuce and tomatoes instead.

Compare:

Regular Hamburger	Double Burger with Sauce
270 calories	825 calories
9 grams fat	42 grams fat

Chicken and fish – Beware the breading

Chicken and fish are often perceived as light fare. They start out very healthful, but battering or breading and deep frying cancel out their usual low-fat advantage. Deep-fried chicken items often have the highest calorie count of any item on a restaurant menu. Fortunately, many restaurants have added grilled chicken sandwiches to their menus. But when mayonnaise-based dressings are added, the calories can double or even triple.

If fried chicken is your only choice, choose regular coating over the extra crispy varieties (which soak up more oil during cooking), and save 70 to 80 calories per piece. Even better, peel off the skin and lose even more calories plus most of the fat and excess sodium. You also can save calories by ordering separate pieces instead of combinations or whole dinners. The same applies for fish items. Also, when eating fish, skip the usual two tablespoons of tartar sauce (200 calories) in favor of cocktail sauce (35 calories) or lemon juice (0 calories).

Compare:

BBQ Chicken Sandwich	Deep-fried Breaded Chicken Sandwich
310 calories	710 calories
6 grams fat	43 grams fat
Roasted Chicken Breast	Extra Crispy Chicken Breast
170 calories	500 calories
5 grams fat	35 grams fat
Baked Fish Sandwich	Deep-fried Breaded Fish Sandwich
290 calories	700 calories
2 grams fat	41 grams fat

Sandwiches – Many low-fat options

Turkey, ham, and roast beef sandwiches can be the best choices at fast-food restaurants, as long as you stay with the regular- and junior-sized versions. Lettuce, tomatoes, peppers, and other fresh vegetables add nutrients as well as a pleasing crunch to make a sandwich healthy and satisfying. Skip the mayonnaise and mayonnaise-based toppings (such as in tuna salad sandwiches) and save 100 calories or more; use mustard, horseradish, or barbecue sauce instead. Croissant sandwiches are deceptively high in fat, averaging 500 to 600 calories. Stick with a sandwich on regular or whole-grain bread, a bun, pita bread, or a tortilla and save 150 to 300 calories.

Compare:

Turkey Wrap Sandwich	Tuna Wrap Sandwich
550 calories	950 calories
12 grams fat	64 grams fat
Junior Roast Beef Sandwich	Giant Roast Beef Sandwich
324 calories	555 calories
14 grams fat	28 grams fat

Pizza – Extra toppings, extra calories

As a snack or a quick meal, pizza fits nicely into a well-balanced diet. It's not necessarily a low-calorie food, but with its calories it also contributes very respectably to nutrition. With a tomato sauce base, mozzarella cheese, and a flour-based crust, pizza offers protein, vitamins, and carbohydrates all in one fairly low-fat package. On average, a serving has about 20 grams of protein – more than one-third of the RDA for most adults. Cheese pizza is a great source of calcium – an average of 400 milligrams per slice, or one-half of the RDA. Meat pizzas average 200 milligrams of calcium – 35 percent of the RDA. Pizza is also a good source of some B vitamins (in the crust) and vitamins A and C (tomato sauce and vegetable toppings). All this is dependent, however, on the choices you make.

Choose thin-crust pizza instead of thick-crust or deep-dish pizza and save up to 200 calories per slice. When choosing toppings, stay with mushrooms, onions, green or hot peppers, and other vegetable toppings. Extra cheese, pepperoni, and sausage mean extra fat and calories – as much as 170 calories per slice. To avoid extra sodium, skip the olives and anchovies.

Compare:

Thin-crust Cheese Pizza (2 slices)	Deep-dish Cheese Pizza (2 slices)
255 calories	465 calories
11 grams fat	20 grams fat

Potatoes – Plain and baked are best

Potatoes are nourishing, filling, and virtually free of fat and sodium. But all of this goodness goes awry when toppings are added. Cheese sauce, crumbled bacon, and sour cream can increase fat content to as much as 40 grams and calories to over 700 – amounts that are hefty even for a whole meal. A baked potato becomes a complete, satisfying, and healthy meal when topped with a low-fat protein, such as one-quarter cup of cottage cheese or one to two tablespoons of grated Swiss, cheddar, or parmesan cheese, and paired with a salad.

Other types of potatoes call for other measures. Go easy on the French fries if you are trying to cut calories. If the fries are just too tempting, limit them to the small size or a once-in-awhile treat, or split an order with a friend. If the choice is between fries and onion rings, remember that breading makes onion rings higher in fat and calories than French fries.

Compare:

Baked potato	Deluxe Baked Potato (with toppings)
355 calories	750 calories
0 grams fat	35 grams fat
Mashed Potatoes and Gravy	Medium French Fries
120 calories	380 calories
6 grams fat	19 grams fat

Southwestern fare – Stay free of fried

Entrees made with soft flour tortillas are generally better choices than those made with fried (hard) corn tortillas. Choose chicken, bean, or beef burritos or other non-fried items, and spice them to your taste. To keep the fat and calories down, skip the guacamole and sour cream and pile on extra salsa, tomatoes, and lettuce. If you prefer corn tortillas, a small taco or tostada accompanied by tomatoes and fresh vegetables can be an excellent choice.

Chili is a surprisingly good choice as well; even a large bowl has only 300 calories and 12 grams of fat. The large amounts of cheese and refried beans commonly served with Mexican entrees are high in fat and need to be eaten in small amounts.

Compare:

Steak Soft Taco	Seven-layer Burrito
200 calories	540 calories
7 grams fat	24 grams fat

Salad – A healthy choice

A trip to the salad bar is a healthy alternative to high-fat fast-food sandwiches, and many restaurants now offer this option on their menus. As you fill your plate, go heavy on raw vegetables and pass on the prepared salads, such as potato salad and pasta salad. A large salad containing a variety of vegetables, one-half cup cottage cheese, and a reduced-fat or nonfat salad dressing has less than 250 calories. However, adding just one tablespoon of regular dressing, a sprinkling of bacon bits, and one-quarter cup macaroni salad or potato salad doubles the calories to 500. In fact, there's no quicker way to cancel out the health advantages of a salad than to drown it in regular salad dressing. Instead, stick with low-calorie, reduced-fat, or nonfat salad dressings.

Some fast-food restaurants also have pre-made salads on their menus. The best choices are grilled chicken or garden salads. Avoid taco salads, Caesar salads, and chef salads, which include meats, cheeses, and eggs that boost the fat content.

Compare:

Grilled Chicken Salad	Taco Salad
240 calories	840 calories
11 grams fat	52 grams fat

Beverages – Watch for hidden sugar and fat

The most popular beverages at fast-food restaurants are shakes and soft drinks. A twelve-ounce can of a regular soft drink contains the equivalent of eight to nine teaspoons of sugar. Better choices are diet beverages, reduced-fat or nonfat milk, fruit juice, or – the best of all beverage choices – water. Coffee and tea are good choices, as long as you drink them without a whitener or use low-fat or skim milk or a nonfat creamer.

Compare:

Orange Juice (6 ounces)	Chocolate Shake (14 ounces)
80 calories	560 calories
0 grams fat	15 grams fat

Dessert – The simpler the better

Low-fat or nonfat frozen yogurt cones can satisfy your sweet tooth with little damage, as can ices, sorbets, and sherbets, which generally have less fat and fewer calories than ice cream or gelato. Use chocolate sprinkles (about 34 calories in two tablespoons) to perk up plain yogurt or ice cream, and skip the hot fudge, sauces, nuts, and whipped toppings.

You can also satisfy your dessert craving by bringing fresh fruit from home. Try eating your "dessert" fruit first; it's a creative way to curb your appetite and avoid overeating.

Compare:

Regular Yogurt Cone	Heath Blizzard®
180 calories	820 calories
less than 1 gram fat	33 grams fat

Breakfast – Proceed with caution

Healthy fast-food lunch or dinner choices may be easier to make than breakfast choices. Morning food options tend to be heavy with fat, calories, and cholesterol. Breakfast sandwiches, especially sausage versions, are very high in fat and calories.

As with fast-food desserts, simpler is better when it comes to fast-food breakfasts. Start your day with low-fat muffins, English muffins, bagels, or toast. Add one scrambled egg, fruit juice, and reduced-fat or skim milk. Pancakes without butter are a surprisingly good breakfast option as well.

Compare:

Low-fat Triple Berry Muffin   Pecan Roll
270 calories   900 calories
3 grams fat   48 grams fat

Pancakes with Syrup   Big Country® Sausage Breakfast
490 calories   1000 calories
7 grams fat   66 grams fat

Fast-food Tips

As you think about fitting fast food into your healthy lifestyle, remember that eating three meals a day is just as important as making healthy food choices. It's tempting to skip breakfast or lunch when you're dieting to lose weight, or when life gets too hectic. This can lead to overeating when you finally do eat, and if you're eating fast food – well, you can imagine where that can lead. And although exercise is important, don't skip lunch in order to find the time to do it. Healthful eating habits and regular exercise are both important! The following tips will help you make the right fast-food choices for you.

Eat mainly at meal times. The average calorie content of a fast-food meal is 685, which is reasonable for many people. However, when you eat fast-food items (such as French fries) as snacks rather than as meals, you can add a hefty average of 427 calories to your usual daily intake. This can easily put you well over your daily calorie limit.

Buy small. Avoid menu choices labeled "jumbo," "giant," or "deluxe." Larger servings mean extra calories and usually more fat, cholesterol, and sodium as well.

Limit high-fat condiments. Each tablespoon of salad dressing, mayonnaise, mayonnaise-based dressing, or another fat-containing sauce adds an extra 100 to 200 calories to a sandwich or salad. If no low-fat versions are available, take just a small amount of the regular condiment. You may find that a little goes a long way and that food tastes even better when it's not smothered in add-ons.

Share. French fries, a large sandwich, or dessert will taste even better when shared with a friend. Or take half home for another meal.

About This Edition

The information in the food lists is presented in four parts or groups:

1) Menu items;

2) Serving sizes and calories;

3) Nutrients in each serving, including grams of fat, grams of saturated fat, milligrams of sodium, grams of protein, and grams of carbohydrate; and

4) Carbohydrate choices and exchange choices.

The information for each menu item stretches across two pages of the open book. The first two parts – often the most used – appear on the left-hand page. The second two parts are on the right-hand page. The exchange and carbohydrate choices – essential information for people following a meal plan for weight loss or for other health reasons – are conveniently located to the far right.

Carbohydrate choices were calculated using the 15-gram equation. Because fiber is a carbohydrate that is not digested, fiber was subtracted from the total grams of carbohydrate before calculating the carbohydrate and exchange choices for items with five or more grams of fiber.

The 15-gram Equation

15 grams of carbohydrate = 1 carbohydrate choice

Exchange choices are based on the *Exchange Lists* published by the American Diabetes Association and The American Dietetic Association. Exchanges include starch; fruit; milk; other carbohydrates; vegetable; very lean, lean, medium fat, or high fat meat; and fat. Some of the nutrient values for food items are based on actual laboratory analysis, and some were calculated from nutrient composition tables. The values listed are averages and may vary from restaurant to restaurant.

Smart Choices are the most healthful menu items offered by each restaurant. They are designated in the lists by a small light bulb in the left margin. The following guidelines were used to determine Smart Choices:

- Entrees (main dishes, main-dish soups and salads, sandwiches): Less than 700 calories; no high fat meat or fat exchanges

- Side orders (vegetables, bread, side soups, salads, salad dressings): 0 to 1 fat exchanges

- Salad bar selections and condiments: Less than 3 grams of fat

- Beverages: Skim or reduced-fat milk or fruit juice

- Desserts: Less than 250 calories; 0 to 1 fat exchanges

SMART MEAL

Smart Meals are menus that appear at the end of most restaurant sections. We used the following guidelines to create Smart Meals:

- Each Smart Meal includes foods from at least three food groups (grains, dairy, vegetables, fruit, or meat).

- A Smart Meal has 700 calories or less and 20 grams or less of fat.

- All menu items selected for Smart Meals are Smart Choices or free foods. (Free foods are foods with less than 20 calories per serving.)

This book is designed to alert you to the nutritive values, carbohydrate choices, and exchange choices for food items and to help you make smart fast-food choices. You can enjoy the taste and convenience of eating at fast-food restaurants and still eat healthfully.

Nutrition Information for 40 Popular Fast-Food Restaurants

MENU ITEM	SERVING SIZE	CALORIES	CALORIES FROM FAT

A&W OF CANADA
SANDWICHES

Cheeseburger	1 (6 oz)	424	133
💡 Chicken Grill®	1 (6 oz)	330	121
Country Chicken Deluxe	1 (10 oz)	551	234
Double Cheeseburger	1 (8 oz)	604	203
Double Mozza Burger®	1 (11 oz)	900	422
Double Teen Burger®	1 (11 oz)	789	305
💡 Hamburger	1 (5.5 oz)	378	103
Mozza Burger®	1 (8 oz)	669	331
Teen Burger®	1 (8.5 oz)	557	214
Whistle Dog®	1 (6 oz)	490	267

CHICKEN CHUNKS

Chicken Chunks, 3-piece	1 order (2.2 oz)	166	98
Chicken Chunks, 6-piece	1 order (4.4 oz)	322	196
Chicken Chunks, 9-piece	1 order (6.6 oz)	498	294

SIDE ORDERS

French Fries, small	1 order (3 oz)	263	123
French Fries, regular	1 order (5 oz)	439	206
French Fries, large	1 order (7 oz)	613	287
Fresh Onion Rings	1 order (3.5 oz)	332	168
💡 Gravy	1 (0.3 oz)	33	9

SALADS

💡 Caesar Salad	1 (8.5 oz)	139	44
💡 Tossed Green Salad	1 (5.5 oz)	54	5

💡 Smart Choice

TOTAL FAT (g)	SATURATED FAT (g)	SODIUM (mg)	PROTEIN (g)	CARBOHYDRATE (g)	CARBOHYDRATE CHOICES	EXCHANGES
15	NA	1153	16	57	3½	3½ starch, 2 med. fat meat, 1 fat
13	NA	660	16	36	2½	2½ starch, 2 med. fat meat
26	NA	410	29	51	3½	3½ starch, 3 med. fat meat, 2 fat
23	NA	1406	24	77	5	5 starch, 3 med. fat meat, 1 fat
47	NA	1360	33	89	6	6 starch, 3 med. fat meat, 6 fat
34	NA	1814	31	92	6	6 starch, 3 med. fat meat, 3 fat
11	NA	930	14	56	3½	3½ starch, 2 med. fat meat
37	NA	1033	22	63	4	4 starch, 2 med. fat meat, 5 fat
24	NA	1397	21	66	4	4 starch, 2 med. fat meat, 2 fat
30	NA	1507	17	39	2½	2½ starch, 2 med. fat meat, 4 fat
11	NA	404	8	9	½	½ starch, 1 med. fat meat, 1 fat
22	NA	807	17	18	1	1 starch, 2 med. fat meat, 2 fat
33	NA	1211	25	27	2	2 starch, 3 med. fat meat, 3 fat
14	NA	139	3	33	2	2 starch, 3 fat
23	NA	231	6	55	3½	3½ starch, 4 fat
32	NA	323	8	77	5	5 starch, 5 fat
19	NA	670	5	38	2½	2½ starch, 3 fat
1	NA	385	1	5	0	free
5	NA	317	9	15	1	3 veg or 1 starch, 1 med. fat meat
1	NA	62	2	11	1	2 veg

1 Carbohydrate Choice = 1 starch or 1 fruit or 1 milk exchange
* Grams of fiber subtracted from total carbohydrate

MENU ITEM	SERVING SIZE	CALORIES	CALORIES FROM FAT
SALAD DRESSINGS			
Creamy Caesar Salad Dressing	1 pkt (1.3 oz)	212	189
French Salad Dressing	1 pkt (1.3 oz)	144	126
💡 French Salad Dressing, Calorie Wise	1 pkt (1.3 oz)	34	27
💡 Italian Salad Dressing, Calorie Wise	1 pkt (1.3 oz)	17	9
Ranch Salad Dressing	1 pkt (1.3 oz)	208	198
Thousand Island Salad Dressing	1 pkt (1.3 oz)	224	219
DESSERTS			
Apple Turnover	1 (3 oz)	193	74
Chocolate Chunk Cookie	1 (3 oz)	360	135
Cinnamon Bun	1 (3.8 oz)	388	101
SHAKES			
A&W Root Beer Milkshake, small	10 oz	434	84
A&W Root Beer Milkshake, large	15 oz	602	121
Chocolate Milkshake, small	10 oz	367	86
Chocolate Milkshake, large	15 oz	519	124
Strawberry Milkshake, small	10 oz	363	84
Strawberry Milkshake, large	15 oz	514	120
SOFT DRINKS			
A&W Cream Soda®	12.5 oz	42	0
A&W Root Beer®, small	10 oz	131	0
A&W Root Beer®, medium	13 oz	173	0
A&W Root Beer®, large	18 oz	230	0
Coca-Cola Classic®, small	10 oz	115	NA
Coca-Cola Classic®, medium	13 oz	152	NA
Coca-Cola Classic®, large	18 oz	202	NA

 Smart Choice

TOTAL FAT (g)	SATURATED FAT (g)	SODIUM (mg)	PROTEIN (g)	CARBOHYDRATE (g)	CARBOHYDRATE CHOICES	EXCHANGES
21	NA	56	1	0	0	4 fat
14	NA	324	0	5	0	3 fat
3	NA	388	0	7	½	½ other carb
1	NA	582	0	2	0	free
22	NA	280	1	2	0	4 fat
24	NA	304	1	2	0	5 fat
8	NA	341	3	29	2	2 other carb, 1½ fat
15	NA	330	5	54	3½	3½ other carb, 3 fat
11	NA	154	7	65	4	4 other carb
9	NA	219	10	74	5	5 other carb, 1 fat
13	NA	310	15	101	7	7 other carb, 2 fat
10	NA	221	10	61	4	4 other carb, 2 fat
14	NA	312	15	86	6	6 other carb, 3 fat
9	NA	190	10	61	4	4 other carb, 2 fat
13	NA	273	15	86	6	6 other carb, 2 fat
0	NA	39	1	42	3	3 other carb
0	NA	36	0	34	2	2 other carb
0	NA	47	0	45	3	3 other carb
0	NA	63	1	60	4	4 other carb
NA	NA	11	NA	32	2	2 other carb
NA	NA	14	NA	42	3	3 other carb
NA	NA	19	NA	56	4	4 other carb

1 Carbohydrate Choice = 1 starch or 1 fruit or 1 milk exchange
* Grams of fiber subtracted from total carbohydrate

MENU ITEM	SERVING SIZE	CALORIES	CALORIES FROM FAT
Diet A&W Cream Soda®	12.5 oz	4	0
Diet A&W Root Beer®, small	10 oz	2	0
Diet A&W Root Beer®, medium	13 oz	2	0
Diet A&W Root Beer®, large	18 oz	3	0
Diet Coke®, small	10 oz	1	NA
Diet Coke®, medium	13 oz	2	NA
Diet Coke®, large	18 oz	2	NA
Orange Soda, small	10 oz	148	0
Orange Soda, medium	13 oz	194	0
Orange Soda, large	18 oz	259	0
Sprite®, small	10 oz	119	NA
Sprite®, medium	13 oz	156	NA
Sprite®, large	18 oz	208	NA

OTHER BEVERAGES

MENU ITEM	SERVING SIZE	CALORIES	CALORIES FROM FAT
Apple Juice, small	6.5 oz	86	1
Apple Juice, large	10.5 oz	141	3
Chocolate Milk, 2%	8 oz	188	48
Hot Chocolate	7 oz	104	25
Milk, 2%	8 oz	124	43
Orange Juice, small	6.5 oz	82	1
Orange Juice, large	10.5 oz	136	2

BREAKFAST

MENU ITEM	SERVING SIZE	CALORIES	CALORIES FROM FAT
Bacon and Eggs (with toast)	1 order (6 oz)	573	364
Bacon N' Egger®	1 (5 oz)	509	311
French Toast with Syrup and Margarine	1 order (9.6 oz)	799	309
Hash Browns	1 order (2.3 oz)	215	112

 Smart Choice

TOTAL FAT (g)	SATURATED FAT (g)	SODIUM (mg)	PROTEIN (g)	CARBOHYDRATE (g)	CARBOHYDRATE CHOICES	EXCHANGES
0	NA	68	0	1	0	free
0	NA	40	1	0	0	free
0	NA	53	1	0	0	free
0	NA	70	1	0	0	free
NA	NA	5	NA	0	0	free
NA	NA	6	NA	0	0	free
NA	NA	8	NA	0	0	free
0	NA	12	0	39	2½	2½ other carb
0	NA	15	0	51	3½	3½ other carb
0	NA	21	0	68	4½	4½ other carb
NA	NA	37	NA	30	2	2 other carb
NA	NA	48	NA	41	3	3 other carb
NA	NA	64	NA	54	3½	3½ other carb
0	NA	6	0	21	1½	1½ fruit
0	NA	9	0	35	2	2 fruit
5	NA	159	9	28	2	1 other carb, 1 2% milk
3	NA	5	1	18	1	1 other carb, ½ fat
5	NA	125	8	12	1	1 2% milk
0	NA	2	1	20	1	1 fruit
0	NA	3	2	33	2	2 fruit
40	NA	1036	23	28	2	2 starch, 2½ med. fat meat, 5 fat
35	NA	938	17	32	2	2 starch, 2 med. fat meat, 5 fat
34	NA	1080	23	98	6½	3½ starch, 3 other carb, 2½ med. fat meat, 4 fat
12	NA	343	2	24	1½	1½ starch, 2 fat

1 Carbohydrate Choice = 1 starch or 1 fruit or 1 milk exchange
* Grams of fiber subtracted from total carbohydrate

MENU ITEM	SERVING SIZE	CALORIES	CALORIES FROM FAT
Toast, 100% whole wheat	1 order (3.7 oz)	364	132
Toast, white	1 order (3.7 oz)	386	133

SMART MEAL, A&W OF CANADA

Hamburger	**Calories:**	451
Tossed Green Salad	**Fat:**	13 grams
Italian Salad Dressing, Calorie Wise (1 pkt)	**Carb Choices:**	4½
	Exchanges:	3½ starch, 2 veg, 2 med. fat meat

ARBY'S

ROAST BEEF SANDWICHES

MENU ITEM	SERVING SIZE	CALORIES	CALORIES FROM FAT
Arby's Melt with Cheddar Sandwich	1 (5.2 oz)	368	162
Arby-Q Sandwich	1 (6.4 oz)	431	162
Bac'n Cheddar Deluxe Sandwich	1 (8.1 oz)	539	306
Beef 'n Cheddar Sandwich	1 (6.7 oz)	487	252
Giant Roast Beef Sandwich	1 (8.1 oz)	555	252
Junior Roast Beef Sandwich	1 (4.4 oz)	324	126
Regular Roast Beef Sandwich	1 (5.4 oz)	388	171
Super Roast Beef Sandwich	1 (8.7 oz)	523	243

CHICKEN

MENU ITEM	SERVING SIZE	CALORIES	CALORIES FROM FAT
Breaded Chicken Fillet	1 (7.2 oz)	536	252
Chicken Cordon Bleu Sandwich	1 (8.5 oz)	623	297
Chicken Fingers	2 pieces (3.6 oz)	290	144
Grilled Chicken BBQ Sandwich	1 (7.1 oz)	388	117
Grilled Chicken Deluxe Sandwich	1 (8.1 oz)	430	180
Roast Chicken Club Sandwich	1 (8.5 oz)	546	279
Roast Chicken Deluxe Sandwich	1 (7.6 oz)	433	198
Roast Chicken Santa Fe Sandwich	1 (6.4 oz)	436	198

 Smart Choice

TOTAL FAT (g)	SATURATED FAT (g)	SODIUM (mg)	PROTEIN (g)	CARBOHYDRATE (g)	CARBOHYDRATE CHOICES	EXCHANGES
15	NA	721	11	41*	3	3 starch, 3 fat
15	NA	688	9	53	3½	3½ starch, 3 fat
18	6	937	18	36	2½	2½ starch, 2 med. fat meat, 1 fat
18	6	1321	22	48	3	3 starch, 2 med. fat meat, 1 fat
34	10	1140	22	38	2½	2½ starch, 2½ med. fat meat, 4 fat
28	9	1216	25	40	2½	2½ starch, 3 med. fat meat, 2 fat
28	11	1561	35	38*	2½	2½ starch, 4 med. fat meat, 1 fat
14	5	779	17	35	2	2 starch, 2 med. fat meat, 1 fat
19	7	1009	23	33	2	2 starch, 3 med. fat meat
27	9	1189	25	45*	3	3 starch, 3 med. fat meat, 2 fat
28	5	1016	28	41*	3	3 starch, 3 med. fat meat, 2 fat
33	8	1594	38	41*	3	3 starch, 4 med. fat meat, 2 fat
16	2	677	16	20	1	1 starch, 2 med. fat meat, 1 fat
13	3	1002	23	47	3	3 starch, 2½ med. fat meat
20	4	848	23	41	3	3 starch, 2½ med. fat meat, 1 fat
31	9	1103	31	37	2½	2½ starch, 3½ med. fat meat, 2 fat
22	5	763	24	36	2½	2½ starch, 2½ med. fat meat, 1 fat
22	6	818	29	35	2½	2½ starch, 3½ med. fat meat

1 Carbohydrate Choice = 1 starch or 1 fruit or 1 milk exchange
* Grams of fiber subtracted from total carbohydrate

MENU ITEM	SERVING SIZE	CALORIES	CALORIES FROM FAT
SUB ROLL SANDWICHES			
French Dip Sandwich	1 (6.8 oz)	475	198
Hot Ham 'n Swiss Sandwich	1 (9.3 oz)	500	207
Italian Sandwich	1 (10.1 oz)	675	324
Philly Beef 'n Swiss Sandwich	1 (10.4 oz)	755	423
Roast Beef Sandwich	1 (10.8 oz)	700	378
Triple Cheese Melt Sandwich	1 (8.4 oz)	720	405
Turkey Sandwich	1 (9.8 oz)	550	243
LIGHT MENU SANDWICHES			
Roast Beef Deluxe Sandwich	1 (6.4 oz)	296	90
Roast Chicken Deluxe Sandwich	1 (6.8 oz)	276	54
Roast Turkey Deluxe Sandwich	1 (6.8 oz)	260	63
OTHER SANDWICHES			
Fish Fillet Sandwich	1 (7.7 oz)	529	243
Ham 'n Cheese Sandwich	1 (5.9 oz)	359	126
Ham 'n Cheese Melt Sandwich	1 (4.9 oz)	329	117
BAKED POTATOES			
Baked Potato, plain	1 (11.5 oz)	355	3
Baked Potato with Margarine & Sour Cream	1 (14 oz)	578	216
Broccoli 'n Cheddar Baked Potato	1 (15.7 oz)	571	180
Deluxe Baked Potato	1 (15.3 oz)	736	324
SIDE ORDERS			
Cheddar Curly Fries	1 order (4.25 oz)	333	163
Curly Fries	1 order (3.5 oz)	300	135
French Fries	1 order (2.5 oz)	246	117

 Smart Choice

TOTAL FAT (g)	SATURATED FAT (g)	SODIUM (mg)	PROTEIN (g)	CARBOHYDRATE (g)	CARBOHYDRATE CHOICES	EXCHANGES
22	8	1411	30	40	2½	2½ starch, 4 med. fat meat
23	7	1664	30	43	3	3 starch, 4 med. fat meat
36	13	2089	30	46	3	3 starch, 4 med. fat meat, 3 fat
47	15	2025	39	48	3	3 starch, 5 med. fat meat, 4 fat
42	14	2034	38	44	3	3 starch, 5 med. fat meat, 3 fat
45	16	1797	37	46	3	3 starch, 5 med. fat meat, 4 fat
27	7	2084	31	47	3	3 starch, 4 med. fat meat, 1 fat
10	3	826	18	27*	2	2 starch, 2 med. fat meat
6	2	777	20	33	2	2 starch, 2 lean meat
7	2	1262	20	33	2	2 starch, 2 lean meat
27	7	864	23	50	3	3 starch, 3 med. fat meat, 2 fat
14	5	1283	24	34	2	2 starch, 3 med. fat meat
13	4	1013	20	34	2	2 starch, 2½ med. fat meat
0	0	26	7	75*	5	5 starch
24	9	209	9	78*	5	5 starch, 4 fat
20	5	565	14	80*	5	5 starch, 1 med. fat meat, 2 fat
36	16	499	19	79*	5	5 starch, 2 med. fat meat, 4 fat
18	4	1016	5	40	2½	2½ starch, 3 fat
15	3	853	4	38	2½	2½ starch, 3 fat
13	3	114	2	30	2	2 starch, 2 fat

1 Carbohydrate Choice = 1 starch or 1 fruit or 1 milk exchange
* Grams of fiber subtracted from total carbohydrate

MENU ITEM	SERVING SIZE	CALORIES	CALORIES FROM FAT
Potato Cakes (2)	1 order (3 oz)	204	108
SOUPS			
☀ Boston Clam Chowder Soup	8 oz	190	81
☀ Cream of Broccoli Soup	8 oz	160	72
☀ Lumberjack Mixed Vegetable Soup	8 oz	90	36
☀ Old Fashion Chicken Noodle Soup	8 oz	80	18
☀ Potato with Bacon Soup	8 oz	170	63
☀ Timberline Chili Soup	8 oz	220	90
Wisconsin Cheese Soup	8 oz	280	162
SALADS			
☀ Garden Salad	1 (11.9 oz)	61	3
☀ Roast Chicken Salad	1 (14.4 oz)	149	18
☀ Side Salad	1 (5 oz)	23	3
SALAD DRESSINGS			
Blue Cheese Salad Dressing	2 oz	290	279
☀ Buttermilk Ranch Salad Dressing, Reduced Calorie	2 oz	50	0
Honey French Salad Dressing	2 oz	280	207
☀ Italian Salad Dressing, Reduced Calorie	2 oz	20	9
☀ Red Ranch Salad Dressing	0.5 oz	75	54
Thousand Island Salad Dressing	2 oz	260	234
CONDIMENTS			
☀ Arby's Sauce	0.5 oz	15	2
☀ Barbeque Sauce	0.5 oz	30	0
☀ Beef Stock Au Jus	2 oz	10	0
Cheddar Cheese Sauce	0.75 oz	35	27

☀ Smart Choice

TOTAL FAT (g)	SATURATED FAT (g)	SODIUM (mg)	PROTEIN (g)	CARBOHYDRATE (g)	CARBOHYDRATE CHOICES	EXCHANGES
12	2	397	2	20	1	1½ starch, 2 fat
9	3	965	9	18	1	1 starch, 1 med. fat meat, 1 fat
8	4	1005	7	15	1	1 starch, 1 high fat meat
4	2	1150	2	10	½	½ starch, 1 fat or 2 veg, 1 fat
2	0	850	6	11	1	1 starch
7	3	905	6	23	1½	1½ starch, 1 fat
10	4	1130	18	10*	1	1 starch, 2 med. fat meat
18	7	1065	10	20	1	1 starch, 1 high fat meat, 2 fat
1	0	40	3	7*	½	2 veg
2	<1	418	20	7*	½	2 veg, 3 very lean meat
0	0	15	1	4	0	1 veg
31	6	580	2	2	0	6 fat
0	0	710	0	12	1	1 other carb
23	3	400	0	18	1	1 other carb, 4 fat
1	0	1000	0	3	0	free
6	1	115	0	5	0	1 fat
26	4	420	0	7	½	½ other carb, 5 fat
0	0	113	0	4	0	free
0	0	185	0	7	½	½ other carb
0	0	440	0	1	0	free
3	1	139	1	1	0	½ fat

1 Carbohydrate Choice = 1 starch or 1 fruit or 1 milk exchange
* Grams of fiber subtracted from total carbohydrate

MENU ITEM	SERVING SIZE	CALORIES	CALORIES FROM FAT
Honey Mayonnaise, Reduced Calorie	0.5 oz	70	63
Horsey Sauce	0.5 oz	60	45
Italian Sub Sauce	0.5 oz	70	63
☀ Ketchup	0.5 oz	16	0
Mayonnaise	0.5 oz	110	108
☀ Mayonnaise, Light Cholesterol Free	0.25 oz	12	9
☀ Mustard, German Style	0.16 oz	5	0
Parmesan Cheese Sauce	0.5 oz	70	63
☀ Table Syrup	1 oz	100	0
Tartar Sauce	1 oz	140	135

DESSERTS

Apple Turnover	1 (3.2 oz)	330	126
Cheesecake, plain	1 (3 oz)	320	207
Cherry Turnover	1 (3.2 oz)	320	117
☀ Chocolate Chip Cookie	1 (1 oz)	125	54
Polar Swirl, Butterfinger	1 (11.6 oz)	457	162
Polar Swirl, Heath	1 (11.6 oz)	543	198
Polar Swirl, Oreo	1 (11.6 oz)	482	198
Polar Swirl, Peanut Butter Cup	1 (11.6 oz)	517	216
Polar Swirl, Snickers	1 (11.6 oz)	511	171

SHAKES

Chocolate Shake	12 oz	451	108
Jamocha Shake	12 oz	384	90
Vanilla Shake	12 oz	360	108

☀ Smart Choice

TOTAL FAT (g)	SATURATED FAT (g)	SODIUM (mg)	PROTEIN (g)	CARBOHYDRATE (g)	CARBOHYDRATE CHOICES	EXCHANGES
7	1	135	0	1	0	1 fat
5	1	150	0	2	0	1 fat
7	1	240	0	1	0	1 fat
0	0	143	0	4	0	free
12	7	80	0	0	0	2 fat
1	0	64	0	0.5	0	free
0	0	70	0	1	0	free
7	1	130	1	2	0	1 fat
0	0	30	0	25	1½	1½ other carb
15	2	220	0	0	0	3 fat
14	7	180	4	48	3	3 other carb, 2 fat
23	14	240	5	23	1½	1½ other carb, 4½ fat
13	5	190	4	46	3	3 other carb, 2 fat
6	2	85	2	16	1	1 other carb, 1 fat
18	8	318	15	62	4	4 other carb, 3 fat
22	5	346	15	76	5	5 other carb, 4 fat
22	10	521	15	66	4	4 other carb, 4 fat
24	8	385	20	61	4	4 other carb, 5 fat
19	7	351	15	73	5	5 other carb, 3 fat
12	3	341	15	76	5	5 other carb, 2 fat
10	3	262	15	62	4	4 other carb, 2 fat
12	4	281	15	50	3	3 other carb, 2 fat

1 Carbohydrate Choice = 1 starch or 1 fruit or 1 milk exchange
* Grams of fiber subtracted from total carbohydrate

MENU ITEM	SERVING SIZE	CALORIES	CALORIES FROM FAT
SOFT DRINKS			
Coca-Cola Classic®	12 oz	140	0
Diet Coke®	12 oz	0	0
Diet Pepsi®	12 oz	0	0
Diet 7 Up®	12 oz	0	0
Dr. Pepper®	12 oz	160	0
Nehi Orange®	12 oz	195	0
Pepsi Cola®	12 oz	150	0
RC Cola®	12 oz	165	0
RC Diet Rite®	12 oz	1	0
7 Up®	12 oz	144	0
Upper Ten®	12 oz	169	0
OTHER BEVERAGES			
Coffee, black	8 oz	3	0
Hot Chocolate	8 oz	110	9
Iced Tea	16 oz	6	0
☀ Orange Juice	6 oz	82	0
BREAKFAST			
Bacon (2 pieces)	1 order (0.53 oz)	90	63
Biscuit, plain	1 (2.9 oz)	280	135
Blueberry Muffin	1 (2.3 oz)	230	81
Cinnamon Nut Danish	1 (3.5 oz)	360	99
Croissant, plain	1 (2 oz)	220	108
Egg Portion	1 (1.6 oz)	95	72
French-Toastix	6 (4.4 oz)	430	189
☀ Ham	1 order (1.5 oz)	45	9

☀ Smart Choice

TOTAL FAT (g)	SATURATED FAT (g)	SODIUM (mg)	PROTEIN (g)	CARBOHYDRATE (g)	CARBOHYDRATE CHOICES	EXCHANGES
0	0	50	0	39	2½	2½ other carb
0	0	40	0	0	0	free
0	0	35	0	0	0	free
0	0	35	0	0	0	free
0	0	55	0	40	3½	3½ other carb
0	0	52	0	52	3½	3½ other carb
0	0	35	0	41	3	3 other carb
0	0	52	0	43	3	3 other carb
0	0	10	0	0	0	free
0	0	34	0	38	2½	2½ other carb
0	0	40	0	42	3	3 other carb
0	0	3	0	0	0	free
1	<1	120	2	23	1½	1½ other carb
0	0	12	0	1	0	free
0	0	2	0	20	1	1 fruit
7	3	220	5	0	0	1½ fat
15	3	730	6	34	2	2 starch, 3 fat
9	2	290	2	35	2	2 starch, 2 fat
11	1	105	6	60	4	4 starch, 2 fat
12	7	230	4	25	1½	1½ starch, 2 fat
8	2	54	0.5	0.5	0	1½ fat
21	5	550	10	52	3½	3½ starch, 4 fat
1	<1	405	7	0	0	1 very lean meat

1 Carbohydrate Choice = 1 starch or 1 fruit or 1 milk exchange
* Grams of fiber subtracted from total carbohydrate

MENU ITEM	SERVING SIZE	CALORIES	CALORIES FROM FAT
Sausage	1 order (1.3 oz)	163	135

SMART MEAL, ARBY'S

Regular Roast Beef Sandwich Side Salad Italian Salad Dressing, Reduced Calorie (2 oz) Iced Tea (unsweetened)	**Calories:** **Fat:** **Carb Choices:** **Exchanges:**	437 20 grams 2½ 2 starch, 1 veg, 3 med. fat meat

Roast Chicken Salad Italian Salad Dressing, Reduced Calorie (2 oz) Lumberjack Mixed Vegetable Soup	**Calories:** **Fat:** **Carb Choices:** **Exchanges:**	259 7 grams 1½ 1 starch, 1 veg, 3 very lean meat, 1 fat

AU BON PAIN

CHEF'S CREATION SANDWICHES

Menu Item	Serving Size	Calories	Calories from Fat
Arizona Chicken Sandwich	1 (12.7 oz)	720	300
California Chicken Sandwich	1 (13.2 oz)	820	390
Fresh Mozzarella, Tomato and Pesto Sandwich	1 (10.5 oz)	650	270
Parmesan Chicken Sandwich	1 (11 oz)	740	220
Steak and Cheese Melt Sandwich	1 (11.8 oz)	750	290
·ᄋ́· Thanksgiving Sub Sandwich	1 (10.4 oz)	520	45

HOT CROISSANTS

Menu Item	Serving Size	Calories	Calories from Fat
Ham and Cheese Croissant	1 (4.3 oz)	380	180
Spinach and Cheese Croissant	1 (3.5 oz)	270	140
Turkey and Cheddar Croissant	1 (4.2 oz)	390	190

WRAPS SANDWICHES

Menu Item	Serving Size	Calories	Calories from Fat
Chicken Caesar Wrap	1 (10 oz)	630	280

·ᄋ́· Smart Choice

TOTAL FAT (g)	SATURATED FAT (g)	SODIUM (mg)	PROTEIN (g)	CARBOHYDRATE (g)	CARBOHYDRATE CHOICES	EXCHANGES
15	6	321	7	0	0	1 med. fat meat, 2 fat

SMART MEAL, ARBY'S

Roast Turkey Deluxe Light Menu Sandwich
Garden Salad
Buttermilk Ranch Salad Dressing,
   Reduced Calorie (2 oz)
Diet Soft Drink

Calories: 371
Fat: 8 grams
Carb Choices: 3½
Exchanges: 2 starch, 1 veg, 1 other carb, 2 lean meat

TOTAL FAT (g)	SATURATED FAT (g)	SODIUM (mg)	PROTEIN (g)	CARBOHYDRATE (g)	CARBOHYDRATE CHOICES	EXCHANGES
33	12	1190	49	57	4	4 starch, 6 med. fat meat
44	12	1200	51	55	3½	3½ starch, 6 med. fat meat, 2 fat
30	12	1090	30	69	4½	4½ starch, 3 med. fat meat, 2 fat
24	9	1620	42	86*	5½	5½ starch, 4½ med. fat meat
32	8	1600	40	79	5	5 starch, 4 med. fat meat, 2 fat
5	1	1340	37	80	5	5 starch, 4 very lean meat
20	12	690	16	36	2½	2½ starch, 2 med. fat meat, 1 fat
16	9	330	9	27	2	2 starch, 3 fat
21	13	650	16	36	2½	2½ starch, 2 med. fat meat, 1 fat
31	8	1140	38	46	3	3 starch, 4½ med. fat meat, 1 fat

1 Carbohydrate Choice = 1 starch or 1 fruit or 1 milk exchange
* Grams of fiber subtracted from total carbohydrate

MENU ITEM	SERVING SIZE	CALORIES	CALORIES FROM FAT
Grilled Vegetable Wrap	1 (11.5 oz)	300	260
Southwestern Tuna Wrap	1 (14.5 oz)	950	570
Summer Turkey Wrap	1 (11.7 oz)	550	100
SANDWICH FILLINGS			
Brie Cheese	½ portion (1.5 oz)	140	110
Cheddar Cheese	½ portion (1.5 oz)	170	130
Chicken Tarragon	1 portion (4 oz)	240	160
Country Ham	1 portion (3.7 oz)	150	60
Cracked Pepper Chicken	1 portion (4 oz)	140	16
Grilled Chicken	1 portion (4 oz)	140	16
Herb Cheese	½ portion (1.5 oz)	150	130
Provolone	½ portion (1.5 oz)	150	100
Roast Beef	1 portion (3.7 oz)	140	40
Swiss Cheese	½ portion (1.5 oz)	160	110
Tuna Salad	1 portion (4.5 oz)	360	260
Turkey Breast	1 portion (3.7 oz)	120	10
FRESH LOAF BREADS/ROLLS			
Baguette	1 slice (1.8 oz)	140	5
Cheese Loaf	1 slice (1.8 oz)	140	25
Country Seed Roll	1 (2.5 oz)	220	35
Four Grain Loaf	1 slice (1.8 oz)	130	10
Hearth Roll	1 (2.8 oz)	220	15
Parisienne	1 slice (1.8 oz)	120	5
Petit Pain	1 (2.5 oz)	200	10
Three-Seed Walnut Raisin Roll	1 (2.8 oz)	250	50
FRESH SANDWICH BREADS			
Braided Roll	1 (1.8 oz)	170	50

 Smart Choice

TOTAL FAT (g)	SATURATED FAT (g)	SODIUM (mg)	PROTEIN (g)	CARBOHYDRATE (g)	CARBOHYDRATE CHOICES	EXCHANGES
29	4	440	3	9	½	½ starch, 6 fat
64	17	1230	41	53	3½	3½ starch, 5 med. fat meat, 7 fat
12	1	1610	29	66*	4½	4½ starch, 3 med. fat meat
12	7	270	9	0	0	1 high fat meat
14	9	260	11	1	0	1½ high fat meat
17	3	170	20	1	0	3 med. fat meat
7	3	1370	21	1	0	3 lean meat
2	0	184	27	2	0	4 very lean meat
2	0	184	27	2	0	4 very lean meat
15	7	220	2	3	0	3 fat
11	7	370	11	1	0	1½ high fat meat
5	0	550	22	1	0	3 lean meat
12	8	110	12	1	0	1½ high fat meat
29	5	520	21	3	0	3 med. fat meat, 3 fat
1	0	1110	24	1	0	3 lean meat
1	0	350	5	29	2	2 starch
3	2	400	6	24	1½	1½ starch, ½ fat
4	<1	450	9	38	2½	2½ starch, ½ fat
1	0	280	5	25	1½	1½ starch
1	0	410	9	43	3	3 starch
1	0	300	4	25	1½	1½ starch
1	0	570	7	41	2½	2½ starch
6	1	240	9	43	3	3 starch, 1 fat
5	1	320	5	26	1½	1½ starch, 1 fat

1 Carbohydrate Choice = 1 starch or 1 fruit or 1 milk exchange
* Grams of fiber subtracted from total carbohydrate

MENU ITEM	SERVING SIZE	CALORIES	CALORIES FROM FAT
☼ French Roll	1 (1.8 oz)	170	50
☼ Hearth Sandwich Bread	1 (1.8 oz)	140	10
☼ Multigrain Loaf	1 slice	130	10
☼ Rye Loaf	1 slice	110	15
Sandwich Croissant	1	310	140

SOUPS

MENU ITEM	SERVING SIZE	CALORIES	CALORIES FROM FAT
☼ Beef Barley Soup, small	8 oz	75	15
☼ Beef Barley Soup, medium	12 oz	112	25
☼ Beef Barley Soup, large	16 oz	150	30
☼ Caribbean Black Bean Soup, small	8 oz	120	10
☼ Caribbean Black Bean Soup, medium	12 oz	180	15
☼ Caribbean Black Bean Soup, large	16 oz	250	20
☼ Chicken Chili, small	8 oz	240	110
☼ Chicken Chili, medium	12 oz	350	160
☼ Chicken Chili, large	16 oz	470	220
☼ Chicken Noodle Soup, small	8 oz	80	10
☼ Chicken Noodle Soup, medium	12 oz	120	20
☼ Chicken Noodle Soup, large	16 oz	170	25
Clam Chowder Soup, small	8 oz	270	180
Clam Chowder Soup, medium	12 oz	400	260
Clam Chowder Soup, large	16 oz	540	350
Cream of Broccoli Soup, small	8 oz	220	170
Cream of Broccoli Soup, medium	12 oz	330	250
Cream of Broccoli Soup, large	16 oz	440	330
☼ French Onion Soup, small	8 oz	80	30
☼ French Onion Soup, medium	12 oz	120	45
☼ French Onion Soup, large	16 oz	170	60

TOTAL FAT (g)	SATURATED FAT (g)	SODIUM (mg)	PROTEIN (g)	CARBOHYDRATE (g)	CARBOHYDRATE CHOICES	EXCHANGES
5	1	320	4	25	1½	1½ starch, 1 fat
1	0	260	6	28	2	2 starch
1	0	340	5	26	2	2 starch, 1 fat
2	0	310	5	21	1½	1½ starch
16	10	290	7	36	2½	2½ starch, 3 fat
2	<1	660	6	11	1	1 starch
3	1	980	9	16	1	1 starch, 1 lean meat
4	1	1310	12	17*	1	1 starch, 1 lean meat
1	0	770	7	14*	1	1 starch, 1 very lean meat
2	0	1150	10	20*	1½	1½ starch, 1 very lean meat
2	0	1540	13	27*	2	2 starch, 1½ very lean meat
12	7	1350	14	17*	1	1 starch, 2 med. fat meat
18	10	2030	21	25*	1½	1½ starch, 3 med. fat meat
24	13	2700	28	33*	2	2 starch, 3½ med. fat meat, 1 fat
1	0	670	8	10	1	1 starch
2	<1	1000	12	14	1	1 starch, 1 very lean meat
3	<1	1340	16	19	1	1 starch, 2 very lean meat
19	9	730	11	16	1	1 starch, 1 med. fat meat, 2 fat
29	14	1090	16	24	1½	1½ starch, 2 med. fat meat, 3 fat
39	18	1460	22	32	2	2 starch, 3 med. fat meat, 4 fat
18	9	770	5	14	1	1 starch, 3 fat
28	13	1160	8	21	1½	1½ starch, 5 fat
37	17	1550	10	28	2	2 starch, 7 fat
3	<1	1280	2	12	1	1 starch
5	1	1910	4	17	1	1 starch, 1 fat
7	1	2550	5	23	1½	1½ starch, 1 fat

1 Carbohydrate Choice = 1 starch or 1 fruit or 1 milk exchange
* Grams of fiber subtracted from total carbohydrate

MENU ITEM	SERVING SIZE	CALORIES	CALORIES FROM FAT
N.E. Potato & Cheese with Ham Soup, small	8 oz	150	70
N.E. Potato & Cheese with Ham Soup, medium	12 oz	220	100
N.E. Potato & Cheese with Ham Soup, large	16 oz	290	140
Tomato Florentine Soup, small	8 oz	61	10
Tomato Florentine Soup, medium	12 oz	90	15
Tomato Florentine Soup, large	16 oz	122	20
Vegetarian Chili, small	8 oz	139	25
Vegetarian Chili, medium	12 oz	210	35
Vegetarian Chili, large	16 oz	278	50

SOUP IN A BREAD BOWL

Beef Barley Soup	21 oz	760	60
Caribbean Black Bean Soup	21 oz	830	45
Chicken Chili	21 oz	990	200
Chicken Noodle Soup	21 oz	760	50
Clam Chowder Soup	21 oz	1050	290
Cream of Broccoli Soup	21 oz	970	280
French Onion Soup	21 oz	760	80
N.E. Potato & Cheese with Ham Soup	21 oz	860	140
Tomato Florentine Soup	21 oz	760	45
Vegetarian Chili	21 oz	870	70

SALADS

Chicken Caesar Salad (without dressing)	1 (11.5 oz)	360	100
Chicken Tarragon Salad	1 (16 oz)	470	210
Grilled Vegetable Salad	1 (11 oz)	60	10
Tuna Salad	1 (15 oz)	490	240

 Smart Choice

TOTAL FAT (g)	SATURATED FAT (g)	SODIUM (mg)	PROTEIN (g)	CARBOHYDRATE (g)	CARBOHYDRATE CHOICES	EXCHANGES
8	5	820	5	14	1	1 starch, 1½ fat
12	8	1220	7	21	1½	1½ starch, 2 fat
15	11	1630	10	23*	1½	1½ starch, 1 med. fat meat, 2 fat
1	1	1030	4	13	1	1 starch
2	1	1550	6	20	1½	1½ starch
2	1	2070	8	27	2	2 starch
3	0	1070	6	27	2	2 starch
4	0	1610	9	40	2½	2½ starch
5	<1	2150	13	53	3½	3½ starch
7	2	2940	36	139*	9	9 starch, 2 very lean meat
5	1	3100	36	146*	10	10 starch, 2 very lean meat
22	11	3970	48	150*	10	10 starch, 3 med. fat meat
6	1	2950	39	139*	9	9 starch, 2 very lean meat
32	15	3040	43	150*	10	10 starch, 3 med. fat meat, 2 fat
31	15	3100	34	145*	9½	9½ starch, 2 med. fat meat, 1 fat
8	2	3860	30	140*	9	9 starch, 2 lean meat
15	9	3170	34	143*	9½	9½ starch, 2 med. fat meat
5	2	3490	33	142*	9	9 starch, 2 lean meat
7	1	3550	36	163*	11	11 starch, 2 lean meat
11	6	910	36	23*	1½	1½ starch, 4 lean meat
23	4	500	32	32*	2	2 starch, 4 med. fat meat
1	0	180	4	6*	0	1 veg
27	5	750	26	33*	2	2 starch, 3 med. fat meat, 2 fat

1 Carbohydrate Choice = 1 starch or 1 fruit or 1 milk exchange
* Grams of fiber subtracted from total carbohydrate

MENU ITEM	SERVING SIZE	CALORIES	CALORIES FROM FAT
SALAD DRESSINGS			
Bleu Cheese Salad Dressing	3 oz	410	370
Buttermilk Ranch Salad Dressing	3 oz	310	290
Caesar Salad Dressing	3 oz	380	350
Greek Salad Dressing	3 oz	440	440
Honey Mustard Salad Dressing	3 oz	380	300
Italian Salad Dressing, Lite	3 oz	230	180
Lemon Basil Vinaigrette Salad Dressing	3 oz	330	280
Mandarin Orange Salad Dressing	3 oz	380	290
Sesame French Salad Dressing	3 oz	370	270
Tomato Basil Salad Dressing, Fat Free	3 oz	70	0
SOURDOUGH BAGELS			
Asiago Cheese Bagel	1 (4.2 oz)	380	50
Cinnamon Raisin Bagel	1 (4.5 oz)	390	10
Everything Bagel	1 (4.2 oz)	360	20
Honey 9 Grain Bagel	1 (4.2 oz)	360	40
Onion Bagel	1 (4.5 oz)	360	10
Plain Bagel	1 (4 oz)	350	10
Sesame Bagel	1 (4.2 oz)	380	20
Wild Blueberry Bagel	1 (4.5 oz)	380	10
SPREADS			
Cream Cheese with Chives, Lite	2 oz	110	80
Honey Walnut Cream Cheese, Lite	2 oz	260	100
Plain Cream Cheese	2 oz	180	160
Plain Cream Cheese, Lite	2 oz	100	80
Raspberry Cream Cheese, Lite	2 oz	200	80
Sun-Dried Tomato Cream Cheese, Lite	2 oz	120	80

 Smart Choice

TOTAL FAT (g)	SATURATED FAT (g)	SODIUM (mg)	PROTEIN (g)	CARBOHYDRATE (g)	CARBOHYDRATE CHOICES	EXCHANGES
41	8	910	4	8	½	½ other carb, 8 fat
32	4	270	3	4	0	6½ fat
39	5	410	5	3	0	8 fat
50	7	820	0	2	0	10 fat
33	3	550	2	22	1½	1½ other carb, 6 fat
20	2	570	0	15	1	1 other carb, 4 fat
32	2	460	0	15	1	1 other carb, 6 fat
33	3	310	0	23	1½	1½ other carb, 6 fat
30	5	1010	1	26	1½	1½ other carb, 6 fat
0	0	650	1	17	1	1 other carb
6	4	690	17	66	4½	4½ starch
1	0	550	14	83	5½	5½ starch
3	0	710	14	72	5	5 starch
2	0	580	14	66*	4½	4½ starch
1	0	540	14	75	5	5 starch
1	0	540	13	71	5	5 starch
4	<1	540	15	71	5	5 starch
2	0	570	14	80	5	5 starch
10	5	280	8	6	0	2 fat
12	5	260	4	8	½	½ other carb, 2 fat
18	11	150	4	2	0	4 fat
8	5	280	6	4	0	2 fat
8	5	280	6	10	½	½ other carb, 2 fat
8	5	320	6	6	0	2 fat

1 Carbohydrate Choice = 1 starch or 1 fruit or 1 milk exchange
* Grams of fiber subtracted from total carbohydrate

MENU ITEM

MENU ITEM	SERVING SIZE	CALORIES	CALORIES FROM FAT
Veggie Cream Cheese, Lite	2 oz	100	80
DESSERT CROISSANTS			
Almond Croissant	1 (4.3 oz)	560	330
Apple Croissant	1 (3.5 oz)	280	90
Chocolate Croissant	1 (3.5 oz)	440	210
Cinnamon Raisin Croissant	1 (3.7 oz)	380	120
Plain Croissant	1 (2 oz)	270	130
Raspberry Cheese Croissant	1 (3.5 oz)	380	170
Strawberry Cheese Croissant	1 (3.5 oz)	370	170
Sweet Cheese Croissant	1 (3.7 oz)	390	200
GOURMET MUFFINS			
Blueberry Muffin	1 (4.5 oz)	410	130
Carrot Walnut Muffin	1 (5 oz)	480	210
Chocolate Chip Muffin	1 (4.5 oz)	490	180
Corn Muffin	1 (4.6 oz)	470	160
Pumpkin with Streusel Topping Muffin	1 (5.6 oz)	470	160
Raisin Bran Muffin	1 (4.7 oz)	390	100
LOW FAT MUFFINS			
☀ Cinnamon Cranapple Muffin	1 (4.6 oz)	310	30
☀ Chocolate Cake Muffin	1 (4 oz)	290	25
☀ Peach Cobbler Muffin	1 (4.4 oz)	310	25
☀ Triple Berry Muffin	1 (4.2 oz)	270	25
PASTRIES			
Blueberry Scone	1 (4 oz)	430	210
Cinnamon Scone	1 (4 oz)	520	250
Danish with Raspberry Filling	1 (3.6 oz)	370	190

 Smart Choice

TOTAL FAT (g)	SATURATED FAT (g)	SODIUM (mg)	PROTEIN (g)	CARBOHYDRATE (g)	CARBOHYDRATE CHOICES	EXCHANGES
10	5	300	6	6	0	2 fat
37	15	260	12	50	3	3 starch, 7 fat
10	6	180	4	46	3	3 starch, 1 fat
23	15	230	7	53	3½	3½ starch, 4 fat
13	8	290	7	61	4	4 starch, 2 fat
15	9	240	6	30	2	2 starch, 3 fat
19	11	300	6	47	3	3 starch, 3 fat
19	11	300	6	47	3	3 starch, 3 fat
22	12	330	7	42	3	3 starch, 4 fat
15	3	380	8	64	4	4 starch, 2 fat
23	5	650	8	61	4	4 starch, 4 fat
20	7	560	8	70	4½	4½ starch, 3 fat
18	3	570	8	70	4½	4½ starch, 3 fat
18	3	550	8	74	5	5 starch, 3 fat
11	4	1030	9	58*	4	4 starch, 2 fat
3	<1	890	5	68	4½	4½ starch
3	<1	630	4	68	4½	4½ starch
3	<1	680	5	69	4½	4½ starch
3	<1	560	5	60	4	4 starch
23	13	250	10	47	3	3 starch, 4 fat
28	14	230	10	60	4	4 starch, 5 fat
21	10	350	7	42	3	3 starch, 4 fat

1 Carbohydrate Choice = 1 starch or 1 fruit or 1 milk exchange
* Grams of fiber subtracted from total carbohydrate

MENU ITEM	SERVING SIZE	CALORIES	CALORIES FROM FAT
Danish with Sweet Cheese Filling	1 (3.6 oz)	420	230
Orange Scone	1 (4 oz)	440	200
Pecan Roll	1 (6.8 oz)	900	440
COOKIES			
Almond Biscotti	1 (1.5 oz)	200	90
Brownie Nut Fudge Cookie	1 (2 oz)	260	130
Chocolate Almond Biscotti	1 (1.7 oz)	240	120
Chocolate Chip Cookie	1 (2 oz)	280	120
Oatmeal Raisin Cookie	1 (2 oz)	250	90
Peanut Butter Cookie	1 (2 oz)	280	140
Shortbread Cookie	1 (2.4 oz)	390	230
COFFEE BEVERAGES			
Hot Mocha Blast, small	9 oz	160	35
Hot Mocha Blast, medium	13 oz	260	50
Hot Mocha Blast, large	17 oz	310	70
Hot Raspberry Mocha Blast, small	10 oz	180	35
Hot Raspberry Mocha Blast, medium	16 oz	300	50
Hot Raspberry Mocha Blast, large	20 oz	350	70
Iced Caffe Latte, small	9 oz	130	45
Iced Caffe Latte, medium	12 oz	150	50
Iced Caffe Latte, large	20.5 oz	270	90
Iced Cocoa, small	9 oz	200	50
Iced Cocoa, medium	12 oz	280	60
Iced Cocoa, large	20.5 oz	440	100
Iced Mocha Blast, small	9 oz	180	40
Iced Mocha Blast, medium	12 oz	260	50
Iced Mocha Blast, large	20.5 oz	360	90

TOTAL FAT (g)	SATURATED FAT (g)	SODIUM (mg)	PROTEIN (g)	CARBOHYDRATE (g)	CARBOHYDRATE CHOICES	EXCHANGES
26	13	380	7	42	3	3 starch, 4 fat
23	13	240	10	53	3½	3½ starch, 4 fat
48	16	480	11	111	7	7 starch, 8 fat
10	4	45	4	24	1½	1½ starch, 2 fat
14	5	130	5	31	2	2 starch, 2 fat
13	6	50	5	28	2	2 starch, 2 fat
13	8	85	3	40	2½	2½ starch, 2 fat
10	4	240	3	40	2½	2½ starch, 1½ fat
15	5	260	7	32	2	2 starch, 3 fat
25	15	190	3	39	2½	2½ starch, 4 fat
4	3	120	8	23	1½	½ carb, 1 2% milk
6	4	180	11	41	3	2 other carb, 1 2% milk
8	5	230	14	45	3	2 other carb, 1½ 2% milk
4	3	115	14	29	2	1 carb, 1 2% milk
6	4	170	11	52	3½	2½ other carb, 1 2% milk
8	5	220	14	57	4	2½ other carb, 1½ 2% milk
5	3	130	9	12	1	1 2% milk
6	4	150	10	15	1	1 2% milk
10	6	270	18	26	2	1 other carb, 1 2% milk
6	4	160	10	27	2	1 other carb, 1 2% milk
6	4	190	12	42	3	2 other carb, 1 2% milk
11	7	320	20	66	4½	4½ other carb, 2 2% milk
5	3	135	9	25	1½	1 other carb, 1 2% milk
6	4	180	11	41	3	2 other carb, 1 2% milk
10	6	280	18	50	3	2 other carb, 1½ 2% milk

1 Carbohydrate Choice = 1 starch or 1 fruit or 1 milk exchange
* Grams of fiber subtracted from total carbohydrate

MENU ITEM	SERVING SIZE	CALORIES	CALORIES FROM FAT
Iced Raspberry Mocha Blast, small	12 oz	160	30
Iced Raspberry Mocha Blast, medium	16 oz	210	45
Iced Raspberry Mocha Blast, large	24 oz	330	60
Whipped Cream	1.2 oz	160	100

SMART MEAL, AU BON PAIN

Vegetarian Chili, medium
Cracked Pepper Chicken on Country
  Seed Roll

Calories:	570
Fat:	10 grams
Carb Choices:	5½
Exchanges:	5 starch, 4 very lean meat, ½ fat

BLIMPIE

SUBS

☀ Blimpie® Best Sub, 6-inch	1	410	120
Cheese Trio Sub, 6-inch	1	510	200
☀ Club Sub, 6-inch	1	450	120
Five Meatball Sub, 6-inch	1	500	200
☀ Grilled Chicken Sub, 6-inch	1	400	80
☀ Ham & Swiss Sub, 6-inch	1	400	120
Ham, Salami, Provolone Sub, 6-inch	1	590	250
☀ Roast Beef Sub, 6-inch	1	340	40
Steak & Cheese Sub, 6-inch	1	550	230
Tuna Sub, 6-inch	1	570	290
☀ Turkey Sub, 6-inch	1	320	40

CHICKEN

Chicken Fajita	1 (9.8 oz)	420	140
☀ Grilled Chicken Salad (without dressing)	1 (16.3 oz)	350	110

☀ Smart Choice

TOTAL FAT (g)	SATURATED FAT (g)	SODIUM (mg)	PROTEIN (g)	CARBOHYDRATE (g)	CARBOHYDRATE CHOICES	EXCHANGES
4	2	100	6	27	2	1 other carb, 1 2% milk
5	3	140	9	32	2	1½ other carb, 1 2% milk
7	4	200	13	54	3½	2 other carb, 1½ 2% milk
11	8	0	0	11	1	1 other carb, 2 fat

SMART MEAL, AU BON PAIN

Thanksgiving Sub
Grilled Vegetable Salad
Tomato Basil Salad Dressing, Fat Free

Calories: 650
Fat: 6 grams
Carb Choices: 7
Exchanges: 5 starch, 1 other carb, 1 veg, 4 very lean meat

TOTAL FAT (g)	SATURATED FAT (g)	SODIUM (mg)	PROTEIN (g)	CARBOHYDRATE (g)	CARBOHYDRATE CHOICES	EXCHANGES
13	5	1480	26	47	3	3 starch, 2½ med. fat meat
23	13	1060	26	51	3½	3½ starch, 2 med. fat meat, 2 fat
13	6	1350	30	53	3½	3½ starch, 3 med. fat meat
22	8	970	23	52	3½	3½ starch, 2 med. fat meat, 2 fat
9	2	950	28	52	3½	3½ starch, 2½ lean meat
13	7	970	25	47	3	3 starch, 2½ med. fat meat
28	11	1880	32	52	3½	3½ starch, 3½ med. fat meat, 1½ fat
5	1	870	27	42*	3	3 starch, 3 very lean meat
26	4	1080	27	51	3½	3½ starch, 3 med. fat meat, 2 fat
32	5	790	21	50	3	3 starch, 1½ med. fat meat, 4 fat
5	1	890	19	51	3½	3½ starch, 2 lean meat
16	6	520	21	48	3	3 starch, 2 med. fat meat, 1 fat
12	0	1190	47	13	1	1 starch, 6 lean meat

1 Carbohydrate Choice = 1 starch or 1 fruit or 1 milk exchange
* Grams of fiber subtracted from total carbohydrate

MENU ITEM	SERVING SIZE	CALORIES	CALORIES FROM FAT
CONDIMENTS			
Salsa	.75 oz	5	0

BOSTON MARKET

ENTREES

MENU ITEM	SERVING SIZE	CALORIES	CALORIES FROM FAT
Chicken (with skin)	½ chicken (10 oz)	630	330
Chicken, Dark Meat (without skin)	¼ chicken (3.7 oz)	210	90
Chicken, Dark Meat (with skin)	¼ chicken (4.7 oz)	330	200
Chicken, White Meat (with skin)	¼ chicken (5.4 oz)	330	150
Chicken, White Meat (without skin or wing)	¼ chicken (3.7 oz)	160	35
Chunky Chicken Salad	¾ cup (5.5 oz)	370	240
Ham with Cinnamon Apples	1 order (8 oz)	350	110
Meat Loaf & Brown Gravy	1 order (7 oz)	390	200
Meat Loaf & Chunky Tomato Sauce	1 order (8 oz)	370	160
Original Chicken Pot Pie	1 pie (15 oz)	750	300
Skinless Rotisserie Turkey Breast	1 order (5 oz)	170	10

SANDWICHES

MENU ITEM	SERVING SIZE	CALORIES	CALORIES FROM FAT
Chicken Sandwich (no cheese or sauce)	1 (11.5 oz)	430	40
Chicken Sandwich (with cheese and sauce)	1 (12 oz)	750	300
Chicken Salad Sandwich	1 (11.5 oz)	680	270
Ham Sandwich (no cheese or sauce)	1 (9.5 oz)	450	80
Ham Sandwich (with cheese and sauce)	1 (11.5 oz)	760	320
Ham & Turkey Club Sandwich (no cheese or sauce)	1 (9.5 oz)	430	60
Ham & Turkey Club Sandwich (with cheese and sauce)	1 (13.5 oz)	890	400
Meat Loaf Sandwich (no cheese)	1 (12.5 oz)	690	190

 Smart Choice

TOTAL FAT (g)	SATURATED FAT (g)	SODIUM (mg)	PROTEIN (g)	CARBOHYDRATE (g)	CARBOHYDRATE CHOICES	EXCHANGES
0	0	210	0	1	0	free
37	10	960	74	2	0	11 lean meat
10	3	320	28	1	0	4 lean meat
22	6	460	31	2	0	4½ med. fat meat
17	5	530	43	2	0	6 lean meat
4	1	350	31	0	0	4 very lean meat
27	5	800	28	3	0	4 med. fat meat, 1 fat
13	5	1750	25	35	2	2 other carb, 3 med. fat meat
22	8	1040	30	19	1	1 starch, 4 med. fat meat
18	8	1170	30	22	1½	1½ starch, 4 med. fat meat
34	9	2380	34	72*	5	5 starch, 3 med. fat meat, 3 fat
1	<1	850	36	1	0	5 very lean meat
5	1	910	34	57*	4	4 starch, 4 very lean meat
33	12	1860	41	67*	5	5 starch, 4½ med. fat meat, 1 fat
30	5	1360	39	63	4	4 starch, 5 med. fat meat
9	3	1600	25	66	4	4 starch, 3 lean meat
35	13	1880	38	71	5	5 starch, 4 med. fat meat, 2 fat
6	2	1330	29	64	4	4 starch, 3 lean meat
44	20	2350	48	76	5	5 starch, 5 med. fat meat, 2 fat
21	7	1610	40	80*	5	5 starch, 4 med. fat meat

1 Carbohydrate Choice = 1 starch or 1 fruit or 1 milk exchange
* Grams of fiber subtracted from total carbohydrate

MENU ITEM	SERVING SIZE	CALORIES	CALORIES FROM FAT
Meat Loaf Sandwich (with cheese)	1 (13.5 oz)	860	290
Turkey Sandwich (no cheese or sauce)	1 (9.5 oz)	400	30
Turkey Sandwich (with cheese and sauce)	1 (11.5 oz)	710	260

HOT SIDE DISHES

BBQ Baked Beans	¾ cup	330	80
Butternut Squash	¾ cup	160	60
Chicken Gravy	1 (1 oz)	15	10
Creamed Spinach	¾ cup	280	190
Green Bean Casserole	¾ cup	90	40
Homestyle Mashed Potatoes & Gravy	¾ cup	200	80
Hot Cinnamon Apples	¾ cup	250	40
Macaroni & Cheese	¾ cup	280	90
Mashed Potatoes	⅔ cup	180	80
New Potatoes	¾ cup	130	20
Rice Pilaf	⅔ cup	180	45
Steamed Vegetables	⅔ cup	35	5
Stuffing	¾ cup	310	110
Whole Kernel Corn	¾ cup	180	40
Zucchini Marinara	¾ cup	80	40

COLD SIDE DISHES

Caesar Side Salad	1 (4 oz)	210	150
Cole Slaw	¾ cup	280	140
Corn Bread, small loaf	1	200	50
Cranberry Relish	¾ cup	370	45
Fruit Salad	¾ cup	70	5
Honey Wheat Roll	½ roll	150	10

 Smart Choice

TOTAL FAT (g)	SATURATED FAT (g)	SODIUM (mg)	PROTEIN (g)	CARBOHYDRATE (g)	CARBOHYDRATE CHOICES	EXCHANGES
33	16	2270	46	89*	6	6 starch, 5 med. fat meat
4	1	1070	32	61	4	4 starch, 4 very lean meat
28	10	1390	45	68	4½	4½ starch, 5 med. fat meat
9	3	630	11	44*	3	3 starch, 2 fat
6	4	580	2	25	1½	1½ starch, 1 fat
1	0	170	0	2	0	free
21	13	820	9	12	1	3 veg or 1 starch, 1 med. fat meat, 3 fat
5	2	580	2	10	½	2 veg, 1 fat
9	5	560	3	27	2	2 starch, 1½ fat
5	<1	45	0	56	4	4 fruit, 1 fat
10	6	760	12	36	2½	2½ starch, 1 high fat meat
8	5	390	3	25	1½	1½ starch, 1½ fat
3	0	150	3	25	1½	1½ starch
5	1	600	5	32	2	2 starch, 1 fat
1	0	35	2	7	½	1 veg
12	2	1140	6	44	3	3 starch, 2 fat
4	<1	170	5	30	2	2 starch, 1 fat
4	<1	470	2	10	½	2 veg, 1 fat
17	5	560	8	6	0	1 veg, 1 med. fat meat, 2 fat
16	3	520	2	32	2	2 starch, 3 fat
6	2	390	3	33	2	2 starch, 1 fat
5	<1	5	2	79*	5	5½ fruit, 1 fat
1	0	10	1	17	1	1 fruit
2	0	280	5	29	2	2 starch

1 Carbohydrate Choice = 1 starch or 1 fruit or 1 milk exchange
* Grams of fiber subtracted from total carbohydrate

MENU ITEM	SERVING SIZE	CALORIES	CALORIES FROM FAT
Mediterranean Pasta Salad	¾ cup	170	90
Tortellini Salad	¾ cup	380	220
SOUPS			
☀ Chicken Soup	¾ cup	80	25
☀ Chicken Tortilla Soup	1 cup	220	100
SALADS			
Caesar Salad Entree	1 (10 oz)	520	390
☀ Caesar Salad without Dressing	1 (8 oz)	240	120
Chicken Caesar Salad	1 (13 oz)	670	420
DESSERTS			
Brownie	1	450	240
Chocolate Chip Cookie	1	340	150
Oatmeal Raisin Cookie	1	320	110

SMART MEAL, BOSTON MARKET

¼ Chicken, White Meat (no skin or wing)
New Potatoes
Zucchini Marinara
Honey Wheat Roll
Margarine (1 pat)

Calories: 565
Fat: 18 grams
Carb Choices: 4½
Exchanges: 3½ starch, 2 veg, 4 very lean meat, 2 fat

Ham & Turkey Club Sandwich
 (no cheese or sauce)
Fruit Salad

Calories: 500
Fat: 7 grams
Carb Choices: 5½
Exchanges: 4 starch, 1 fruit, 3 lean meat

☀ Smart Choice

TOTAL FAT (g)	SATURATED FAT (g)	SODIUM (mg)	PROTEIN (g)	CARBOHYDRATE (g)	CARBOHYDRATE CHOICES	EXCHANGES
10	3	490	4	16	1	1 starch, 2 fat
24	5	530	14	29	2	2 starch, 1½ med. fat meat, 3 fat
3	1	470	9	4	0	1 veg, 1 lean meat
11	4	1410	10	19	1	1 starch, 1 med. fat meat, 1 fat
43	12	1420	20	16	1	3 veg or 1 starch, 2½ med. fat meat, 6 fat
13	7	780	19	14	1	3 veg or 1 starch, 2½ med. fat meat
47	13	1860	45	16	1	3 veg or 1 starch, 6 med. fat meat, 3 fat
27	7	190	6	47	3	3 other carb, 5 fat
17	6	240	4	48	3	3 other carb, 3 fat
13	3	260	4	48	3	3 other carb, 2½ fat

SMART MEAL, BOSTON MARKET

Skinless Rotisserie Turkey Breast
Homestyle Mashed Potatoes & Gravy
Steamed Vegetables
Fruit Salad

Calories: 475
Fat: 12 grams
Carb Choices: 3½
Exchanges: 2 starch, 1 fruit, 1 veg, 5 very lean meat, 1½ fat

1 Carbohydrate Choice = 1 starch or 1 fruit or 1 milk exchange
* Grams of fiber subtracted from total carbohydrate

MENU ITEM	SERVING SIZE	CALORIES	CALORIES FROM FAT

BRUEGGER'S BAGEL BAKERY
SPECIALTY SANDWICHES (ON PLAIN BAGEL)

MENU ITEM	SERVING SIZE	CALORIES	CALORIES FROM FAT
☼ Chicken Fajita Sandwich	1 (8.8 oz)	460	90
☼ Garden Veggie Sandwich	1 (7.7 oz)	330	20
☼ Herby Turkey™ Sandwich	1 (8.3 oz)	510	120
☼ Hot Shot Turkey™ Sandwich	1 (8.3 oz)	450	70
☼ Leonardo da Veggie™ Sandwich	1 (7.8 oz)	420	100
☼ Roast Turkey Sandwich	1 (10.2 oz)	370	25
☼ Santa Fe Turkey Sandwich	1 (9.3 oz)	450	80

BAGELS

MENU ITEM	SERVING SIZE	CALORIES	CALORIES FROM FAT
☼ Blueberry Bagel	1 (3.6 oz)	300	20
☼ Cinnamon Raisin Bagel	1 (3.6 oz)	290	10
☼ Cranberry Orange Bagel	1 (3.6 oz)	290	10
☼ Egg Bagel	1 (3.6 oz)	280	5
☼ Everything Bagel	1 (3.7 oz)	290	20
☼ Garlic Bagel	1 (3.6 oz)	280	10
☼ Honey Grain Bagel	1 (3.6 oz)	300	25
☼ Onion Bagel	1 (3.6 oz)	280	10
☼ Pesto Bagel	1 (3.6 oz)	280	15
☼ Plain Bagel	1 (3.6 oz)	280	15
☼ Poppyseed Bagel	1 (3.6 oz)	280	15
☼ Pumpernickel Bagel	1 (3.6 oz)	280	15
☼ Salt Bagel	1 (3.6 oz)	270	15
☼ Sesame Bagel	1 (3.6 oz)	290	20
☼ Spinach Bagel	1 (3.6 oz)	280	10
☼ Sun Dried Tomato Bagel	1 (3.6 oz)	280	15
☼ Wheat Bran Bagel	1 (3.6 oz)	280	20

☼ Smart Choice

TOTAL FAT (g)	SATURATED FAT (g)	SODIUM (mg)	PROTEIN (g)	CARBOHYDRATE (g)	CARBOHYDRATE CHOICES	EXCHANGES
10	5	830	28	66	4	4 starch, 3 lean meat
2	0	460	13	65	4	4 starch, 1 very lean meat
13	5	1100	30	67	4½	4½ starch, 3 lean meat
8	4	1090	26	68	4½	4½ starch, 2 lean meat
11	6	690	19	62	4	4 starch, 2 med. fat meat
3	<1	1140	26	61	4	4 starch, 3 very lean meat
9	4	1040	27	63	4	4 starch, 3 lean meat
2	0	480	10	60	4	4 starch
2	0	400	10	60	4	4 starch
1	0	470	10	61	4	4 starch
1	<1	510	10	57	4	4 starch
2	0	700	11	58	4	4 starch
2	0	440	10	57	4	4 starch
3	<1	390	11	58	4	4 starch
2	0	430	10	57	4	4 starch
2	0	480	10	55	4	4 starch
2	0	430	10	56	4	4 starch
2	0	440	11	57	4	4 starch
2	0	390	11	56	4	4 starch
2	0	1670	10	55	4	4 starch
3	<1	440	11	57	4	4 starch
1	0	490	11	56	4	4 starch
2	0	490	10	56	4	4 starch
2	0	410	10	50*	3½	3½ starch

1 Carbohydrate Choice = 1 starch or 1 fruit or 1 milk exchange
* Grams of fiber subtracted from total carbohydrate

MENU ITEM	SERVING SIZE	CALORIES	CALORIES FROM FAT
CREAM CHEESE			
Bacon Scallion Cream Cheese	1 oz	100	70
Chive Cream Cheese	1 oz	100	80
Garden Veggie Cream Cheese	1 oz	100	70
☀ Garden Veggie Cream Cheese, Light	1 oz	50	30
☀ Herb Garlic Cream Cheese, Light	1 oz	60	35
Honey Walnut Cream Cheese	1 oz	100	70
Jalapeno Cream Cheese	1 oz	100	80
Plain Cream Cheese	1 oz	100	80
☀ Plain Cream Cheese, Light	1 oz	70	40
Salmon Cream Cheese	1 oz	100	80
☀ Strawberry Cream Cheese, Light	1 oz	60	30
Wildberry Cream Cheese	1 oz	100	80
SANDWICH MEATS			
☀ Oven Roasted Beef	1 serving (2.5 oz)	150	13
☀ Oven Roasted Turkey	1 serving (2.5 oz)	63	13
☀ Smoked Honey Ham	1 serving (2.5 oz)	75	25
☀ Smoked Turkey Breast	1 serving (2.5 oz)	63	13

☀ Smart Choice

TOTAL FAT (g)	SATURATED FAT (g)	SODIUM (mg)	PROTEIN (g)	CARBOHYDRATE (g)	CARBOHYDRATE CHOICES	EXCHANGES
8	5	95	2	3	0	2 fat
9	5	85	2	2	0	2 fat
8	5	100	2	4	0	2 fat
4	3	60	3	2	0	1 fat
4	2	75	3	2	0	1 fat
8	5	95	2	3	0	2 fat
9	5	100	2	3	0	2 fat
9	6	65	2	2	0	2 fat
5	3	95	4	3	0	1 fat
9	4	100	2	2	0	2 fat
4	2	70	3	3	0	1 fat
9	5	85	2	4	0	2 fat
1	0	375	13	0	0	2 very lean meat
1	0	725	10	0	0	1½ very lean meat
3	0	950	13	0	0	2 very lean meat
1	0	725	10	0	0	1½ very lean meat

1 Carbohydrate Choice = 1 starch or 1 fruit or 1 milk exchange
* Grams of fiber subtracted from total carbohydrate

MENU ITEM	SERVING SIZE	CALORIES	CALORIES FROM FAT

BURGER KING
SANDWICHES

BK Big Fish™ Sandwich	1 (8.9 oz)	700	370
BK Broiler® Chicken Sandwich	1 (8.7 oz)	550	260
Cheeseburger	1 (4.8 oz)	380	170
Chicken Sandwich	1 (8 oz)	710	390
Double Cheeseburger	1 (7.4 oz)	600	320
Double Cheeseburger with Bacon	1 (7.6 oz)	640	350
Double Whopper® Sandwich	1 (12.3 oz)	870	500
Double Whopper® with Cheese Sandwich	1 (13.1 oz)	960	570
Hamburger	1 (4.4 oz)	330	140
Whopper Jr.® Sandwich	1 (5.7 oz)	420	220
Whopper Jr.® with Cheese Sandwich	1 (6.2 oz)	460	250
Whopper® Sandwich	1 (9.5 oz)	640	350
Whopper® with Cheese Sandwich	1 (10.1 oz)	730	410

OTHER ENTREES

☀ Chicken Tenders®	8 (4.1 oz)	310	150

SIDE ORDERS

Coated French Fries, medium (salted)	1 order (3.6 oz)	340	150
French Fries, medium (salted)	1 order (4.1 oz)	370	180
Onion Rings	1 order (4.3 oz)	310	130

SALADS

☀ Broiled Chicken Salad	1 (10.6 oz)	200	90
☀ Garden Salad	1 (7.5 oz)	100	45
☀ Side Salad	1 (4.7 oz)	60	25

☀ Smart Choice

TOTAL FAT (g)	SATURATED FAT (g)	SODIUM (mg)	PROTEIN (g)	CARBOHYDRATE (g)	CARBOHYDRATE CHOICES	EXCHANGES
41	6	980	26	56	4	4 starch, 2½ med. fat meat, 5 fat
29	6	480	30	41	3	3 starch, 3½ med. fat meat, 2 fat
19	9	770	23	28	2	2 starch, 2½ med. fat meat, 1 fat
43	9	1400	26	54	3½	3½ starch, 3 med. fat meat, 5 fat
36	17	1060	41	28	2	2 starch, 5 med. fat meat, 2 fat
39	18	1240	44	28	2	2 starch, 5½ med. fat meat, 2 fat
56	19	940	46	45	3	3 starch, 5½ med. fat meat, 4 fat
63	24	1420	52	46	3	3 starch, 6½ med. fat meat, 5½ fat
15	6	530	20	28	2	2 starch, 2 med. fat meat, 1 fat
24	8	530	21	29	2	2 starch, 2½ med. fat meat, 2 fat
28	10	770	23	29	2	2 starch, 2½ med. fat meat, 2½ fat
39	11	870	27	45	3	3 starch, 3 med. fat meat, 4 fat
46	16	1350	33	46	3	3 starch, 4 med. fat meat, 4 fat
17	4	710	21	19	1	1 starch, 3 med. fat meat
17	5	680	0	43	3	3 starch, 2½ fat
20	5	240	5	43	3	3 starch, 3 fat
14	2	810	4	35*	2	2½ starch, 2½ fat
10	4	110	21	7	½	½ starch or 2 veg, 3 lean meat
5	3	110	6	7	½	½ starch or 2 veg, 1 med. fat meat
3	2	55	3	4	0	1 veg, 1 fat

1 Carbohydrate Choice = 1 starch or 1 fruit or 1 milk exchange
* Grams of fiber subtracted from total carbohydrate

MENU ITEM	SERVING SIZE	CALORIES	CALORIES FROM FAT
SALAD DRESSINGS			
Bleu Cheese Salad Dressing	1.1 oz	160	140
French Salad Dressing	1.1 oz	140	90
Ranch Salad Dressing	1.1 oz	180	170
🔆 Italian Salad Dressing, Reduced Calorie Light	1.1 oz	15	5
Thousand Island Salad Dressing	1.1 oz	140	110
CONDIMENTS			
🔆 Bacon Bits	0.1 oz	15	10
🔆 Barbecue Dipping Sauce	1 oz	35	0
🔆 Bull's Eye® Barbecue Sauce	0.5 oz	20	0
🔆 Croutons	0.2 oz	30	10
🔆 Dip, A.M. Express®	1 oz	80	0
🔆 Grape Jam, A.M. Express®	0.4 oz	30	0
🔆 Honey Dipping Sauce	1 oz	90	0
🔆 Ketchup	0.5 oz	15	0
Land O'Lakes® Whipped Classic Blend	0.4 oz	65	65
🔆 Lettuce	0.7 oz	0	0
Mayonnaise	1 oz	210	210
🔆 Mustard	0.1 oz	0	0
🔆 Onion	0.5 oz	5	0
🔆 Pickles	0.5 oz	0	0
Processed American Cheese	0.9 oz	90	70
Ranch Dipping Sauce	1 oz	170	160
🔆 Strawberry Jam, A.M. Express®	0.4 oz	30	0
🔆 Sweet & Sour Dipping Sauce	1 oz	45	0
Tartar Sauce	1 oz	180	175
🔆 Tomato	1 oz	5	0

 Smart Choice

TOTAL FAT (g)	SATURATED FAT (g)	SODIUM (mg)	PROTEIN (g)	CARBOHYDRATE (g)	CARBOHYDRATE CHOICES	EXCHANGES
16	4	260	2	1	0	3 fat
10	2	190	0	11	1	1 other carb, 2 fat
19	4	170	<1	2	0	4 fat
1	0	50	0	3	0	free
12	3	190	0	7	½	½ other carb, 2 fat
1	<1	0	1	0	0	free
0	0	400	0	9	½	½ other carb
0	0	140	0	5	0	free
1	0	75	<1	4	0	free
0	0	20	0	21	1½	1½ other carb
0	0	0	0	7	½	½ other carb
0	0	10	0	23	1½	1½ other carb
0	0	180	0	4	0	free
7	1	75	0	0	0	1 fat
0	0	0	0	0	0	free
23	3	160	0	<1	0	5 fat
0	0	40	0	0	0	free
0	0	0	0	1	0	free
0	0	140	0	0	0	free
8	5	420	6	0	0	1 high fat meat
17	3	200	0	2	0	3 fat
0	0	5	0	8	½	½ other carb
0	0	50	0	11	1	1 other carb
19	3	220	0	0	0	4 fat
0	0	0	0	1	0	free

1 Carbohydrate Choice = 1 starch or 1 fruit or 1 milk exchange
* Grams of fiber subtracted from total carbohydrate

MENU ITEM	SERVING SIZE	CALORIES	CALORIES FROM FAT
DESSERTS			
Dutch Apple Pie	1 (4 oz)	300	140
SHAKES			
Chocolate Shake, medium	10 oz	320	60
Strawberry Shake, medium	12 oz	420	50
Vanilla Shake, medium	10 oz	300	50
SOFT DRINKS			
Coca-Cola Classic®, medium	22 oz	280	0
Diet Coke®, medium	22 oz	1	0
Sprite®, medium	22 oz	260	0
OTHER BEVERAGES			
Coffee, black	12.4 oz	5	0
Milk, 2%	8.5 oz	130	45
Orange Juice, Tropicana®	10.9 oz	140	0
BREAKFAST			
Biscuit with Bacon, Egg and Cheese	6 oz	510	280
Biscuit with Sausage	5.3 oz	590	360
Croissan'wich® with Sausage, Egg & Cheese	6.2 oz	600	410
French Toast Sticks	4.9 oz	500	240
Hash Browns	2.5 oz	220	110

SMART MEAL, BURGER KING

Hamburger with lettuce, tomato, pickles, ketchup
Side Salad
Italian Salad Dressing, Reduced Calorie Light (1.1 oz)
Diet Soft Drink

Calories: 425
Fat: 19 grams
Carb Choices: 2½
Exchanges: 2 starch, 1 veg, 2 med. fat meat, 2 fat

Smart Choice

TOTAL FAT (g)	SATURATED FAT (g)	SODIUM (mg)	PROTEIN (g)	CARBOHYDRATE (g)	CARBOHYDRATE CHOICES	EXCHANGES
15	3	230	3	39	2½	2½ other carb, 3 fat
7	4	230	9	54	3½	3½ other carb, 1 fat
6	4	260	9	83	5½	5½ other carb, 1 fat
6	4	230	9	53	3½	3½ other carb, 1 fat
0	0	NA	0	70	4½	4½ other carb
0	0	NA	0	<1	0	free
0	0	NA	0	66	4½	4½ other carb
0	0	5	0	1	0	free
5	3	120	8	12	1	1 2% milk
0	0	0	2	33	2	2 fruit
31	10	1530	19	39	2½	2½ starch, 2 med. fat meat, 4 fat
40	13	1390	16	41	3	3 starch, 1½ med. fat meat, 6 fat
46	16	1140	22	25	1½	1½ starch, 3 med. fat meat, 6 fat
27	7	490	4	60	4	4 starch, 4 fat
12	3	320	2	25	1½	1½ starch, 2 fat

1 Carbohydrate Choice = 1 starch or 1 fruit or 1 milk exchange
* Grams of fiber subtracted from total carbohydrate

MENU ITEM	SERVING SIZE	CALORIES	CALORIES FROM FAT

CARL'S JR.

SANDWICHES

	MENU ITEM	SERVING SIZE	CALORIES	CALORIES FROM FAT
☀	BBQ Chicken Sandwich	1 (6.75 oz)	310	50
☀	Big Burger	1 (6.75 oz)	470	180
	Carl's Catch Fish Sandwich™	1 (7.5 oz)	560	270
	Chicken Club Sandwich	1 (8.75 oz)	550	260
	Double Western Bacon Cheeseburger®	1 (11.5 oz)	970	510
	Famous Big Star™ Hamburger	1 (8.5 oz)	610	340
	Hamburger	1 (3 oz)	200	70
	Hot & Crispy Sandwich	1 (5 oz)	400	200
	Santa Fe Chicken Sandwich	1 (8 oz)	530	260
	Super Star® Hamburger	1 (11.25 oz)	820	480
	Western Bacon Cheeseburger®	1 (8 oz)	870	315

GREAT STUFF™ POTATOES

	MENU ITEM	SERVING SIZE	CALORIES	CALORIES FROM FAT
	Bacon & Cheese Stuffed Potato	1 (14.5 oz)	630	260
	Broccoli & Cheese Stuffed Potato	1 (14.5 oz)	530	190
☀	Plain Potato	1 (9.5 oz)	290	0
	Sour Cream & Chive Stuffed Potato	1 (11 oz)	430	130

SIDE ORDERS

MENU ITEM	SERVING SIZE	CALORIES	CALORIES FROM FAT
Chicken Stars, 6-piece	1 order (3 oz)	230	130
CrissCut Fries®, large	1 order (5.75 oz)	550	310
French Fries, regular	1 order (4.5 oz)	370	180
Hash Brown Nuggets	1 order (3.25 oz)	270	150
Onion Rings	1 order (5.25 oz)	520	230
Zucchini	1 order (6 oz)	380	210

☀ Smart Choice

TOTAL FAT (g)	SATURATED FAT (g)	SODIUM (mg)	PROTEIN (g)	CARBOHYDRATE (g)	CARBOHYDRATE CHOICES	EXCHANGES
6	2	830	31	34	2	2 starch, 4 very lean meat
20	8	810	25	46	3	3 starch, 3 med. fat meat
30	7	1220	17	49*	3	3 starch, 2 med. fat meat, 4 fat
29	8	1160	35	37	2½	2½ starch, 4 med. fat meat, 2 fat
57	27	1810	56	58	4	4 starch, 7 med. fat meat, 4 fat
38	11	890	26	42	3	3 starch, 3 med. fat meat, 4 fat
8	4	500	11	23	1½	1½ starch, 1 high fat meat
22	5	980	14	35	2	2 starch, 2 med. fat meat, 2 fat
30	7	1230	30	36	2½	2½ starch, 3½ med. fat meat, 2 fat
53	20	1030	43	41	3	3 starch, 5 med. fat meat, 5 fat
35	16	1490	34	59	4	4 starch, 4 med. fat meat, 3 fat
29	7	1720	20	70*	4½	4½ starch, 2 med. fat meat, 3 fat
22	5	930	11	68*	4½	4½ starch, 4 fat
0	0	40	6	62*	4	4 starch
14	3	160	8	64*	4	4 starch, 3 fat
14	3	450	13	11	1	1 starch, 1½ med. fat meat, 1 fat
34	9	1280	7	55	3½	3½ starch, 6 fat
20	7	240	4	44	3	3 starch, 3 fat
17	4	410	3	27	2	2 starch, 3 fat
26	6	840	8	63	4	4 starch, 5 fat
23	6	1040	7	38	2½	2½ starch, 4 fat

1 Carbohydrate Choice = 1 starch or 1 fruit or 1 milk exchange
* Grams of fiber subtracted from total carbohydrate

MENU ITEM	SERVING SIZE	CALORIES	CALORIES FROM FAT
SALADS			
☼ Charbroiled Chicken Salad-To-Go™	1 (12 oz)	260	80
☼ Garden Salad-To-Go™	1 (4.75 oz)	50	25
SALAD DRESSINGS			
Blue Cheese Salad Dressing	2 oz	310	310
☼ French Salad Dressing, Fat Free	2 oz	70	0
House Salad Dressing	2 oz	220	200
☼ Italian Salad Dressing, Fat Free	2 oz	15	0
Thousand Island Salad Dressing	2 oz	250	220
CONDIMENTS			
American Cheese	1 slice (0.5 oz)	60	45
☼ BBQ Sauce	1 oz	50	0
☼ Breadsticks	0.25 oz	35	5
☼ Croutons	0.25 oz	35	10
☼ Grape Jelly	0.5 oz	35	0
☼ Honey Sauce	1 oz	90	0
☼ Mustard Sauce	1 oz	45	5
☼ Salsa	1 oz	10	0
☼ Strawberry Jam	0.5 oz	35	0
☼ Sweet N'Sour Sauce	1 oz	50	0
Swiss Cheese	1 slice (0.5 oz)	45	30
☼ Table Syrup	1 oz	90	0
DESSERTS			
Cheese Danish	1 (4 oz)	400	200
Cheesecake (Strawberry Swirl)	1 (3.5 oz)	300	160
Chocolate Cake	1 (3 oz)	300	90

☼ Smart Choice

TOTAL FAT (g)	SATURATED FAT (g)	SODIUM (mg)	PROTEIN (g)	CARBOHYDRATE (g)	CARBOHYDRATE CHOICES	EXCHANGES
9	5	530	28	11	1	2 veg or 1 starch, 3½ lean meat
3	2	75	3	4	0	1 veg
34	6	360	2	1	0	7 fat
0	0	760	0	18	1	1 other carb
22	4	440	1	3	0	4 fat
0	0	800	0	4	0	free
24	4	540	<1	7	½	½ other carb, 4 fat
5	3	270	3	0	0	1 fat
0	0	270	<1	11	1	1 other carb
<1	0	60	1	7	½	½ starch
1	0	65	<1	5	0	free
0	0	0	0	9	½	½ other carb
0	0	5	0	23	1½	1½ other carb
<1	0	150	0	10	½	½ other carb
0	0	160	0	2	0	free
0	0	0	0	9	½	½ other carb
0	0	60	0	11	1	1 other carb
4	3	220	3	0	0	1 fat
0	0	5	0	22	1½	1½ other carb
22	5	390	5	49	3	3 other carb, 4 fat
17	9	220	6	31	2	2 other carb, 3 fat
10	3	260	3	49	3	3 other carb, 2 fat

1 Carbohydrate Choice = 1 starch or 1 fruit or 1 milk exchange
* Grams of fiber subtracted from total carbohydrate

MENU ITEM	SERVING SIZE	CALORIES	CALORIES FROM FAT
Chocolate Chip Cookie	1 (2.5 oz)	370	170
SHAKES			
Chocolate Shake, small	13.5 oz	390	60
Strawberry Shake, small	13.5 oz	400	60
Vanilla Shake, small	13.5 oz	330	70
SOFT DRINKS			
Coca-Cola Classic®, regular	16 oz	190	0
Diet 7 Up®, regular	16 oz	0	0
Diet Coke®, regular	16 oz	0	0
Dr. Pepper®, regular	16 oz	200	0
Minute Maid® Orange Soda, regular	16 oz	230	0
Ramblin® Root Beer, regular	16 oz	230	0
Sprite®, regular	16 oz	190	0
OTHER BEVERAGES			
Coffee, black	12 oz	10	0
Hot Chocolate, regular	12 oz	110	10
Iced Tea, regular	14 oz	5	0
Orange Juice	6 oz	90	0
Milk, 1%	10 oz	150	30
BREAKFAST			
Bacon	2 pieces	40	35
Blueberry Muffin	1 (4.25 oz)	340	120
Bran Muffin	1 (4.75 oz)	370	120
Breakfast Burrito	1 (5.25 oz)	430	230
Breakfast Quesadilla	1 (5 oz)	300	130
Cinnamon Roll	1 (4.25 oz)	420	120

 Smart Choice

TOTAL FAT (g)	SATURATED FAT (g)	SODIUM (mg)	PROTEIN (g)	CARBOHYDRATE (g)	CARBOHYDRATE CHOICES	EXCHANGES
19	8	350	3	49	3	3 other carb, 3 fat
7	5	280	9	74	5	5 other carb, 1 fat
7	5	240	9	77	5	5 other carb, 1 fat
8	5	250	11	54	3½	3½ other carb, 1 fat
0	0	50	0	51	3½	3½ other carb
0	0	90	0	1	0	free
0	0	40	0	0	0	free
0	0	30	0	52	3½	3½ other carb
0	0	30	0	59	4	4 other carb
0	0	75	0	61	4	4 other carb
0	0	90	0	48	3	3 other carb
0	0	25	1	1	0	free
1	0	125	1	24	1½	1½ other carb
0	0	55	0	0	0	free
0	0	0	1	20	1	1 fruit
3	2	180	14	18	1	1 1% milk
4	2	125	3	0	0	1 fat
14	2	340	5	49	3	3 starch, 3½ fat
13	2	410	7	55*	3½	3½ starch, 2 fat
26	12	810	22	29	2	2 starch, 2½ med. fat meat, 2 fat
14	6	750	14	27	2	2 starch, 2 med. fat meat
13	4	570	9	68	4½	4½ other carb, 2 fat

1 Carbohydrate Choice = 1 starch or 1 fruit or 1 milk exchange
* Grams of fiber subtracted from total carbohydrate

MENU ITEM	SERVING SIZE	CALORIES	CALORIES FROM FAT
English Muffin with Margarine	1 (2.5 oz)	230	90
French Toast Dips® (syrup not included)	1 order (3.75 oz)	410	230
Sausage	1 patty	200	160
Scrambled Eggs	1 order (3.5 oz)	160	100
Sunrise Sandwich®	1 (4.5 oz)	370	190

SMART MEAL, CARL'S JR.

BBQ Chicken Sandwich
Garden Salad-To-Go™
Italian Salad Dressing, Fat Free (2 oz)
Milk, 1% (10 oz)

Calories: 525
Fat: 12 grams
Carb Choices: 4
Exchanges: 2 starch, 1 veg,
1 1% milk,
4 very lean meat

 Smart Choice

Total Fat (g)	Saturated Fat (g)	Sodium (mg)	Protein (g)	Carbohydrate (g)	Carbohydrate Choices	Exchanges
10	2	330	5	30	2	2 starch, 2 fat
25	6	380	6	40	2½	2½ starch, 5 fat
18	7	530	7	0	0	1 high fat meat, 2 fat
11	4	125	13	1	0	2 med. fat meat
21	6	710	14	31	2	2 starch, 2 med. fat meat, 2 fat

SMART MEAL, CARL'S JR.

Breakfast Quesadilla
Orange Juice (6 oz)

Calories: 390
Fat: 14 grams
Carb Choices: 3
Exchanges: 2 starch, 1 fruit, 2 med. fat meat

1 Carbohydrate Choice = 1 starch or 1 fruit or 1 milk exchange
* Grams of fiber subtracted from total carbohydrate

MENU ITEM	SERVING SIZE	CALORIES	CALORIES FROM FAT
CHICK-FIL-A			
SANDWICHES			
Chargrilled Chicken Club Sandwich (no dressing)	1 (8.2 oz)	390	110
Chargrilled Chicken Deluxe Sandwich	1 (7.4 oz)	290	30
Chicken Deluxe Sandwich	1 (8 oz)	300	80
Chick-fil-A Chargrilled Chicken Sandwich®	1 (5.3 oz)	280	30
Chick-fil-A® Chicken Salad Sandwich (on whole wheat)	1 (5.9 oz)	320	40
Chick-fil-A® Chicken Sandwich	1 (5.9 oz)	290	80
Chick-n-Q® Sandwich	1 (6.1 oz)	370	120
OTHER ENTREES			
Chick-fil-A Chick-n-Strips®	4 (4.2 oz)	230	70
Chick-fil-A Nuggets®	8 (3.9 oz)	290	130
SIDE ORDERS			
Chick-fil-A Waffle Potato Fries®, small (salted)	1 order (3 oz)	290	90
Chick-fil-A Waffle Potato Fries®, small (unsalted by request)	1 order (3 oz)	290	90
SOUPS			
Hearty Breast of Chicken Soup	1 cup	110	10
SALADS			
Carrot & Raisin Salad, small	1 (2.7 oz)	150	20
Chargrilled Chicken Garden Salad	1 (14 oz)	170	30
Chicken Salad Plate	1 (16.5 oz)	290	40
Chick-n-Strips Salad	1 (15.9 oz)	290	80
Tossed Salad	1 (4.6 oz)	70	0

 Smart Choice

TOTAL FAT (g)	SATURATED FAT (g)	SODIUM (mg)	PROTEIN (g)	CARBOHYDRATE (g)	CARBOHYDRATE CHOICES	EXCHANGES
12	5	980	33	38	2½	2½ starch, 4 lean meat
3	1	640	28	38	2½	2½ starch, 3 very lean meat
9	2	870	25	31	2	2 starch, 3 lean meat
3	1	640	27	36	2½	2½ starch, 3 very lean meat
5	2	810	25	42	3	3 starch, 3 very lean meat
9	2	870	24	29	2	2 starch, 3 lean meat
13	3	1040	25	36	2½	2½ starch, 2½ med. fat meat
8	2	380	29	10	½	½ starch, 4 lean meat
14	3	770	28	12	1	1 starch, 4 lean meat
10	4	960	1	49	3	3 starch, 2 fat
10	4	80	1	49	3	3 starch, 2 fat
1	0	760	16	10	½	½ starch, 1 very lean meat
2	0	650	5	28	2	2 starch or 2 veg, 1 fruit
3	1	650	26	5*	0	1 veg, 4 very lean meat
5	0	570	21	34*	2	2 starch, 3 lean meat
9	2	430	32	16*	1	1 starch, 4 lean meat
0	0	0	5	13	1	1 starch or 3 veg

1 Carbohydrate Choice = 1 starch or 1 fruit or 1 milk exchange
* Grams of fiber subtracted from total carbohydrate

MENU ITEM	SERVING SIZE	CALORIES	CALORIES FROM FAT
☀ Cole Slaw, small	1 (2.8 oz)	130	50
DESSERTS			
Cheesecake	1 slice (3.1 oz)	270	190
Cheesecake with Blueberry Topping	1 slice (4.1 oz)	290	210
Cheesecake with Strawberry Topping	1 slice (4.1 oz)	290	210
Fudge Nut Brownie	1 (2.6 oz)	350	140
☀ Icedream®, small cone	1 (4.5 oz)	140	35
Icedream®, small cup	1 (7.5 oz)	350	90
Lemon Pie	1 slice (3.5 oz)	280	200
SOFT DRINKS			
Coca-Cola Classic®	9 oz	110	0
Diet Coke®	9 oz	0	0
OTHER BEVERAGES			
Iced Tea (sweetened)	9 oz	150	0
Iced Tea (unsweetened)	9 oz	0	0
Lemonade	9 oz	90	0
Lemonade, Diet	9 oz	5	0

SMART MEAL, CHICK-FIL-A

Chargrilled Chicken Deluxe Sandwich
Carrot & Raisin Salad
Icedream® cone, small
Iced Tea (unsweetened)

Calories: 580
Fat: 9 grams
Carb Choices: 5½
Exchanges: 4½ starch,
1 other carb,
3 very lean meat,
1 fat

☀ Smart Choice

TOTAL FAT (g)	SATURATED FAT (g)	SODIUM (mg)	PROTEIN (g)	CARBOHYDRATE (g)	CARBOHYDRATE CHOICES	EXCHANGES
6	1	430	6	11	1	1 starch or 3 veg, 1 fat
21	9	510	13	7	½	½ other carb, 2 med. fat meat, 2 fat
23	10	550	14	9	½	½ other carb, 2 med. fat meat, 2 fat
23	10	580	14	8	½	½ other carb, 2 med. fat meat, 2 fat
16	3	650	10	41	3	3 other carb, 3 fat
4	1	240	11	16	1	1 other carb, 1 fat
10	3	390	16	50	3	3 other carb, 2 fat
22	6	550	1	19	1	1 other carb, 4 fat
0	0	10	0	28	2	2 other carb
0	0	10	0	0	0	free
0	0	50	0	38	2½	2½ other carb
0	0	50	0	0	0	free
0	0	4	0	23	1½	1½ other carb
0	0	4	0	2	0	free

SMART MEAL, CHICK-FIL-A

Hearty Breast of Chicken Soup
Chicken Salad Plate
Diet Lemonade

Calories: 405
Fat: 6 grams
Carb Choices: 3
Exchanges: 2½ starch, 4 lean meat

1 Carbohydrate Choice = 1 starch or 1 fruit or 1 milk exchange
* Grams of fiber subtracted from total carbohydrate

MENU ITEM	SERVING SIZE	CALORIES	CALORIES FROM FAT

CHURCH'S CHICKEN
CHICKEN PIECES

☀ Breast	1 (2.8 oz)	200	112
☀ Leg	1 (2 oz)	140	82
Thigh	1 (2.8 oz)	230	146
☀ Wing	1 (3.1 oz)	250	145

CHICKEN TENDER STRIPS™

☀ Chicken Tender Strips™, 4-piece	4.4 oz	320	144
☀ Chicken Tender Strips™, 5-piece	5.5 oz	400	180
Chicken Tender Strips™, 15-piece	16.5 oz	1,200	540

SIDE ORDERS

☀ Cajun Rice	1 order (3.1 oz)	130	63
☀ Potatoes & Gravy	1 order (3.7 oz)	90	30

SMART MEAL, CHURCH'S CHICKEN

Chicken Tender Strips, 4-piece
Potatoes & Gravy
(Add fresh vegetables or fruit)

Calories: 410
Fat: 19 grams
Carb Choices: 2½
Exchanges: 2 starch,
3 med. fat meat

☀ Smart Choice

TOTAL FAT (g)	SATURATED FAT (g)	SODIUM (mg)	PROTEIN (g)	CARBOHYDRATE (g)	CARBOHYDRATE CHOICES	EXCHANGES
12	NA	510	19	4	0	3 med. fat meat
9	NA	160	12	2	0	2 med. fat meat
16	NA	520	16	5	0	2 med. fat meat, 1 fat
16	NA	540	19	8	½	½ starch, 2½ med. fat meat
16	NA	560	24	18	1	1 starch, 3 med. fat meat
20	NA	700	30	23	1½	1½ starch, 4 med. fat meat
60	NA	2100	90	68	4½	4½ starch, 12 med. fat meat
7	NA	260	1	16	1	1 starch, 1 fat
3	NA	520	1	14	1	1 starch

1 Carbohydrate Choice = 1 starch or 1 fruit or 1 milk exchange
* Grams of fiber subtracted from total carbohydrate

MENU ITEM	SERVING SIZE	CALORIES	CALORIES FROM FAT

DAIRY QUEEN/ BRAZIER

SANDWICHES

☀ Chicken Breast Fillet Sandwich	1 (6.75 oz)	430	180
Chicken Breast Fillet Sandwich with Cheese	1 (7.25 oz)	480	230
DQ® Homestyle® Bacon Double Cheeseburger	1 (9 oz)	610	320
DQ® Homestyle® Cheeseburger	1 (5.4 oz)	340	150
☀ DQ® Homestyle® Hamburger	1 (4.9 oz)	290	110
☀ DQ® Homestyle® Deluxe Double Hamburger	1 (7.5 oz)	440	200
DQ® Homestyle® Deluxe Double Cheeseburger	1 (8.5 oz)	540	280
DQ® Homestyle® Double Cheeseburger	1 (7.75 oz)	540	280
DQ® Homestyle® Ultimate Burger	1 (9.5 oz)	670	390
Fish Fillet Sandwich	1 (6 oz)	370	150
Fish Fillet Sandwich with Cheese	1 (6.5 oz)	420	190
☀ Grilled Chicken Breast Fillet Sandwich	1 (6.5 oz)	310	90

HOT DOGS/CHILI DOGS

Cheese Dog	1 (4 oz)	290	160
Chili Dog	1 (4.5 oz)	280	150
Chili 'n Cheese Dog	1 (5 oz)	330	190
Hot Dog	1 (3.5 oz)	240	120

CHICKEN STRIPS

Chicken Strip Basket with BBQ Sauce	1 basket (10.25 oz)	810	330
Chicken Strip Basket with Gravy	1 (13 oz)	860	380

SIDE ORDERS

French Fries, small	1 order (2.5 oz)	210	90

☀ Smart Choice

TOTAL FAT (g)	SATURATED FAT (g)	SODIUM (mg)	PROTEIN (g)	CARBOHYDRATE (g)	CARBOHYDRATE CHOICES	EXCHANGES
20	4	760	24	37	2½	2½ starch, 3 med. fat meat
25	7	980	27	38	2½	2½ starch, 3 med. fat meat, 2 fat
36	18	1380	41	31	2	2 starch, 5 med. fat meat, 2 fat
17	8	850	20	29	2	2 starch, 2 med. fat meat, 1 fat
12	5	630	17	29	2	2 starch, 2 med. fat meat
22	10	680	30	29	2	2 starch, 4 med. fat meat
31	16	1130	36	31	2	2 starch, 4 med. fat meat, 2 fat
31	16	1130	35	30	2	2 starch, 4 med. fat meat, 2 fat
43	19	1210	40	29	2	2 starch, 5 med. fat meat, 3 fat
16	4	630	16	39	2½	2½ starch, 2 med. fat meat, 1 fat
21	6	850	19	40	2½	2½ starch, 2 med. fat meat, 2 fat
10	3	1040	24	30	2	2 starch, 3 lean meat
18	8	950	12	20	1	1 starch, 1 med. fat meat, 3 fat
16	6	870	12	21	1½	1½ starch, 1 med. fat meat, 2 fat
21	9	1090	14	22	1½	1½ starch, 1 med. fat meat, 3 fat
14	5	730	9	19	1	1 starch, 1 med. fat meat, 2 fat
37	9	1590	33	83*	5½	5½ starch, 3 med. fat meat, 3 fat
42	11	1820	35	83*	6	6 starch, 3 med. fat meat, 4 fat
10	2	115	3	29	2	2 starch, 2 fat

1 Carbohydrate Choice = 1 starch or 1 fruit or 1 milk exchange
* Grams of fiber subtracted from total carbohydrate

MENU ITEM	SERVING SIZE	CALORIES	CALORIES FROM FAT
French Fries, regular	1 order (3.5 oz)	300	120
French Fries, large	1 order (4.5 oz)	390	160
Onion Rings	1 order (3 oz)	240	110
ICE CREAM			
DQ® Chocolate Soft Serve	½ cup (3.3 oz)	150	45
DQ® Vanilla Soft Serve	½ cup (3.3 oz)	140	40
NONFAT FROZEN YOGURT			
Cup of Yogurt, regular	1 (7 oz)	230	5
Yogurt Cone, regular	1 (7.5 oz)	280	10
CONES			
Chocolate Cone, small	1 (5 oz)	240	70
Chocolate Cone, regular	1 (7.5 oz)	360	100
Dipped Cone, small	1 (5.5 oz)	340	150
Dipped Cone, regular	1 (8.25 oz)	510	220
Vanilla Cone, small	1 (5 oz)	230	60
Vanilla Cone, regular	1 (7.5 oz)	350	90
Vanilla Cone, large	1 (9 oz)	410	110
SUNDAES			
Chocolate Sundae, small	1 (6 oz)	290	60
Chocolate Sundae, regular	1 (8.5 oz)	410	90
Yogurt Strawberry Sundae, regular	1 (8 oz)	300	5
MISTY®			
Misty® Slush, small	16 oz	220	0
Misty® Slush, regular	20 oz	290	0
Strawberry Misty® Cooler	12 oz	190	0

 Smart Choice

TOTAL FAT (g)	SATURATED FAT (g)	SODIUM (mg)	PROTEIN (g)	CARBOHYDRATE (g)	CARBOHYDRATE CHOICES	EXCHANGES
14	3	160	4	40	2½	2½ starch, 2½ fat
18	4	200	5	46*	3	3 starch, 3 fat
12	3	135	4	29	2	2 starch, 2 fat
5	4	75	4	22	1½	1½ other carb, 1 fat
5	3	70	3	22	1½	1½ other carb, 1 fat
<1	0	160	8	49	3	3 other carb
1	<1	170	9	59	4	4 other carb
8	5	115	6	37	2½	2½ other carb, 1 fat
11	8	180	9	56	4	4 other carb, 2 fat
17	9	130	6	42	3	3 other carb, 3 fat
25	13	200	9	63	4	4 other carb, 5 fat
7	5	115	6	38	2½	2½ other carb, 1 fat
10	7	170	8	57	4	4 other carb, 2 fat
12	8	200	10	65	4	4 other carb, 2 fat
7	5	150	6	51	3½	3½ other carb, 1 fat
10	6	210	8	73	4½	4½ other carb, 2 fat
<1	<1	180	9	66	4	4 other carb
0	0	20	0	56	3½	3½ other carb
0	0	30	0	74	5	5 other carb
0	0	25	0	49	3	3 other carb

1 Carbohydrate Choice = 1 starch *or* 1 fruit *or* 1 milk exchange
* Grams of fiber subtracted from total carbohydrate

MENU ITEM	SERVING SIZE	CALORIES	CALORIES FROM FAT
MALTS/SHAKES			
Chocolate Malt, small	15 oz	650	150
Chocolate Malt, regular	20 oz	880	200
Chocolate Shake, small	14 oz	560	140
Chocolate Shake, regular	19 oz	770	180
BLIZZARD®			
Butterfinger® Blizzard®, small	12 oz	520	160
Butterfinger® Blizzard®, regular	16 oz	750	240
Chocolate Chip Cookie Dough Blizzard®, small	12 oz	660	220
Chocolate Chip Cookie Dough Blizzard®, regular	16 oz	950	320
Chocolate Sandwich Cookie Blizzard®, small	12 oz	520	160
Chocolate Sandwich Cookie Blizzard®, regular	16 oz	640	210
Heath® Blizzard®, small	12 oz	560	190
Heath® Blizzard®, regular	16 oz	820	300
Reeses® Peanut Butter Cup Blizzard®, small	12 oz	590	210
Reeses® Peanut Butter Cup Blizzard®, regular	16 oz	790	300
Strawberry Blizzard®, small	12 oz	400	100
Strawberry Blizzard®, regular	16 oz	570	140
BREEZE®			
Heath® Breeze®, small	12 oz	470	90
Heath® Breeze®, regular	16 oz	710	170
Strawberry Breeze®, small	12 oz	320	5
Strawberry Breeze®, regular	16 oz	460	10

TOTAL FAT (g)	SATURATED FAT (g)	SODIUM (mg)	PROTEIN (g)	CARBOHYDRATE (g)	CARBOHYDRATE CHOICES	EXCHANGES
16	10	370	15	111	7½	7½ other carb, 3 fat
22	14	500	19	153	10	10 other carb, 4 fat
15	10	310	13	94	6	6 other carb, 3 fat
20	13	420	17	130	8½	8½ other carb, 4 fat
18	11	250	11	80	5	5 other carb, 3 fat
26	16	360	16	115	7½	7½ other carb, 5 fat
24	13	440	12	99	6½	6½ other carb, 4 fat
36	19	660	17	143	9½	9½ other carb, 6 fat
18	9	380	10	79	5	5 other carb, 3 fat
23	11	500	12	97	6½	6½ other carb, 4 fat
21	14	380	10	82	5½	5½ other carb, 4 fat
33	20	580	14	119	8	8 other carb, 6 fat
24	13	320	14	81	5½	5½ other carb, 4 fat
33	17	430	19	105	7	7 other carb, 6 fat
11	7	190	9	66	4½	4½ other carb, 2 fat
16	11	260	12	95	6	6 other carb, 3 fat
10	6	380	11	85	5½	5½ other carb, 2 fat
18	11	580	15	123	8	8 other carb, 3 fat
<1	<1	190	10	68	4½	4½ other carb
1	1	270	13	99	6½	6½ other carb

1 Carbohydrate Choice = 1 starch or 1 fruit or 1 milk exchange
* Grams of fiber subtracted from total carbohydrate

MENU ITEM	SERVING SIZE	CALORIES	CALORIES FROM FAT
DQ® TREATZZA PIZZA™			
🔆 Heath®	⅛ pizza (2.4 oz)	180	60
🔆 M&M	⅛ pizza (2.4 oz)	190	70
Peanut Butter Fudge	⅛ pizza (2.5 oz)	220	90
🔆 Strawberry-Banana	⅛ pizza (2.7 oz)	180	50
DQ® FROZEN CAKES			
Heart Cake (undecorated)	¹⁄₁₀ cake (4.8 oz)	270	80
Log Cake	⅛ cake (4.75 oz)	280	80
Round Cake (8", undecorated)	⅛ cake (6.25 oz)	340	100
Round Cake (10", undecorated)	¹⁄₁₂ cake (6.5 oz)	360	110
Sheet Cake	¹⁄₂₀ cake (6 oz)	350	110
OTHER FROZEN TREATS			
Banana Split	1 (13 oz)	510	100
Buster Bar®	1 (5.25 oz)	450	260
Chocolate Dilly® Bar	1 (3 oz)	210	120
Chocolate Mint Dilly® Bar	1 (2.75 oz)	190	100
🔆 DQ® Fudge Bar	1 (2.3 oz)	50	0
🔆 DQ® Lemon Freez'r™	½ cup (3.25 oz)	80	0
🔆 DQ® Sandwich (ice cream)	1 (2 oz)	150	45
🔆 DQ® Vanilla Orange Bar	1 (2.3 oz)	60	0
Fudge Nut Bar™	1 (5 oz)	410	220
Peanut Buster® Parfait	1 (5.25 oz)	730	280
Queen's Choice® Chocolate Big Scoop®	1 (4 oz)	250	120
Queen's Choice® Vanilla Big Scoop®	1 (4 oz)	250	120
🔆 Starkiss®	1 (3 oz)	80	0

🔆 Smart Choice

TOTAL FAT (g)	SATURATED FAT (g)	SODIUM (mg)	PROTEIN (g)	CARBOHYDRATE (g)	CARBOHYDRATE CHOICES	EXCHANGES
7	4	160	3	28	2	2 other carb, 1 fat
7	4	160	3	29	2	2 other carb, 1 fat
10	5	200	4	28	2	2 other carb, 2 fat
6	3	140	3	29	2	2 other carb, 1 fat
9	6	190	5	41	3	3 other carb, 1 fat
9	6	220	5	43	3	3 other carb, 1½ fat
12	7	250	7	53	3½	3½ other carb, 2 fat
12	8	260	7	55	3½	3½ other carb, 2 fat
12	7	270	7	54	3½	3½ other carb, 2 fat
12	8	180	8	96	6½	6½ other carb, 2 fat
28	12	280	10	41	3	3 other carb, 5 fat
13	7	75	3	21	1½	1½ other carb, 2 fat
12	9	100	3	20	1	1 other carb, 2 fat
0	0	70	4	13	1	1 other carb
0	0	10	0	20	1	1 other carb
5	2	115	3	24	1½	1½ other carb, 1 fat
0	0	40	2	17	1	1 other carb
25	11	250	8	40	2½	2½ other carb, 5 fat
31	17	400	16	99	6½	6½ other carb, 6 fat
14	9	95	4	28	2	2 other carb, 2½ fat
14	9	100	4	27	2	2 other carb, 2½ fat
0	0	10	0	21	1½	1½ other carb

1 Carbohydrate Choice = 1 starch or 1 fruit or 1 milk exchange
* Grams of fiber subtracted from total carbohydrate

MENU ITEM	SERVING SIZE	CALORIES	CALORIES FROM FAT
Strawberry Shortcake	1 (8.5 oz)	430	120
Toffee Dilly® Bar with Heath® Pieces	1 (2.8 oz)	210	110

SMART MEAL, DAIRY QUEEN/BRAZIER

Grilled Chicken Breast Fillet Sandwich (request lettuce and tomato) Strawberry Misty® Cooler (12 oz)	**Calories:**	500
	Fat:	10 grams
	Carb Choices:	5½
	Exchanges:	2 starch, 3 other carb, 3 lean meat

DEL TACO
TACOS

Chicken Soft Taco	1	197	99
Chicken Taco	1	186	117
Deluxe Double Beef Soft Taco	1	211	99
Deluxe Double Beef Taco	1	205	117
Double Beef Soft Taco	1	178	72
Double Beef Taco	1	172	90
☀ Soft Taco	1	146	54
☀ Taco	1	140	72
☀ Tostada	1	140	72

BURRITOS

Chicken Burrito	1	264	90
Combination Burrito	1	413	153
Del Beef Burrito	1	440	180
Deluxe Chicken Burrito	1	549	306
Deluxe Combo Burrito	1	453	180
Deluxe Del Beef Burrito	1	479	207

☀ Smart Choice

TOTAL FAT (g)	SATURATED FAT (g)	SODIUM (mg)	PROTEIN (g)	CARBOHYDRATE (g)	CARBOHYDRATE CHOICES	EXCHANGES
14	9	360	7	70	4½	4½ other carb, 3 fat
12	9	100	3	24	1½	1½ other carb, 2 fat

SMART MEAL, DAIRY QUEEN/BRAZIER

DQ® Homestyle® Hamburger (request lettuce and tomato)
DQ® Sandwich (ice cream)

Calories: 440
Fat: 17 grams
Carb Choices: 3½
Exchanges: 2 starch, 1½ other carb, 2 med. fat meat, 1 fat

TOTAL FAT (g)	SATURATED FAT (g)	SODIUM (mg)	PROTEIN (g)	CARBOHYDRATE (g)	CARBOHYDRATE CHOICES	EXCHANGES
11	3	401	7	16	1	1 starch, 1 med. fat meat, 1 fat
13	3	276	8	10	½	½ starch, 1 med. fat meat, 1½ fat
11	5	283	8	20	1	1 starch, 1 med. fat meat, 1 fat
13	5	159	9	13	1	1 starch, 1 high fat meat, 1 fat
8	3	274	7	18	1	1 starch, 1 high fat meat
10	3	150	8	12	1	1 starch, 1 high fat meat
6	3	223	5	17	1	1 starch, 1 med. fat meat
8	3	99	6	10	½	½ starch, 1 med. fat meat
8	3	333	6	12	1	1 starch, 1 med. fat meat
10	4	771	13	32	2	2 starch, 1 med. fat meat, 1 fat
17	7	1035	21	46	3	3 starch, 2 med. fat meat, ½ fat
20	9	878	23	43	3	3 starch, 2½ med. fat meat, 1 fat
34	10	978	21	40	2½	2½ starch, 2 med. fat meat, 4½ fat
20	9	1047	22	49	3	3 starch, 2 med. fat meat, 1½ fat
23	10	890	25	45	3	3 starch, 2½ med. fat meat, 1½ fat

1 Carbohydrate Choice = 1 starch or 1 fruit or 1 milk exchange
* Grams of fiber subtracted from total carbohydrate

MENU ITEM	SERVING SIZE	CALORIES	CALORIES FROM FAT
🔆 Green Burrito, small	1	229	72
Green Burrito, regular	1	330	99
Macho Beef Burrito	1	893	369
Macho Combo Burrito	1	774	279
🔆 Red Burrito, small	1	235	72
Red Burrito, regular	1	342	108
Spicy Chicken Burrito	1	392	99
"The Works" Burrito	1	448	162
QUESADILLAS			
Chicken Quesadilla	1	544	279
Chicken Spicy Jack Quesadilla	1	537	270
Quesadilla, small	1	257	108
Quesadilla, regular	1	483	243
Spicy Jack Quesadilla, small	1	254	108
Spicy Jack Quesadilla, regular	1	476	243
BURGERS			
Cheeseburger	1	284	117
Del Burger	1	385	180
Del Cheeseburger	1	439	225
Double Del Cheeseburger	1	618	351
🔆 Hamburger	1	231	72
KIDS' MEALS			
Hamburger Meal	1	617	180
Taco Meal	1	532	153
SIDE ORDERS			
🔆 Beans and Cheese	1 order	122	27

🔆 Smart Choice

TOTAL FAT (g)	SATURATED FAT (g)	SODIUM (mg)	PROTEIN (g)	CARBOHYDRATE (g)	CARBOHYDRATE CHOICES	EXCHANGES
8	3	714	9	32	2	2 starch, 1 med. fat meat
11	5	1149	14	46	3	3 starch, 1 med. fat meat, ½ fat
41	18	1969	49	84	5½	5½ starch, 5 med. fat meat, 2 fat
31	15	2180	38	87	6	6 starch, 3 med. fat meat, 2 fat
8	4	656	10	32	2	2 starch, 1 med. fat meat
12	5	1033	15	46	3	3 starch, 1 med. fat meat, 1 fat
11	3	1243	16	59	4	4 starch, 1 med. fat meat, ½ fat
18	6	1248	15	60	4	4 starch, 1 med. fat meat, 1½ fat
31	16	1147	30	38	2½	2½ starch, 3½ med. fat meat, 2 fat
30	17	1214	31	38	2½	2½ starch, 3½ med. fat meat, 2 fat
12	6	455	11	26	2	2 starch, 1 med. fat meat, 1 fat
27	16	871	23	37	2½	2½ starch, 2½ med. fat meat, 2 fat
12	6	482	11	26	2	2 starch, 1 med. fat meat, 1 fat
27	16	938	23	37	2½	2½ starch, 2½ med. fat meat, 2 fat
13	6	852	14	26	2	2 starch, 1½ med. fat meat, 1 fat
20	6	1065	14	35	2	2 starch, 1½ med. fat meat, 2 fat
25	9	1268	18	35	2	2 starch, 2 med. fat meat, 3 fat
39	16	1638	29	36	2½	2½ starch, 3 med. fat meat, 4 fat
8	3	649	11	26	2	2 starch, 1½ med. fat meat
20	7	799	14	96	6½	6½ starch, 1 med. fat meat, 1 fat
17	6	373	8	87	6	6 starch, 2 fat
3	2	892	7	17	1	1 starch, ½ med. fat meat

1 Carbohydrate Choice = 1 starch or 1 fruit or 1 milk exchange
* Grams of fiber subtracted from total carbohydrate

MENU ITEM	SERVING SIZE	CALORIES	CALORIES FROM FAT
Chili Cheese Fries	1 order	562	270
Deluxe Chili Cheese Fries	1 order	600	297
French Fries, small	1 order	242	99
French Fries, regular	1 order	404	171
French Fries, large	1 order	566	234
Macho Nachos	1 order	1089	549
Nacho Fries	1 order	669	306
Nachos	1 order	390	207
SALADS			
Chicken Salad	1	254	171
Deluxe Chicken Salad	1	716	423
Deluxe Taco Salad	1	741	441
Taco Salad	1	235	171
CONDIMENTS			
American Cheese	1 slice	53	36
Guacamole	1 oz	60	54
Hot Sauce	1 pkt	2	NA
Nacho Cheese Sauce	1 order	100	72
Salsa	2 oz	14	NA
Salsa Dressing	1 oz	33	27
Sour Cream	1 oz	60	54
SHAKES			
Chocolate Shake, small	1	549	144
Chocolate Shake, medium	1	755	198
Oreos® Toppers (topping only)	1 serving	257	90
Strawberry Shake, small	1	486	144
Strawberry Shake, medium	1	668	198

 Smart Choice

TOTAL FAT (g)	SATURATED FAT (g)	SODIUM (mg)	PROTEIN (g)	CARBOHYDRATE (g)	CARBOHYDRATE CHOICES	EXCHANGES
30	13	846	15	58	4	4 starch, 1 med. fat meat, 4 fat
33	15	855	16	61	4	4 starch, 1 med. fat meat, 5 fat
11	4	136	3	32	2	2 starch, 2 fat
19	6	227	5	54	3½	3½ starch, 3 fat
26	9	318	8	76	5	5 starch, 4 fat
61	13	1740	26	110	7	7 starch, 2 med. fat meat, 9 fat
34	11	926	10	80	5	5 starch, 6 fat
23	4	504	6	39	2½	2½ starch, 4 fat
19	6	476	12	8	½	2 veg, 1½ med. fat meat, 2 fat
47	15	1419	26	55	3½	3½ starch, 2½ med. fat meat, 6 fat
49	16	1280	26	57	4	4 starch, 2½ med. fat meat, 6 fat
19	6	268	9	9	½	2 veg, 1 med. fat meat, 2½ fat
4	3	203	3	<1	0	1 fat
6	0	130	1	2	0	1 fat
<1	0	38	<1	<1	0	free
8	2	401	2	4	0	2 fat
<1	0	308	<1	3	0	free
3	2	85	<1	1	0	½ fat
6	4	15	<1	<1	0	1 fat
16	10	302	2	98	6½	6½ other carb, 2 fat
22	14	415	3	135	9	9 other carb, 3 fat
10	4	188	1	42	3	3 other carb, 1 fat
16	10	222	2	87	6	6 other carb, 2 fat
22	14	305	3	120	8	8 other carb, 3 fat

1 Carbohydrate Choice = 1 starch or 1 fruit or 1 milk exchange
* Grams of fiber subtracted from total carbohydrate

MENU ITEM	SERVING SIZE	CALORIES	CALORIES FROM FAT
Vanilla Shake, small	1	514	162
Vanilla Shake, medium	1	707	225

SOFT DRINKS

MENU ITEM	SERVING SIZE	CALORIES	CALORIES FROM FAT
Coca-Cola Classic®, small	1	144	0
Coca-Cola Classic®, medium	1	198	0
Coca-Cola Classic®, large	1	287	0
Coca-Cola Classic®, Best Value	1	395	0
Diet Coke®, small	1	1	0
Diet Coke®, medium	1	1	0
Diet Coke®, large	1	2	0
Diet Coke®, Best Value	1	2	0
Iced Tea, small	1	3	NA
Iced Tea, medium	1	4	NA
Iced Tea, large	1	6	NA
Iced Tea, Best Value	1	8	NA
Mr. Pibb®, small	1	142	0
Mr. Pibb®, medium	1	195	0
Mr. Pibb®, large	1	283	0
Mr. Pibb®, Best Value	1	390	0
Sprite®, small	1	144	0
Sprite®, medium	1	198	0
Sprite®, large	1	287	0
Sprite®, Best Value	1	395	0

OTHER BEVERAGES

MENU ITEM	SERVING SIZE	CALORIES	CALORIES FROM FAT
Coffee, black	1	6	NA
☀ Milk, 1%	8 oz	126	27
☀ Orange Juice	6 oz	83	NA

☀ Smart Choice

TOTAL FAT (g)	SATURATED FAT (g)	SODIUM (mg)	PROTEIN (g)	CARBOHYDRATE (g)	CARBOHYDRATE CHOICES	EXCHANGES
18	12	257	2	88	6	6 other carb, 2 fat
25	17	353	3	121	8	8 other carb, 3 fat
0	0	17	0	38	2½	2½ other carb
0	0	24	0	52	3½	3½ other carb
0	0	35	0	76	5	5 other carb
0	0	48	0	104	7	7 other carb
0	0	20	0	<1	0	free
0	0	27	0	<1	0	free
0	0	39	0	<1	0	free
0	0	53	0	<1	0	free
<1	0	13	<1	<1	0	free
<1	0	18	<1	1	0	free
<1	0	26	<1	2	0	free
<1	0	36	<1	2	0	free
0	0	23	0	36	2½	2½ other carb
0	0	32	0	49	3	3 other carb
0	0	47	0	72	5	5 other carb
0	0	64	0	99	6½	6½ other carb
0	0	35	0	36	2½	2½ other carb
0	0	49	0	49	3	3 other carb
0	0	71	0	72	5	5 other carb
0	0	97	0	99	6½	6½ other carb
<1	<1	4	<1	1	0	free
3	2	152	10	15	1	1 1% milk
<1	0	19	1	20	1	1 fruit

1 Carbohydrate Choice = 1 starch or 1 fruit or 1 milk exchange
* Grams of fiber subtracted from total carbohydrate

MENU ITEM	SERVING SIZE	CALORIES	CALORIES FROM FAT
BREAKFAST			
Beef and Egg Burrito	1	529	243
Breakfast Burrito	1	256	99
Egg and Bean Burrito	1	470	198
Egg and Cheese Burrito	1	443	198
Steak and Egg Burrito	1	500	225

SMART MEAL, DEL TACO

Soft Taco
Tostada
Beans and Cheese
Hot Sauce or Salsa
Orange Juice (6 oz)

Calories: 505
Fat: 18 grams
Carb Choices: 4½
Exchanges: 3 starch, 1 fruit, 2½ med. fat meat

DOMINO'S
LARGE (14") CHEESE PIZZAS

MENU ITEM	SERVING SIZE	CALORIES	CALORIES FROM FAT
Deep Dish Pizza	2 slices (6.2 oz)	464	177
☀ Hand Tossed Pizza	2 slices (4.8 oz)	319	88
☀ Thin Crust Pizza	⅙ pizza (3.5 oz)	255	98

"ADD A TOPPING" FOR LARGE PIZZA, PER SLICE

MENU ITEM	SERVING SIZE	CALORIES	CALORIES FROM FAT
☀ Anchovies	NA	23	9
Bacon	NA	75	58
☀ Banana Peppers	NA	3	0
☀ Canned Mushrooms	NA	3	0
Cheddar Cheese	NA	48	35
Extra Cheese	NA	46	31
☀ Fresh Mushrooms	NA	3	0
☀ Green Olives	NA	11	11
☀ Green Peppers	NA	2	0

☀ Smart Choice

TOTAL FAT (g)	SATURATED FAT (g)	SODIUM (mg)	PROTEIN (g)	CARBOHYDRATE (g)	CARBOHYDRATE CHOICES	EXCHANGES
27	10	929	29	43	3	3 starch, 3 med. fat meat, 2 fat
11	4	409	9	30	2	2 starch, ½ med. fat meat, 1½ fat
22	8	1035	24	45	3	3 starch, 2½ med. fat meat, 1 fat
22	8	792	22	40	2½	2½ starch, 2 med. fat meat, 2 fat
25	9	1068	30	41	3	3 starch, 3 med. fat meat, 1 fat
20	7	978	18	55	3½	3½ starch, 1½ med. fat meat, 2 fat
10	4	622	14	44	3	3 starch, 1 med. fat meat
11	4	710	11	28	2	2 starch, 1 med. fat meat, ½ fat
1	<1	395	3	0	0	free
6	2	207	4	0	0	1 fat
0	0	81	0	1	0	free
0	<1	50	0	1	0	free
4	2	73	3	0	0	1 fat
3	2	116	3	0	0	1 fat
0	<1	0	0	1	0	free
1	<1	227	0	0	0	free
0	0	0	0	1	0	free

1 Carbohydrate Choice = 1 starch or 1 fruit or 1 milk exchange
* Grams of fiber subtracted from total carbohydrate

MENU ITEM	SERVING SIZE	CALORIES	CALORIES FROM FAT
☼ Ham	NA	17	6
Italian Sausage	NA	44	31
☼ Onion	NA	3	0
Pepperoni	NA	55	45
☼ Pineapple Tidbits	NA	8	0
Pre-Cooked Beef	NA	44	36
☼ Ripe Olives	NA	12	10

MEDIUM (12") PIZZAS

Deep Dish Pizza	2 slices (6.2 oz)	467	192
Hand Tossed Pizza	2 slices (4.9 oz)	349	95
Thin Crust Pizza	¼ pizza (3.7 oz)	273	105

"ADD A TOPPING" FOR MEDIUM PIZZA, PER SLICE

☼ Anchovies	NA	23	9
Bacon	NA	82	63
☼ Banana Peppers	NA	3	0
☼ Canned Mushrooms	NA	4	0
Cheddar Cheese	NA	57	42
Extra Cheese	NA	49	33
☼ Fresh Mushrooms	NA	4	0
☼ Green Olives	NA	12	12
☼ Green Peppers	NA	3	0
☼ Ham	NA	18	7
Italian Sausage	NA	55	39
☼ Onion	NA	4	0
Pepperoni	NA	62	51
☼ Pineapple Tidbits	NA	10	0
Pre-cooked beef	NA	55	44

☼ Smart Choice

TOTAL FAT (g)	SATURATED FAT (g)	SODIUM (mg)	PROTEIN (g)	CARBOHYDRATE (g)	CARBOHYDRATE CHOICES	EXCHANGES
1	<1	156	2	0	0	free
3	1	137	2	1	0	1 fat
0	0	0	0	1	0	free
5	2	177	2	0	0	1 fat
0	0	1	0	2	0	free
4	2	123	2	0	0	1 fat
1	<1	63	0	1	0	free
21	8	998	18	52	3½	3½ starch, 1½ med. fat meat, 2 fat
11	5	673	15	49	3	3 starch, 1 med. fat meat, 1 fat
12	5	759	12	30	2	2 starch, 1 med. fat meat, 1 fat
1	<1	395	3	0	0	free
7	2	226	4	0	0	1½ fat
0	0	92	0	1	0	free
0	<1	73	0	1	0	free
5	3	88	4	0	0	1 fat
4	2	125	3	0	0	1 fat
0	<1	1	0	1	0	free
1	<1	255	0	0	0	free
0	0	0	0	1	0	free
1	<1	162	2	0	0	free
4	2	171	2	2	0	1 fat
0	0	0	0	1	0	free
6	2	199	3	0	0	1 fat
0	0	1	0	2	0	free
5	2	154	3	0	0	1 fat

1 Carbohydrate Choice = 1 starch *or* 1 fruit *or* 1 milk exchange
* Grams of fiber subtracted from total carbohydrate

MENU ITEM	SERVING SIZE	CALORIES	CALORIES FROM FAT
🔅 Ripe Olives	NA	14	11
6" DEEP DISH			
Cheese Pizza	1 pizza (7.5 oz)	591	245
"ADD A TOPPING" FOR 6" DEEP DISH, PER SLICE			
🔅 Anchovies	NA	45	19
Bacon	NA	82	63
🔅 Banana Peppers	NA	3	0
🔅 Canned Mushrooms	NA	2	0
Cheddar Cheese	NA	86	63
Extra Cheese	NA	59	40
🔅 Fresh Mushrooms	NA	2	0
🔅 Green Olives	NA	10	10
🔅 Green Peppers	NA	2	0
🔅 Ham	NA	17	6
Italian Sausage	NA	44	31
🔅 Onion	NA	3	0
Pepperoni	NA	50	40
🔅 Pineapple Tidbits	NA	5	0
Pre-Cooked Beef	NA	44	36
🔅 Ripe Olives	NA	11	9
SIDE ORDERS			
🔅 Barbecue Wings	1 piece (1 oz)	50	22
🔅 Breadsticks	1 piece	78	30
🔅 Cheesy Bread	1 piece	103	49
🔅 Hot Wings	1 piece (1 oz)	45	22

🔅 Smart Choice

Total Fat (g)	Saturated Fat (g)	Sodium (mg)	Protein (g)	Carbohydrate (g)	Carbohydrate Choices	Exchanges
1	<1	71	0	1	0	free
27	10	1208	23	65	4	4 starch, 2 med. fat meat, 3 fat
2	<1	730	6	0	0	free
7	2	226	4	0	0	1½ fat
0	0	73	0	0	0	free
0	0	36	0	0	0	free
7	4	132	5	0	0	1 fat
4	3	150	4	0	0	1 fat
0	0	0	0	0	0	free
1	<1	204	0	0	0	free
0	0	0	0	0	0	free
1	<1	156	2	0	0	free
3	1	137	2	1	0	1 fat
0	0	0	0	1	0	free
5	2	159	2	0	0	1 fat
0	0	0	0	1	0	free
4	2	123	2	0	0	1 fat
1	<1	57	0	0	0	free
2	<1	175	6	2	0	1 lean meat
3	<1	158	2	11	1	1 starch
5	2	182	3	11	1	1 starch, 1 fat
2	<1	354	5	1	0	1 lean meat

1 Carbohydrate Choice = 1 starch or 1 fruit or 1 milk exchange
* Grams of fiber subtracted from total carbohydrate

MENU ITEM	SERVING SIZE	CALORIES	CALORIES FROM FAT
SALADS			
☀ Garden Salad, small	1	22	2
☀ Garden Salad, large	1	39	4
MARZETTI® SALAD DRESSINGS			
Blue Cheese Salad Dressing	1.5 oz	220	216
Creamy Caesar Salad Dressing	1.5 oz	200	198
Honey French Salad Dressing	1.5 oz	210	162
House Italian Salad Dressing	1.5 oz	220	216
☀ Italian Salad Dressing, Light	1.5 oz	20	9
Ranch Salad Dressing	1.5 oz	266	261
☀ Ranch Salad Dressing, Fat-Free	1.5 oz	40	0
Thousand Island Salad Dressing	1.5 oz	200	180

SMART MEAL, DOMINO'S

2 slices of Large Hand Tossed Cheese Pizza
  with fresh mushrooms, ham, and onion
Garden Salad, large
Italian Salad Dressing, Light (1.5 oz)

Calories:	424
Fat:	13 grams
Carb Choices:	4
Exchanges:	3 starch, 1 veg, 1 med. fat meat

☀ Smart Choice

TOTAL FAT (g)	SATURATED FAT (g)	SODIUM (mg)	PROTEIN (g)	CARBOHYDRATE (g)	CARBOHYDRATE CHOICES	EXCHANGES
0	<1	14	1	4	0	1 veg
0	<1	26	2	8	½	1 veg
24	4	440	2	2	0	5 fat
22	3	470	1	2	0	4 fat
18	3	300	0	14	1	1 other carb, 3 fat
24	3	440	0	1	0	5 fat
1	0	780	0	2	0	free
29	4	380	0	1	0	6 fat
0	0	560	0	10	½	½ other carb
20	3	320	0	5	0	4 fat

1 Carbohydrate Choice = 1 starch or 1 fruit or 1 milk exchange
* Grams of fiber subtracted from total carbohydrate

MENU ITEM	SERVING SIZE	CALORIES	CALORIES FROM FAT
DUNKIN' DONUTS			
BAGELS/BREAD			
💡 Blueberry Bagel	1 (4.4 oz)	330	10
💡 Cinnamon Raisin Bagel	1 (4.4 oz)	340	10
💡 Egg Bagel	1 (4.4 oz)	340	15
💡 English Muffin	1 (2 oz)	130	10
💡 Everything Bagel	1 (4.4 oz)	340	20
💡 French Roll	1 (2 oz)	140	5
💡 Garlic Bagel	1 (4.4 oz)	330	10
💡 Onion Bagel	1 (4.4 oz)	320	10
💡 Plain Bagel	1 (4.4 oz)	330	10
💡 Poppy Bagel	1 (4.4 oz)	340	25
💡 Pumpernickel Bagel	1 (4.4 oz)	340	15
💡 Salt Bagel	1 (4.4 oz)	320	10
💡 Sesame Bagel	1 (4.4 oz)	350	40
💡 Whole Wheat Bagel	1 (4.4 oz)	320	10
CREAM CHEESE			
💡 Classic Lite	2 Tbsp (1 oz)	60	45
Classic Plain	2 Tbsp (1 oz)	100	90
Garden Veggie	2 Tbsp (1 oz)	90	80
Savory Chive	2 Tbsp (1 oz)	100	90
Smoked Salmon	2 Tbsp (1 oz)	100	80
Strawberry	2 Tbsp (1 oz)	100	80
CROISSANTS			
Almond Croissant	1 (2.8 oz)	360	190
Cheese Croissant	1 (2.5 oz)	240	140

💡 Smart Choice

TOTAL FAT (g)	SATURATED FAT (g)	SODIUM (mg)	PROTEIN (g)	CARBOHYDRATE (g)	CARBOHYDRATE CHOICES	EXCHANGES
1	0	640	11	70	4½	4½ starch
1	0	470	11	72	4½	4½ starch
2	0	670	12	69	4½	4½ starch
1	<1	520	4	26	2	2 starch
2	0	680	12	68	4½	4½ starch
1	0	220	5	27	2	2 starch
1	0	670	12	69	4½	4½ starch
1	0	650	12	66	4½	4½ starch
1	0	690	12	68	4½	4½ starch
3	0	680	12	68	4½	4½ starch
2	0	660	11	70	4½	4½ starch
1	0	3170	11	65	4	4 starch
4	0	660	13	66	4½	4½ starch
2	0	630	12	58*	4	4 starch
5	3	115	3	3	0	1 fat
10	6	110	2	1	0	2 fat
9	5	200	2	2	0	2 fat
10	6	125	2	2	0	2 fat
9	5	95	2	1	0	2 fat
9	5	100	1	5	0	2 fat
21	5	300	6	38	2½	2½ other carb, 4 fat
15	3	260	6	28	2	2 other carb, 2 fat

1 Carbohydrate Choice = 1 starch or 1 fruit or 1 milk exchange
* Grams of fiber subtracted from total carbohydrate

MENU ITEM	SERVING SIZE	CALORIES	CALORIES FROM FAT
Chocolate Croissant	1 (2.5 oz)	370	200
Plain Croissant	1 (2 oz)	270	150

CRULLERS/STICKS

Dunkin' Donut Cruller	1 (2 oz)	240	130
Glazed Cruller	1 (3 oz)	340	130
Glazed Chocolate Cruller	1 (3 oz)	410	220
Jelly Stick	1 (3 oz)	330	130
Plain Cruller	1 (2 oz)	260	130
Powdered Cruller	1 (2.3 oz)	290	130
Sugar Cruller	1 (2.2 oz)	270	130

DONUTS, CAKE

Blueberry Donut	1 (2.4 oz)	230	90
Blueberry Crumb Donut	1 (2.6 oz)	260	100
Butternut Donut	1 (2.6 oz)	340	180
Chocolate Donut	1 (2 oz)	210	120
Chocolate Coconut Donut	1 (2.4 oz)	250	140
Chocolate Glazed Donut	1 (2.5 oz)	250	120
Cinnamon Donut	1 (2.3 oz)	300	170
Coconut Donut	1 (2.5 oz)	320	180
Double Chocolate Donut	1 (2.5 oz)	260	130
Old Fashioned Donut	1 (2.1 oz)	280	170
Peanut Donut	1 (2.6 oz)	340	200
Powdered Donut	1 (2.4 oz)	310	170
Sugared Donut	1 (2.4 oz)	310	180
Toasted Coconut Donut	1 (2.5 oz)	320	170
Whole Wheat Glazed Donut	1 (2.7 oz)	230	100

TOTAL FAT (g)	SATURATED FAT (g)	SODIUM (mg)	PROTEIN (g)	CARBOHYDRATE (g)	CARBOHYDRATE CHOICES	EXCHANGES
23	8	260	5	40	2½	2½ other carb, 4 fat
17	4	260	4	27	2	2 other carb, 3 fat
14	3	370	4	26	2	2 other carb, 2½ fat
14	3	320	3	49	3	3 other carb, 2½ fat
24	6	350	4	46	3	3 other carb, 4 fat
14	3	350	3	48	3	3 other carb, 2½ fat
14	3	300	3	29	2	2 other carb, 2½ fat
15	3	300	3	35	2½	2½ other carb, 2½ fat
14	3	300	3	31	2	2 other carb, 2½ fat
10	3	240	4	30	2	2 other carb, 2 fat
11	3	260	4	36	2½	2½ other carb, 2 fat
20	5	360	4	35	2	2 other carb, 4 fat
14	3	270	3	19	1	1 other carb, 3 fat
15	5	270	3	25	1½	1½ other carb, 3 fat
14	3	280	3	29	2	2 other carb, 2 fat
19	4	350	3	29	2	2 other carb, 3 fat
20	5	360	3	32	2	2 other carb, 4 fat
14	3	280	3	30	2	2 other carb, 2 fat
19	4	350	3	24	1½	1½ other carb, 3 fat
22	4	360	5	32	2	2 other carb, 4 fat
19	4	350	3	30	2	2 other carb, 3 fat
20	4	380	4	28	2	2 other carb, 3 fat
19	5	360	3	33	2	2 other carb, 4 fat
11	3	340	3	31	2	2 other carb, 2 fat

1 Carbohydrate Choice = 1 starch or 1 fruit or 1 milk exchange
* Grams of fiber subtracted from total carbohydrate

MENU ITEM	SERVING SIZE	CALORIES	CALORIES FROM FAT
DONUTS, YEAST			
Apple 'n Spice Donut	1 (2.5 oz)	230	90
Apple Crumb Donut	1 (2.6 oz)	250	100
Bavarian Kreme Donut	1 (2.5 oz)	250	100
Black Raspberry Donut	1 (2.4 oz)	240	90
Boston Kreme Donut	1 (2.8 oz)	270	100
Chocolate Frosted Donut	1 (2 oz)	210	70
Chocolate Kreme Filled Donut	1 (2.6 oz)	320	140
☀ Glazed Donut	1 (1.6 oz)	160	60
Jelly Filled Donut	1 (2.4 oz)	240	90
Lemon Donut	1 (2.5 oz)	240	100
Maple Frosted Donut	1 (2.1 oz)	210	70
Marble Frosted Donut	1 (2 oz)	210	70
Strawberry Donut	1 (2.4 oz)	240	90
Strawberry Frosted Donut	1 (2.1 oz)	220	70
☀ Sugar Raised Donut	1 (1.6 oz)	170	70
Vanilla Frosted Donut	1 (2.1 oz)	220	70
DONUT HOLES, CAKE MUNCHKINS®			
Butternut Donut Hole	3 (2 oz)	230	100
Chocolate Glazed Donut Hole	3 (2 oz)	180	90
Cinnamon Donut Hole	4 (2 oz)	240	110
Coconut Donut Hole	3 (1.7 oz)	200	100
Glazed Cake Donut Hole	3 (2 oz)	220	80
Plain Donut Hole	4 (1.7 oz)	200	110
Powdered Sugar Donut Hole	4 (2 oz)	240	110
Toasted Coconut Donut Hole	3 (1.8 oz)	210	100

☀ Smart Choice

TOTAL FAT (g)	SATURATED FAT (g)	SODIUM (mg)	PROTEIN (g)	CARBOHYDRATE (g)	CARBOHYDRATE CHOICES	EXCHANGES
10	3	250	4	31	2	2 other carb, 2 fat
11	3	270	4	34	2	2 other carb, 2 fat
11	3	250	4	33	2	2 other carb, 2 fat
10	3	260	4	32	2	2 other carb, 2 fat
11	3	260	4	38	2½	2½ other carb, 2 fat
8	2	230	4	31	2	2 other carb, 1½ fat
16	4	250	4	39	2½	2½ other carb, 3 fat
7	2	200	3	23	1½	1½ other carb, 1 fat
10	3	260	4	32	2	2 other carb, 2 fat
11	3	250	4	31	2	2 other carb, 2 fat
8	2	230	4	32	2	2 other carb, 1½ fat
8	2	230	4	32	2	2 other carb, 1½ fat
10	3	250	4	32	2	2 other carb, 2 fat
8	2	230	4	32	2	2 other carb, 1½ fat
7	2	220	4	23	1½	1½ other carb, 1 fat
8	2	230	4	32	2	2 other carb, 1½ fat
11	4	210	2	30	2	2 other carb, 2 fat
10	2	240	2	22	1½	1½ other carb, 2 fat
13	3	290	3	29	2	2 other carb, 2 fat
11	4	220	2	22	1½	1½ other carb, 2 fat
9	2	220	2	32	2	2 other carb, 2 fat
12	3	290	3	21	1½	1½ other carb, 2 fat
13	3	290	3	28	2	2 other carb, 2 fat
11	3	220	2	26	2	2 other carb, 2 fat

1 Carbohydrate Choice = 1 starch or 1 fruit or 1 milk exchange
* Grams of fiber subtracted from total carbohydrate

MENU ITEM	SERVING SIZE	CALORIES	CALORIES FROM FAT
DONUT HOLES, YEAST MUNCHKINS®			
💡 Glazed Raised Donut Hole	4 (2 oz)	210	60
💡 Jelly Donut Hole	3 (1.9 oz)	170	45
💡 Lemon Donut Hole	3 (2 oz)	160	50
💡 Sugar Raised Donut Hole	6 (1.9 oz)	210	90
FANCIES			
Apple Fritter	1 (3.4 oz)	300	120
Apple Tart	1 (3.5 oz)	290	90
Apple Turnover	1 (3.8 oz)	350	130
Bismark	1 (2.8 oz)	310	120
Blueberry Tart	1 (3.5 oz)	300	90
Blueberry Turnover	1 (3.8 oz)	370	130
Bow Tie	1 (2.5 oz)	250	90
Chocolate Frosted Coffee Roll	1 (2.7 oz)	290	120
Cinnamon Raisin Coffee Roll	1 (3 oz)	330	120
Coffee Roll	1 (2.6 oz)	280	120
Eclair	1 (3 oz)	290	110
Glazed Fritter	1 (2.7 oz)	290	120
Lemon Tart	1 (3.5 oz)	280	100
Lemon Turnover	1 (3.8 oz)	350	140
Maple Frosted Coffee Roll	1 (2.7 oz)	300	120
Raspberry Tart	1 (3.5 oz)	310	90
Raspberry Turnover	1 (3.8 oz)	380	130
Strawberry Tart	1 (3.5 oz)	310	90
Strawberry Turnover	1 (3.8 oz)	380	130
Vanilla Frosted Coffee Roll	1 (2.7 oz)	300	120

💡 Smart Choice

TOTAL FAT (g)	SATURATED FAT (g)	SODIUM (mg)	PROTEIN (g)	CARBOHYDRATE (g)	CARBOHYDRATE CHOICES	EXCHANGES
7	2	170	3	36	2½	2½ other carb, 1 fat
5	1	170	2	28	2	2 other carb, 1 fat
6	1	160	2	23	1½	1½ other carb, 1 fat
10	3	250	4	26	2	2 other carb, 1 fat
13	3	320	5	41	3	3 other carb, 2 fat
10	3	330	5	45	3	3 other carb, 1½ fat
15	4	340	5	49	3	3 other carb, 2½ fat
14	4	260	4	42	3	3 other carb, 2 fat
10	3	320	5	48	3	3 other carb, 1½ fat
15	4	330	5	54	3	3 other carb, 2½ fat
10	3	300	5	35	2	2 other carb, 2 fat
14	3	300	5	38	2½	2½ other carb, 2 fat
13	3	300	5	48	3	3 other carb, 2 fat
13	3	300	5	35	2	2 other carb, 2 fat
12	3	280	4	42	3	3 other carb, 2 fat
13	3	300	5	39	2½	2½ other carb, 2 fat
11	3	340	5	43	3	3 other carb, 1½ fat
15	4	360	5	48	3	3 other carb, 2½ fat
13	3	300	5	42	3	3 other carb, 2 fat
10	3	350	5	51	3½	3½ other carb, 1½ fat
15	4	370	5	57	4	4 other carb, 2½ fat
10	3	340	5	51	3½	3½ other carb, 1½ fat
15	4	360	5	57	4	4 other carb, 2½ fat
13	3	300	5	40	2½	2½ other carb, 2 fat

1 Carbohydrate Choice = 1 starch or 1 fruit or 1 milk exchange
* Grams of fiber subtracted from total carbohydrate

MENU ITEM	SERVING SIZE	CALORIES	CALORIES FROM FAT
MUFFINS			
Apple 'n Spice Muffin	1 (3.4 oz)	330	90
Apple 'n Spice Muffin, lowfat	1 (3.4 oz)	220	15
Banana Muffin, lowfat	1 (3.4 oz)	240	15
Banana Nut Muffin	1 (3.4 oz)	340	110
Blueberry Muffin	1 (3.4 oz)	310	90
Blueberry Muffin, lowfat	1 (3.4 oz)	230	15
Bran Muffin, lowfat	1 (3.4 oz)	260	15
Chocolate Chip Muffin	1 (3.4 oz)	400	140
Cherry Muffin	1 (3.4 oz)	330	100
Cherry Muffin, lowfat	1 (3.4 oz)	230	15
Corn Muffin	1 (3.4 oz)	350	130
Corn Muffin, lowfat	1 (3.4 oz)	250	15
Cranberry Orange Nut Muffin	1 (3.5 oz)	310	100
Cranberry Orange Muffin, lowfat	1 (3.4 oz)	230	15
Honey Raisin Bran Muffin	1 (3.3 oz)	330	90
Oat Bran Muffin	1 (3.3 oz)	290	100
SANDWICHES (ON CROISSANT)			
Broccoli & Cheese Sandwich	1 (6 oz)	370	190
Chicken Salad Sandwich	1 (7.5 oz)	540	280
Ham & Cheese Sandwich	1 (6.8 oz)	540	290
Roast Beef & Cheese Sandwich	1 (6 oz)	490	240
Seafood Salad Sandwich	1 (7.5 oz)	480	240
Tuna Salad Sandwich	1 (7.5 oz)	540	270
SOUPS			
Beef Barley Soup	8 oz	90	5
Beef Noodle Soup	8 oz	90	10

 Smart Choice

TOTAL FAT (g)	SATURATED FAT (g)	SODIUM (mg)	PROTEIN (g)	CARBOHYDRATE (g)	CARBOHYDRATE CHOICES	EXCHANGES
10	3	330	5	54	3½	3½ other carb, 1½ fat
2	0	480	3	50	3	3 other carb
2	0	380	3	54	3½	3½ other carb
12	3	210	6	53	3½	3½ other carb, 2 fat
10	3	190	5	51	3½	3½ other carb, 1 fat
2	0	370	3	51	3½	3½ other carb
2	0	440	4	59	4	4 other carb
16	6	190	5	63	4	4 other carb, 2 fat
11	3	210	5	53	3½	3½ other carb, 1 fat
2	0	380	3	53	3½	3½ other carb
14	1	310	6	51	3½	3½ other carb, 2 fat
2	0	460	4	55	3½	3½ other carb
11	3	180	5	51	3½	3½ other carb, 1 fat
2	0	380	3	53	3½	3½ other carb
10	0	360	5	57	4	4 other carb, 1 fat
11	1	330	4	44	3	3 other carb, 1½ fat
21	6	680	10	36	2½	2½ starch, 1 med. fat meat, 3 fat
31	7	710	27	37	2½	2½ starch, 3 med. fat meat, 3 fat
32	13	1840	33	29	2	2 starch, 4 med. fat meat, 2 fat
27	8	680	31	28	2	2 starch, 4 med. fat meat, 1 fat
26	6	1020	16	45	3	3 starch, 1½ med. fat meat, 3 fat
30	6	1140	30	39	2½	2½ starch, 3½ med. fat meat, 2 fat
1	0	970	7	15	1	1 starch
1	0	980	8	12	1	1 starch

1 Carbohydrate Choice = 1 starch or 1 fruit or 1 milk exchange
* Grams of fiber subtracted from total carbohydrate

MENU ITEM

MENU ITEM	SERVING SIZE	CALORIES	CALORIES FROM FAT
☼ Chicken Noodle Soup	8 oz	80	15
☼ Chili	8 oz	170	60
☼ Chili con Carne with Beans	8 oz	300	140
Cream of Broccoli Soup	8 oz	200	100
Cream of Potato Soup	8 oz	190	90
☼ Harvest Vegetable Soup	8 oz	80	20
☼ Manhattan Clam Chowder Soup	8 oz	70	5
☼ Minestrone Soup	8 oz	100	10
☼ New England Clam Chowder Soup	8 oz	200	90
☼ Split Pea with Ham Soup	8 oz	190	80
DESSERTS			
Blondie with Chocolate Chips Brownie	1 (10.5 oz)	300	120
Chocolate Chocolate Chunk Cookie	1 (1.5 oz)	200	100
Chocolate Chunk Cookie	1 (1.5 oz)	200	90
Chocolate Chunk with Nuts Cookie	1 (1.5 oz)	200	100
Chocolate White Chocolate Chunk Cookie	1 (1.5 oz)	200	100
Fudge Brownie	1 (10.2 oz)	290	120
☼ Oatmeal Raisin Pecan Cookie	1 (1.5 oz)	190	80
Peanut Butter Blondie Brownie	1 (11.6 oz)	330	160
Peanut Butter Chocolate Chunk with Nuts Cookie	1 (1.5 oz)	210	120
Peanut Butter Chocolate Chunk with Peanuts Cookie	1 (1.5 oz)	210	110
BREAKFAST SANDWICHES (ON CROISSANT)			
Egg & Cheese Sandwich	1 (5 oz)	430	250
Egg, Bacon & Cheese Sandwich	1 (5.4 oz)	500	300
Egg, Ham & Cheese Sandwich	1 (6 oz)	530	260

☼ Smart Choice

TOTAL FAT (g)	SATURATED FAT (g)	SODIUM (mg)	PROTEIN (g)	CARBOHYDRATE (g)	CARBOHYDRATE CHOICES	EXCHANGES
2	0	890	6	12	1	1 starch
6	3	860	8	20	1	1 starch, 1 med. fat meat
15	0	690	17	25	1½	1½ starch, 2 med. fat meat
11	6	1050	8	17	1	1 starch, 2 fat
10	5	770	6	19	1	1 starch, 2 fat
2	0	1120	4	12	1	1 starch
1	0	890	5	11	1	1 starch
1	0	900	5	16	1	1 starch
10	3	1050	10	16	1	1 starch, 1 med. fat meat, 1 fat
9	3	830	8	20	1	1 starch, 1 med. fat meat, 1 fat
13	3	150	4	41	3	3 other carb, 2 fat
11	6	160	2	26	1½	1½ other carb, 2 fat
10	6	150	2	26	1½	1½ other carb, 2 fat
11	6	150	2	25	1½	1½ other carb, 2 fat
11	6	160	2	25	1½	1½ other carb, 2 fat
13	3	85	5	37	2½	2½ other carb, 2 fat
9	5	150	2	27	2	2 other carb, 1 fat
18	4	300	6	36	2½	2½ other carb, 3 fat
13	6	110	4	23	1½	1½ other carb, 2 fat
12	5	140	4	22	1½	1½ other carb, 2 fat
27	9	640	16	30	2	2 starch, 2 med. fat meat, 3 fat
34	12	930	20	30	2	2 starch, 2 med. fat meat, 4 fat
29	9	1080	23	30	2	2 starch, 2½ med. fat meat, 3 fat

1 Carbohydrate Choice = 1 starch or 1 fruit or 1 milk exchange
* Grams of fiber subtracted from total carbohydrate

MENU ITEM	SERVING SIZE	CALORIES	CALORIES FROM FAT
Egg, Sausage & Cheese Sandwich	1 (7 oz)	630	440

SMART MEAL, DUNKIN' DONUTS

Harvest Vegetable Soup	**Calories:**	460
Whole Wheat Bagel	**Fat:**	9 grams
Classic Lite Cream Cheese (1 oz)	**Carb Choices:**	5
	Exchanges:	5 starch, 1 fat

EL POLLO LOCO
CHICKEN

MENU ITEM	SERVING SIZE	CALORIES	CALORIES FROM FAT
☼ Breast	1 (3 oz)	160	54
☼ Leg	1 (1.75 oz)	90	45
☼ Thigh	1 (2 oz)	180	108
☼ Wing	1 (1.5 oz)	110	54

BURRITOS

MENU ITEM	SERVING SIZE	CALORIES	CALORIES FROM FAT
BRC Burrito	1 (9.3 oz)	482	135
Classic Chicken Burrito	1 (9.3 oz)	556	198
Grilled Steak Burrito	1 (11.3 oz)	705	288
Loco Grande Burrito	1 (13.1 oz)	632	234
Smokey Black Bean Burrito	1 (9.3 oz)	566	198
Spicy Hot Chicken Burrito	1 (9.8 oz)	559	198
Whole Wheat Chicken Burrito	1 (10.8 oz)	592	234

SPECIALTIES

MENU ITEM	SERVING SIZE	CALORIES	CALORIES FROM FAT
☼ Chicken Soft Taco	1 (4 oz)	224	108
☼ Pollo Bowl	1 (19 oz)	504	117
Taco al Carbon, Chicken	1 (4.4 oz)	265	108
Taco al Carbon, Steak	1 (4.4 oz)	394	198
Taquito	1 (5 oz)	370	153

 Smart Choice

TOTAL FAT (g)	SATURATED FAT (g)	SODIUM (mg)	PROTEIN (g)	CARBOHYDRATE (g)	CARBOHYDRATE CHOICES	EXCHANGES
49	15	1180	24	30	2	2 starch, 3 med. fat meat, 6 fat

SMART MEAL, DUNKIN' DONUTS

Chili
French Roll
Oatmeal Raisin Pecan Cookie

Calories: 500
Fat: 16 grams
Carb Choices: 5
Exchanges: 3 starch, 2 other carb, 1 med. fat meat, 1 fat

TOTAL FAT (g)	SATURATED FAT (g)	SODIUM (mg)	PROTEIN (g)	CARBOHYDRATE (g)	CARBOHYDRATE CHOICES	EXCHANGES
6	2	390	26	0	0	3½ lean meat
5	2	150	11	0	0	1½ lean meat
12	4	230	16	0	0	2 med. fat meat
6	2	220	12	0	0	2 lean meat
15	5	1250	16	63*	4½	4½ starch, 1 med. fat meat, 2 fat
22	7	1499	30	53*	3½	3½ starch, 3 med. fat meat, 1 fat
32	13	1689	39	58*	4	4 starch, 4½ med. fat meat, 2 fat
26	7	1649	33	59*	4	4 starch, 3½ med. fat meat, 1 fat
22	8	1337	16	69*	4½	4½ starch, 1 med. fat meat, 3 fat
22	7	1503	30	53*	3½	3½ starch, 3 med. fat meat, 1 fat
26	9	1199	31	52*	3½	3½ starch, 3 med. fat meat, 2 fat
12	4	585	16	15	1	1 starch, 2 med. fat meat
13	2	2068	37	60*	4	4 starch, 4 lean meat
12	2	223	10	30	2	2 starch, 1 med. fat meat, 1 fat
22	7	473	20	30	2	2 starch, 2 med. fat meat, 2 fat
17	4	690	15	43	3	3 starch, 1 med. fat meat, 2 fat

1 Carbohydrate Choice = 1 starch or 1 fruit or 1 milk exchange
* Grams of fiber subtracted from total carbohydrate

MENU ITEM	SERVING SIZE	CALORIES	CALORIES FROM FAT
TORTILLAS			
☼ Corn Tortilla, 6"	1 (1.1 oz)	70	9
☼ Flour Tortilla, 6"	1 (1 oz)	90	27
SIDE ORDERS			
Cole Slaw	1 order (5 oz)	206	144
☼ Corn on the cob, 5½"	1 ear (5.5 oz)	146	18
French Fries	1 order (4.4 oz)	323	126
☼ Pinto Beans	1 order (6 oz)	185	36
Potato Salad	1 order (6 oz)	256	126
Smokey Black Beans	1 order (5 oz)	255	117
☼ Spanish Rice	1 order (4 oz)	130	27
SIDE BUFFET (SELECTED RESTAURANTS)			
Broccoli Slaw	5 oz	203	153
☼ Crispy Green Beans	5 oz	41	18
☼ Cucumber Salad	4.2 oz	34	0
Cornbread Stuffing	6 oz	281	108
☼ Fiesta Corn	5 oz	152	54
☼ Gravy	1 oz	14	0
☼ Honey Glazed Carrots	5 oz	104	54
☼ Lime Parfait	5 oz	125	27
☼ Macaroni & Cheese	6 oz	238	108
☼ Mashed Potatoes	5 oz	97	9
☼ Rainbow Pasta Salad	5 oz	157	9
Southwest Cole Slaw	5 oz	178	117
☼ Spiced Apples	5 oz	146	0
SALADS			
☼ Chicken Tostada Salad	1 (14.7 oz)	332	126

☼ Smart Choice

TOTAL FAT (g)	SATURATED FAT (g)	SODIUM (mg)	PROTEIN (g)	CARBOHYDRATE (g)	CARBOHYDRATE CHOICES	EXCHANGES
1	0	35	1	14	1	1 starch
3	0	224	3	13	0	1 starch
16	3	358	2	12	1	2 veg, 3 fat
2	0	18	5	33	2	2 starch
14	3	330	5	44	3	3 starch, 2 fat
4	0	744	11	21*	1½	1½ starch, 1 lean meat
14	2	527	3	30	2	2 starch, 2 fat
13	5	609	6	29	2	2 starch, 2 fat
3	1	397	2	24	1½	1½ starch
17	0	365	3	14	1	3 veg or 1 starch, 3 fat
2	1	667	1	6	½	1 veg
0	0	11	2	7	½	1 veg
12	2	832	6	34*	2	2 starch, 2 fat
6	1	397	4	19*	1	1 starch, 1 fat
0	0	139	0	2	0	free
6	1	403	1	14	1	1 starch, 1 fat
3	3	107	1	25	2	2 other carb
12	5	919	10	22	1½	1½ starch, 1 med. fat meat, 1 fat
1	0	369	3	21	1½	1½ starch
1	0	533	6	30	2	2 starch
13	2	267	2	15	1	1 starch, 2½ fat
0	0	139	0	39	2½	2½ fruit
14	5	1280	35	26	2	2 starch, 4½ lean meat

1 Carbohydrate Choice = 1 starch or 1 fruit or 1 milk exchange
* Grams of fiber subtracted from total carbohydrate

MENU ITEM	SERVING SIZE	CALORIES	CALORIES FROM FAT
💡 Flame-Broiled Chicken Salad	1 (14.9 oz)	167	45
💡 Garden Salad	1 (6.4 oz)	29	0
Steak Tostada Salad	1 (13.2 oz)	525	279
Tostada Salad Shell	1 (5.6 oz)	440	243
SALAD DRESSINGS			
Bleu Cheese Salad Dressing	2 oz	300	288
💡 Italian Salad Dressing, Light	2 oz	25	9
Ranch Salad Dressing	2 oz	350	351
Thousand Island Salad Dressing	2 oz	270	243
CONDIMENTS			
Guacamole	1.75 oz	52	27
💡 Jalapeno Hot Sauce	1 pkt (2 tsp)	5	0
💡 Pico de Gallo	1 oz	11	9
💡 Salsa, Chipotle	1 oz	8	0
💡 Salsa, House	1 oz	6	0
💡 Salsa Picante	1 oz	5	0
💡 Salsa Verde	1 oz	6	0
Sour Cream, Light	1 oz	45	27
DESSERTS			
Churro	1 (1.4 oz)	149	72
💡 Flan	1 (5.5 oz)	220	18

SMART MEAL, EL POLLO LOCO

Chicken Breast
Spanish Rice
Corn on the Cob, 5½"
Garden Salad
Italian Salad Dressing, Light (2 oz)

Calories: 490
Fat: 12 grams
Carb Choices: 4½
Exchanges: 3½ starch, 1 veg, 3½ lean meat

💡 Smart Choice

TOTAL FAT (g)	SATURATED FAT (g)	SODIUM (mg)	PROTEIN (g)	CARBOHYDRATE (g)	CARBOHYDRATE CHOICES	EXCHANGES
5	0	765	27	11	1	2 veg, 3½ very lean meat
0	0	20	3	6	½	1 veg
31	14	1206	40	26	2	2 starch, 5 med. fat meat, 1 fat
27	4	610	7	42	3	3 starch, 5 fat
32	6	590	2	2	0	6 fat
1	1	990	0	3	0	free
39	6	500	1	2	0	8 fat
27	4	460	1	9	½	½ other carb, 5 fat
3	0	280	0	5	0	1 fat
0	0	110	0	1	0	free
1	0	131	0	2	0	free
0	0	156	0	2	0	free
0	0	96	0	1	0	free
0	0	66	0	2	0	free
0	0	90	0	1	0	free
3	0	25	2	2	0	1 fat
8	2	160	2	18	1	1 other carb, 1½ fat
2	2	140	6	46	3	3 other carb

SMART MEAL, EL POLLO LOCO

Chicken Soft Taco
Pinto Beans
Garden Salad
Italian Salad Dressing, Light (2 oz)

Calories: 463
Fat: 17 grams
Carb Choices: 3
Exchanges: 2½ starch, 1 veg, 2 med fat meat, 1 lean meat

1 Carbohydrate Choice = 1 starch or 1 fruit or 1 milk exchange
* Grams of fiber subtracted from total carbohydrate

MENU ITEM	SERVING SIZE	CALORIES	CALORIES FROM FAT

GODFATHER'S PIZZA
CHEESE PIZZA

Golden Crust, medium	⅛ pizza	212	72
Golden Crust, large	⅒ pizza	242	81
☀ Original Crust, mini	¼ pizza	131	27
☀ Original Crust, medium	⅛ pizza	231	45
☀ Original Crust, large	⅒ pizza	258	54
☀ Original Crust, jumbo	⅒ pizza	382	81

COMBO PIZZA

Golden Crust, medium	⅛ pizza	271	108
Golden Crust, large	⅒ pizza	305	126
☀ Original Crust, mini	¼ pizza	176	63
☀ Original Crust, medium	⅛ pizza	306	99
☀ Original Crust, large	⅒ pizza	338	108
☀ Original Crust, jumbo	⅒ pizza	503	162

TOTAL FAT (g)	SATURATED FAT (g)	SODIUM (mg)	PROTEIN (g)	CARBOHYDRATE (g)	CARBOHYDRATE CHOICES	EXCHANGES
8	NA	311	10	26	2	2 starch, 1 high fat meat
9	NA	363	12	28	2	2 starch, 1 high fat meat
3	NA	183	7	19	1	1 starch, 1 lean meat
5	NA	338	13	34	2	2 starch, 1½ lean meat
6	NA	396	15	36	2½	2½ starch, 1½ lean meat
9	NA	580	22	53	3½	3½ starch, 2 lean meat
12	NA	562	13	28	2	2 starch, 1 med. fat meat, 1 fat
14	NA	674	16	31	2	2 starch, 1½ med. fat meat, 1 fat
7	NA	382	10	21	1½	1½ starch, 1 med. fat meat
11	NA	660	17	36	2½	2½ starch, 2 med. fat meat
12	NA	740	19	38	2½	2½ starch, 2 med. fat meat
18	NA	1096	29	56	3½	3½ starch, 3 med. fat meat

1 Carbohydrate Choice = 1 starch or 1 fruit or 1 milk exchange
* Grams of fiber subtracted from total carbohydrate

MENU ITEM	SERVING SIZE	CALORIES	CALORIES FROM FAT
HARDEE'S			
SANDWICHES			
Big Roast Beef™ Sandwich	1 (6.5 oz)	460	210
Cheeseburger	1 (4.3 oz)	310	130
☼ Chicken Fillet Sandwich	1 (7.5 oz)	480	160
Cravin' Bacon™ Cheeseburger	1 (8 oz)	690	410
Fisherman's Fillet™	1 (8.3 oz)	560	240
Frisco™ Burger	1 (8 oz)	720	410
☼ Grilled Chicken Sandwich	1 (7 oz)	350	100
☼ Hamburger	1 (4 oz)	270	100
☼ Hot Ham 'N' Cheese™	1 (5 oz)	310	100
Mesquite Bacon Cheeseburger	1 (4.5 oz)	370	160
Mushroom 'N' Swiss™ Burger	1 (6.8 oz)	490	220
Quarter Pound Double Cheeseburger	1 (6 oz)	470	240
Regular Roast Beef	1 (4.3 oz)	320	140
The Boss™	1 (7 oz)	570	300
The Works Burger	1 (8 oz)	530	270
FRIED CHICKEN			
☼ Breast	1 (5 oz)	370	130
☼ Leg	1 (2.5 oz)	170	60
Thigh	1 (4 oz)	330	130
Wing	1 (2.3 oz)	200	70
SIDE ORDERS			
☼ Baked Beans, small	1 order (5 oz)	170	10
Cole Slaw	1 order (4 oz)	240	180
French Fries, small	1 order (3.4 oz)	240	90

☼ Smart Choice

Total Fat (g)	Saturated Fat (g)	Sodium (mg)	Protein (g)	Carbohydrate (g)	Carbohydrate Choices	Exchanges
24	9	1230	26	35	2	2 starch, 3 med. fat meat, 2 fat
14	6	890	16	30	2	2 starch, 2 med. fat meat, 1 fat
18	3	1280	26	54	3½	3½ starch, 3 med. fat meat
46	15	1150	30	38	2½	2½ starch, 4 med. fat meat, 4 fat
27	7	1330	26	54	3½	3½ starch, 3 med. fat meat, 2 fat
46	16	1340	33	43	3	3 starch, 4 med. fat meat, 4 fat
11	2	950	25	38	2½	2½ starch, 3 lean meat
11	3	670	14	29	2	2 starch, 2 med. fat meat
12	6	1410	16	34	2	2 starch, 2 med. fat meat
18	7	970	19	32	2	2 starch, 2 med. fat meat, 1½ fat
25	12	1100	28	39	2½	2½ starch, 3½ med. fat meat, 1 fat
27	11	1290	27	31	2	2 starch, 3½ med. fat meat, 1½ fat
16	6	820	17	26	2	2 starch, 2 med. fat meat, 1 fat
33	12	910	27	42	3	3 starch, 3 med. fat meat, 3 fat
30	12	1030	25	41	3	3 starch, 3 med. fat meat, 2 fat
15	4	1190	29	29	2	2 starch, 3 med. fat meat
7	2	570	13	15	1	1 starch, 1½ med. fat meat
15	4	100	19	30	2	2 starch, 2 med. fat meat, 1 fat
8	2	740	10	23	1½	1½ starch, 1 high fat meat
1	0	600	8	32	2	2 starch
20	3	340	2	13	1	3 veg or 1 starch, 4 fat
10	3	100	4	33	2	2 starch, 2 fat

1 Carbohydrate Choice = 1 starch or 1 fruit or 1 milk exchange
* Grams of fiber subtracted from total carbohydrate

MENU ITEM	SERVING SIZE	CALORIES	CALORIES FROM FAT
French Fries, medium	1 order (5 oz)	350	130
French Fries, large	1 order (6.1 oz)	430	160
☀ Gravy	1 (1.5 oz)	20	0
☀ Mashed Potatoes	1 order (4 oz)	70	0

SALADS

Garden Salad	1 (10 oz)	220	120
☀ Grilled Chicken Salad	1 (11.5 oz)	150	30
☀ Side Salad	1 (4.6 oz)	25	0

SALAD DRESSINGS

☀ French Salad Dressing, Fat Free	2 oz	70	0
Ranch Salad Dressing	2 oz	290	260
Thousand Island Salad Dressing	2 oz	250	210

DESSERTS

Big Cookie™	1 (2 oz)	280	110
☀ Chocolate Cone	1 (4 oz)	180	20
☀ Cool Twist™ Cone (Vanilla/Chocolate)	1 (4 oz)	180	20
Hot Fudge Sundae	1 (5.5 oz)	290	50
Peach Cobbler	1 (6 oz)	310	60
☀ Strawberry Sundae	1 (5.8 oz)	210	20
☀ Vanilla Cone	1 (4 oz)	170	20

SHAKES

Vanilla Shake	12.3 oz	350	50
Chocolate Shake	12.3 oz	370	50
Strawberry Shake	12.8 oz	420	40
Peach Shake	12 oz	390	40

☀ Smart Choice

TOTAL FAT (g)	SATURATED FAT (g)	SODIUM (mg)	PROTEIN (g)	CARBOHYDRATE (g)	CARBOHYDRATE CHOICES	EXCHANGES
15	4	150	5	49	3	3 starch, 3 fat
18	5	190	06	59	4	4 starch, 3½ fat
trace	trace	260	trace	3	0	free
trace	trace	330	2	14	1	1 starch
13	9	350	12	11	1	2 veg, 1 med. fat meat, 2 fat
3	1	610	20	11	1	2 veg, 3 very lean meat
trace	trace	45	1	4	0	1 veg
0	0	580	0	17	1	1 other carb
29	4	510	1	6	0	6 fat
23	3	540	1	9	½	½ other carb, 4½ fat
12	4	150	4	41	3	3 other carb, 2 fat
2	1	110	5	34	2	2 other carb
2	1	120	4	34	2	2 other carb
6	3	310	7	51	3½	3½ other carb, 1 fat
7	1	360	2	60	4	4 other carb, 1 fat
2	1	140	5	43	3	3 other carb
2	1	130	4	34	2	2 other carb
5	3	300	12	65	4	4 other carb, 1 fat
5	3	270	13	67	4½	4½ other carb, 1 fat
4	3	270	11	83	5½	5½ other carb, 1 fat
4	3	290	10	77	5	5 other carb, 1 fat

1 Carbohydrate Choice = 1 starch or 1 fruit or 1 milk exchange
* Grams of fiber subtracted from total carbohydrate

MENU ITEM	SERVING SIZE	CALORIES	CALORIES FROM FAT
BREAKFAST			
Apple Cinnamon 'N' Raisin™ Biscuit	1 (2 oz)	200	70
Bacon and Egg Biscuit	1 (5.5 oz)	570	300
Bacon, Egg and Cheese Biscuit	1 (6 oz)	610	330
Big Country® Breakfast with Bacon	1 (9.5 oz)	820	440
Big Country® Breakfast with Sausage	1 (11.5 oz)	1000	590
Biscuit 'N' Gravy™	1 (7.8 oz)	510	250
Country Ham Biscuit	1 (3.8 oz)	430	200
Frisco Breakfast Sandwich with Ham	1 (7.5 oz)	500	220
Ham Biscuit	1 (4 oz)	400	180
Ham, Egg and Cheese Biscuit	1 (6.5 oz)	540	270
Jelly Biscuit	1 (3.5 oz)	440	190
☀ Orange Juice	1 (12 oz)	140	0
☀ Pancakes	3 (4.8 oz)	280	20
Regular Hash Rounds™	16 (2.8 oz)	230	130
Rise 'N' Shine® Biscuit	1 (3 oz)	390	190
Sausage and Egg Biscuit	1 (12 oz)	630	360
Sausage Biscuit	1 (4 oz)	510	280
Ultimate Omelet™ Biscuit	1 (5.8 oz)	570	270

SMART MEAL, HARDEE'S

Hamburger
Baked Beans
Side Salad
French Salad Dressing, Fat Free (2 oz)

Calories:	535
Fat:	12 grams
Carb Choices:	5½
Exchanges:	4 starch, 1 veg, 1 other carb, 2 med. fat meat

☀ Smart Choice

TOTAL FAT (g)	SATURATED FAT (g)	SODIUM (mg)	PROTEIN (g)	CARBOHYDRATE (g)	CARBOHYDRATE CHOICES	EXCHANGES
8	2	350	2	30	2	2 starch, 1 fat
33	11	1400	22	45	3	3 starch, 2 med. fat meat, 4 fat
37	13	1630	24	45	3	3 starch, 2½ med. fat meat, 4 fat
49	15	1870	33	62	4	4 starch, 3½ med. fat meat, 6 fat
66	38	2310	41	62	4	4 starch, 5 med. fat meat, 7 fat
28	9	1500	10	55	3½	3½ starch, 5½ fat
22	6	1930	15	45	3	3 starch, 1½ med. fat meat, 2 fat
25	9	1370	24	46	3	3 starch, 3 med. fat meat, 1 fat
20	6	1340	9	47	3	3 starch, 1 med. fat meat, 2 fat
30	11	1660	20	48	3	3 starch, 2 med. fat meat, 4 fat
21	6	1000	6	57	4	3 starch, 1 other carb, 4 fat
trace	trace	5	2	34	2	2 fruit
2	1	890	8	56	4	4 starch
14	3	560	3	24	1½	1½ starch, 3 fat
21	6	1000	6	44	3	3 starch, 4 fat
40	22	1480	23	45	3	3 starch, 2 med. fat meat, 6 fat
31	10	1360	14	44	3	3 starch, 1 med. fat meat, 3½ fat
33	12	1370	22	45	3	3 starch, 2 med. fat meat, 4 fat

SMART MEAL, HARDEE'S

Hot Ham 'N' Cheese™ Sandwich	**Calories:**	585
Side Salad	**Fat:**	14 grams
French Salad Dressing, Fat Free (2 oz)	**Carb Choices:**	6
Cool Twist™ Cone	**Exchanges:**	2 starch, 1 veg, 3 other carb, 2 med. fat meat

1 Carbohydrate Choice = 1 starch or 1 fruit or 1 milk exchange
* Grams of fiber subtracted from total carbohydrate

MENU ITEM	SERVING SIZE	CALORIES	CALORIES FROM FAT

HARVEY'S
SANDWICHES

Charbroiled Chicken Sandwich	1 (5 oz)	264	42
Cheeseburger	1 (5.2 oz)	418	198
Chicken Strips	5 pieces (4.4 oz)	364	198
Double Burger	1 (7.5 oz)	609	349
Fish Sandwich	1 (5.5 oz)	393	138
Hamburger	1 (4.5 oz)	357	158
Hot Dog	1 (4 oz)	313	105
Ultra Burger	1 (5.4 oz)	409	171
Ultra Burger with Cheese	1 (5.9 oz)	464	200
Value Burger	1 (3.7 oz)	300	117
Value Burger with Cheese	1 (4.2 oz)	352	144
Value Double Burger	1 (5.9 oz)	473	224

CHURCH'S CHICKEN

Chicken Breast Portion	1 (4.8 oz)	399	239
Chicken Breast Sandwich	1 (5.4 oz)	401	127
Chicken Leg Portion	1 (7 oz)	198	104
Chicken Thigh Portion	1 (4.1 oz)	360	241
Chicken Wing Portion	1 (4.7 oz)	363	212
Chunky Chicken Sandwich	1 (6.7 oz)	354	52

SIDE ORDERS

Church's Cole Slaw, small	1 order (2.5 oz)	96	58
Church's Cole Slaw, large	1 order (5.4 oz)	210	126
Church's Fried Zucchini	1 order (2.6 oz)	219	135
French Fries, junior	1 order (3.1 oz)	234	89

 Smart Choice

TOTAL FAT (g)	SATURATED FAT (g)	SODIUM (mg)	PROTEIN (g)	CARBOHYDRATE (g)	CARBOHYDRATE CHOICES	EXCHANGES
5	1	285	19	36	2	2 starch, 2 lean meat
22	10	1087	22	33	2	2 starch, 2½ med. fat meat, 2 fat
22	5	620	17	24	1½	1½ starch, 2 med. fat meat, 2 fat
39	14	1540	33	32	2	2 starch, 4 med. fat meat, 3½ fat
15	2	750	15	49	3	3 starch, 1 med. fat meat, 2 fat
18	7	1000	18	32	2	2 starch, 2 med. fat meat, 1 fat
12	4	220	13	39	2½	2½ starch, 1 med. fat meat, 1 fat
19	8	746	28	33	2	2 starch, 3½ med. fat meat
22	8	1210	30	36	2	2 starch, 3½ med. fat meat, 1 fat
13	5	452	17	30	2	2 starch, 2 med. fat meat
16	7	694	21	31	2	2 starch, 2 med. fat meat, 1 fat
25	11	862	31	31	2	2 starch, 4 med. fat meat, 1 fat
27	6	795	29	11	1	1 starch, 4 med. fat meat, 1 fat
14	2	775	23	45	3	3 starch, 2½ med. fat meat
12	3	353	18	6	½	½ starch, 2½ med. fat meat
27	6	538	22	8	½	½ starch, 3 med. fat meat, 2 fat
24	5	620	29	8	½	½ starch, 4 med. fat meat, ½ fat
6	2	946	44	32	2	2 starch, 6 very lean meat
6	1	247	1	8	½	2 veg, 1 fat
14	1	540	2	18	1	1 starch, 3 fat
15	2	281	3	18	1	1 starch, 3 fat
10	1	152	3	33	2	2 starch, 2 fat

1 Carbohydrate Choice = 1 starch or 1 fruit or 1 milk exchange
* Grams of fiber subtracted from total carbohydrate

MENU ITEM	SERVING SIZE	CALORIES	CALORIES FROM FAT
French Fries, regular	1 order (4 oz)	308	117
French Fries, large	1 order (5.7 oz)	430	164
Onion Rings, regular	1 order (2.9 oz)	286	179
Onion Rings, large	1 order (4.3 oz)	431	269

SOUPS

MENU ITEM	SERVING SIZE	CALORIES	CALORIES FROM FAT
Chicken Noodle Soup	10 oz	87	13
Vegetable Soup	10 oz	99	11

SALADS

MENU ITEM	SERVING SIZE	CALORIES	CALORIES FROM FAT
Garden Salad	1 (7.4 oz)	103	60

SALAD DRESSINGS

MENU ITEM	SERVING SIZE	CALORIES	CALORIES FROM FAT
Feta Cheese Salad Dressing	1.5 oz	170	153
French Salad Dressing, Light	1.5 oz	68	38
Italian Salad Dressing, Fat Free	1.5 oz	14	0
Ranch Salad Dressing	1.5 oz	205	189

CONDIMENTS

MENU ITEM	SERVING SIZE	CALORIES	CALORIES FROM FAT
Bacon	1 slice (0.4 oz)	52	37
BBQ Sauce	1 pkt (1 oz)	56	1
Honey	0.7 oz	64	0
Honey Mustard Sauce	1 pkt (1 oz)	78	4
Hot Peppers	0.4 oz	4	0
Ketchup	1 pkt (0.3 oz)	12	0
Mayonnaise	0.2 oz	43	190
Mustard	1 pkt (0.3 oz)	3	0
Onions	0.4 oz	8	0
Orange Marmalade	0.7 oz	56	0
Peanut Butter	0.6 oz	115	86

 Smart Choice

TOTAL FAT (g)	SATURATED FAT (g)	SODIUM (mg)	PROTEIN (g)	CARBOHYDRATE (g)	CARBOHYDRATE CHOICES	EXCHANGES
13	2	200	4	44	3	3 starch, 2 fat
18	2	280	6	61	4	4 starch, 3 fat
20	2	580	4	23	1½	1½ starch, 4 fat
30	3	870	6	34	2	2 starch, 6 fat
1	<1	1092	8	11	1	1 starch
1	<1	1349	1	21	1½	1½ starch
7	NA	137	6	5	0	1 veg, 1 med. fat meat
17	2	396	1	2	0	3 fat
4	0	457	0	8	½	½ other carb
0	0	462	0	3	0	free
21	2	343	1	3	0	4 fat
4	1	160	4	0	0	1 fat
0	0	380	1	14	1	1 other carb
0	0	1	0	17	1	1 other carb
0	0	160	0	19	1	1 other carb
0	0	194	0	2	0	free
0	0	119	0	3	0	free
5	<1	28	0	1	0	1 fat
0	0	54	0	0	0	free
0	0	0	0	2	0	free
0	0	9	0	14	1	1 other carb
10	2	86	4	3	0	1 high fat meat

1 Carbohydrate Choice = 1 starch or 1 fruit or 1 milk exchange
* Grams of fiber subtracted from total carbohydrate

MENU ITEM	SERVING SIZE	CALORIES	CALORIES FROM FAT
Pickle	1 (0.5 oz)	18	2
Plum Sauce	1 pkt (1 oz)	69	0
Process Cheese Food	1 slice (0.7 oz)	61	41
Relish	0.5 oz	21	0
Strawberry Jam	0.7 oz	50	0
Sweet & Sour Sauce	1 pkt (1 oz)	49	0
Tomato	0.5 oz	3	0
DESSERTS			
Apple Turnover	2.9 oz	243	131
SHAKES			
Chocolate Shake	10 oz	364	83
Strawberry Shake	10 oz	356	83
Vanilla Shake	10 oz	370	89
SOFT DRINKS			
Coca-Cola Classic®	12 oz	149	0
Diet Coke®	12 oz	1	0
Minute Maid® Orange Soda	12 oz	172	0
Sprite®	12 oz	136	0
OTHER BEVERAGES			
Apple Juice (from concentrate)	6 oz	87	2
Milk, 2%	8 oz	128	45
Orange Juice (from concentrate)	6 oz	78	3
BREAKFAST			
Bacon	1 order (0.8 oz)	103	73
Bacon, Egg, Tomato Sandwich	1 (6.7 oz)	500	250
Blueberry Muffin	1 (3.5 oz)	476	168

 Smart Choice

TOTAL FAT (g)	SATURATED FAT (g)	SODIUM (mg)	PROTEIN (g)	CARBOHYDRATE (g)	CARBOHYDRATE CHOICES	EXCHANGES
0	0	216	0	0	0	free
0	0	345	0	17	1	1 other carb
5	3	87	4	1	0	½ high fat meat
0	0	93	0	5	0	free
0	0	5	0	13	1	1 other carb
0	0	63	0	13	1	1 other carb
0	0	1	0	1	0	free
15	4	310	3	25	1½	1½ other carb, 3 fat
9	5	190	11	59	4	4 other carb, 1½ fat
9	5	130	12	56	4	4 other carb, 1½ fat
10	5	120	11	59	4	4 other carb, 1½ fat
0	0	9	0	39	2½	2½ other carb
0	0	19	0	0	0	free
0	0	46	0	44	3	3 other carb
0	0	42	0	35	2	2 other carb
0	0	5	0	22	1½	1½ fruit
5	3	129	9	12	1	1 2% milk
0	0	4	1	19	1	1 fruit
8	3	320	8	0	0	1 high fat meat
28	11	882	23	40	2½	2½ starch, 4 med. fat meat, 1 fat
19	NA	321	6	62	4	4 starch, 4 fat

1 Carbohydrate Choice = 1 starch or 1 fruit or 1 milk exchange
* Grams of fiber subtracted from total carbohydrate

MENU ITEM	SERVING SIZE	CALORIES	CALORIES FROM FAT
Bran Muffin	1 (3.5 oz)	436	156
☼ Breakfast Club Sandwich	1 (3.9 oz)	310	135
Home Fries	1 order (4.6 oz)	272	100
☼ Pancake Syrup	1 (1.5 oz)	166	0
Sausage	1 order (1.6 oz)	137	95
Sausage, Egg, Tomato Sandwich	1 (6.7 oz)	534	272
Toast	1 order (2.7 oz)	306	118
Toasted Western Sandwich	1 (4.9 oz)	370	132
Fried Eggs (2)	1 order (3.5 oz)	174	118
☼ Pancakes (2)	1 order (4 oz)	223	27

SMART MEAL, HARVEY'S

Value Burger
Vegetable Soup
Church's Cole Slaw, small
Apple Juice (6 oz)

Calories: 582
Fat: 20 grams
Carb Choices: 5½
Exchanges: 3½ starch,
1½ fruit, 2 veg,
2 med. fat meat,
1 fat

☼ Smart Choice

TOTAL FAT (g)	SATURATED FAT (g)	SODIUM (mg)	PROTEIN (g)	CARBOHYDRATE (g)	CARBOHYDRATE CHOICES	EXCHANGES
17	NA	380	6	57	4	4 starch, 3 fat
15	8	560	17	26	2	2 starch, 2 med. fat meat
11	1	923	5	38	2½	2½ starch, 2 fat
0	0	1	0	42	3	3 other carb
11	5	270	8	3	0	1 high fat meat, 1 fat
30	13	832	23	43	3	3 starch, 4 med. fat meat, 1 fat
13	7	490	9	38	2½	2½ starch, 2½ fat
15	6	731	8	52	3½	3½ starch, 2 fat
13	3	140	13	2	0	2 med. fat meat, 1 fat
3	<1	870	7	42	3	3 starch

1 Carbohydrate Choice = 1 starch or 1 fruit or 1 milk exchange
* Grams of fiber subtracted from total carbohydrate

MENU ITEM	SERVING SIZE	CALORIES	CALORIES FROM FAT

JACK IN THE BOX
SANDWICHES

Bacon Ultimate Cheeseburger	1 (10.5 oz)	1150	800
Cheeseburger	1 (4 oz)	330	140
Chicken Caesar Sandwich	1 (8.4 oz)	520	230
Chicken Fajita Pita	1 (6.5 oz)	280	80
Chicken Sandwich	1 (6 oz)	450	230
Chicken Supreme	1 (8.3 oz)	680	400
Double Cheeseburger	1 (5.4 oz)	450	220
Grilled Chicken Fillet	1 (8.1 oz)	520	230
Hamburger	1 (3.6 oz)	280	100
Jumbo Jack®	1 (7.8 oz)	560	320
Jumbo Jack® with Cheese	1 (8.7 oz)	650	390
Philly Cheesesteak	1 (7.6 oz)	520	230
Quarter Pound Burger	1 (6 oz)	510	240
Sourdough Jack®	1 (7.9 oz)	670	390
Spicy Crispy Chicken	1 (7.9 oz)	560	240
Ultimate Cheeseburger	1 (9.8 oz)	1030	710

CHICKEN/FISH

Chicken & Fries	1 order (9.4 oz)	730	310
Chicken Breast Pieces, 5-piece	1 order (5.3 oz)	360	150
Chicken Teriyaki Bowl	1 (17.7 oz)	670	40
Fish & Chips	1 order (9 oz)	720	320

TACOS

Monster Taco	1 (4 oz)	290	160
Taco	1 (2.8 oz)	190	100

 Smart Choice

TOTAL FAT (g)	SATURATED FAT (g)	SODIUM (mg)	PROTEIN (g)	CARBOHYDRATE (g)	CARBOHYDRATE CHOICES	EXCHANGES
89	30	1770	57	31	2	2 starch, 7½ med. fat meat, 10 fat
15	6	760	15	32	2	2 starch, 2 med. fat meat, ½ fat
26	6	1050	27	44	3	3 starch, 3 med. fat meat, 2 fat
9	4	840	24	25	1½	1½ starch, 3 lean meat
26	5	1030	16	38	2½	2½ starch, 2 med. fat meat, 3 fat
45	11	1500	23	46	3	3 starch, 2½ med. fat meat, 6 fat
24	12	970	24	35	2	2 starch, 3 med. fat meat, 1½ fat
26	6	1240	27	42	3	3 starch, 3 med. fat meat, 2½ fat
12	4	560	13	32	2	2 starch, 1½ med. fat meat
36	12	680	28	31	2	2 starch, 3½ med. fat meat, 3 fat
43	16	1090	32	32	2	2 starch, 4 med. fat meat, 4 fat
25	9	1980	33	41	3	3 starch, 4 med. fat meat
27	10	1080	26	39	2½	2½ starch, 3 med. fat meat, 2 fat
43	16	1180	32	39	2½	2½ starch, 4 med. fat meat, 4 fat
27	5	1020	24	55	3½	3½ starch, 3 med. fat meat, 2½ fat
79	26	1200	50	30	2	2 starch, 6½ med. fat meat, 9 fat
34	7	1690	26	79	5	5 starch, 2 med. fat meat, 4 fat
17	3	970	27	24	1½	1½ starch, 3½ med. fat meat
4	1	1620	29	123*	8	8 starch, 2 very lean meat
35	8	1580	19	81	5½	5½ starch, 1 med. fat meat, 5 fat
18	6	550	11	21	1½	1½ starch, 1½ med. fat meat, 1½ fat
11	4	410	7	15	1	1 starch, 1 med. fat meat, 1 fat

1 Carbohydrate Choice = 1 starch or 1 fruit or 1 milk exchange
* Grams of fiber subtracted from total carbohydrate

MENU ITEM	SERVING SIZE	CALORIES	CALORIES FROM FAT
SIDE ORDERS			
Bacon & Cheddar Potato Wedges	1 order (9.4 oz)	800	520
Chili Cheese Curly Fries	1 order (8.1 oz)	650	370
Egg Rolls, 3-piece	1 order (6 oz)	440	220
Egg Rolls, 5-piece	1 order (10 oz)	730	370
Onion Rings	1 order (4.2 oz)	460	230
French Fries, regular	1 order (4.1 oz)	360	150
French Fries, jumbo	1 order (5 oz)	430	180
French Fries, Super Scoop	1 order (7 oz)	610	250
Seasoned Curly Fries	1 order (4.5 oz)	420	220
Stuffed Jalapenos, 7-piece	1 order (5.3 oz)	470	250
Stuffed Jalapenos, 10-piece	1 order (7.6 oz)	680	360
SALADS			
Garden Chicken Salad	1 (8.9 oz)	200	80
Side Salad	1 (3 oz)	50	30
SALAD DRESSINGS			
Blue Cheese Salad Dressing	2 oz	210	160
Buttermilk House Salad Dressing	2 oz	290	270
Italian Salad Dressing, Low Calorie	2 oz	25	15
Thousand Island Salad Dressing	2 oz	250	220
CONDIMENTS			
American Cheese	1 slice (0.4 oz)	45	35
Barbeque Dipping Sauce	1 oz	45	0
Buttermilk House Dipping Sauce	1 oz	130	110
Country Crock Spread	1 pat (0.2 oz)	25	25
Croutons	0.4 oz	50	15

 Smart Choice

TOTAL FAT (g)	SATURATED FAT (g)	SODIUM (mg)	PROTEIN (g)	CARBOHYDRATE (g)	CARBOHYDRATE CHOICES	EXCHANGES
58	16	1470	20	49	3	3 starch, 2 med. fat meat, 9 fat
41	12	1640	12	47*	3	3 starch, 8 fat
24	6	1020	15	40	2½	2½ starch, 1½ med. fat meat, 3 fat
41	10	1700	25	67	4½	4½ starch, 2 med. fat meat, 5 fat
25	5	780	7	50	3	3 starch, 5 fat
17	4	740	4	48	3	3 starch, 3 fat
20	5	890	4	58	4	4 starch, 3 fat
28	6	1250	6	77*	5½	5½ starch, 4 fat
24	5	1030	6	46	3	3 starch, 4 fat
28	11	1560	14	41	3	3 starch, 1 med. fat meat, 4 fat
40	15	2220	20	59	4	4 starch, 2 med. fat meat, 5 fat
9	4	420	23	8	½	1 veg, 3 lean meat
3	2	75	2	3	0	1 veg
18	4	750	1	11	1	1 other carb, 3 fat
30	11	560	1	6	½	½ other carb, 6 fat
2	0	670	0	2	0	free
24	4	570	1	10	½	½ other carb, 5 fat
4	3	200	2	0	0	1 fat
0	0	300	1	11	1	1 other carb
13	5	240	<1	3	0	3 fat
3	<1	40	0	0	0	½ fat
2	<1	105	1	8	½	½ starch

1 Carbohydrate Choice = 1 starch or 1 fruit or 1 milk exchange
* Grams of fiber subtracted from total carbohydrate

MENU ITEM	SERVING SIZE	CALORIES	CALORIES FROM FAT
🔅 Ketchup	0.3 oz	10	0
🔅 Pancake Syrup	1 pkt (1.5 oz)	120	0
🔅 Salsa	1 oz	10	0
Sour Cream	1 pkt (1 oz)	60	50
🔅 Soy Sauce	0.3 oz	5	0
🔅 Sweet & Sour Dipping Sauce	1 oz	40	0
Swiss-Style Cheese	1 slice (0.4 oz)	40	25
Tartar Dipping Sauce	1.5 oz	220	210

DESSERTS

Carrot Cake	1 (3.5 oz)	370	140
Cheesecake	1 (3.5 oz)	310	160
Double Fudge Cake	1 (3 oz)	300	90
Hot Apple Turnover	1 (3.8 oz)	340	160

SHAKES

Cappucino Classic Ice Cream Shake, regular	10.8 oz	630	260
Chocolate Classic Ice Cream Shake, regular	10.9 oz	630	240
Oreo Cookie Classic Ice Cream Shake, regular	11.7 oz	740	320
Strawberry Classic Ice Cream Shake, regular	10.5 oz	640	250
Vanilla Classic Ice Cream Shake, regular	10.8 oz	610	280

SOFT DRINKS

Barq's Root Beer®, regular	20 oz	180	0
Coca-Cola Classic®, regular	20 oz	170	0
Diet Coke®, regular	20 oz	0	0

🔅 Smart Choice

TOTAL FAT (g)	SATURATED FAT (g)	SODIUM (mg)	PROTEIN (g)	CARBOHYDRATE (g)	CARBOHYDRATE CHOICES	EXCHANGES
0	0	100	0	3	0	free
0	0	5	0	30	2	2 other carb
0	0	200	0	2	0	free
6	4	30	1	1	0	1 fat
0	0	480	<1	<1	0	free
0	0	160	<1	11	1	1 other carb
3	2	190	3	0	0	1 fat
23	4	240	1	2	0	5 fat
16	3	340	3	54	3½	3½ other carb, 2½ fat
18	9	210	8	29	2	2 other carb, 3 fat
10	3	320	3	50	3	3 other carb, 2 fat
18	4	510	4	41	3	3 other carb, 3 fat
29	17	320	11	80	5	5 other carb, 5 fat
27	16	330	11	85	5½	5½ other carb, 5 fat
36	19	490	13	91	6	6 other carb, 6 fat
28	15	300	10	85	5½	5½ other carb, 5 fat
31	18	320	12	73	5	5 other carb, 5 fat
0	0	40	0	50	3	3 other carb
0	0	8	0	46	3	3 other carb
0	0	15	0	0	0	free

1 Carbohydrate Choice = 1 starch or 1 fruit or 1 milk exchange
* Grams of fiber subtracted from total carbohydrate

MENU ITEM	SERVING SIZE	CALORIES	CALORIES FROM FAT
Dr. Pepper®, regular	20 oz	190	0
Sprite®, regular	20 oz	160	0
OTHER BEVERAGES			
☼ Milk, 2%	8 oz	130	45
Minute Maid® Lemonade, regular	20 oz	190	0
☼ Orange Juice	10.5 oz	150	0
BREAKFAST			
☼ Breakfast Jack	1 (4.3 oz)	300	110
☼ Grape Jelly	0.5 oz	40	0
Hash Brown	1 (2 oz)	160	100
Pancakes with Bacon	1 (5.6 oz)	400	110
Sausage Croissant	1 (6.4 oz)	670	430
Sourdough Breakfast Sandwich	1 (5.2 oz)	380	190
Supreme Croissant	1 (6 oz)	570	320
Ultimate Breakfast Sandwich	1 (8.5 oz)	620	320

SMART MEAL, JACK IN THE BOX

Hamburger
Side Salad
Italian Salad Dressing, Low Calorie (2 oz)
Diet Soft Drink

Calories: 355
Fat: 17 grams
Carb Choices: 2½
Exchanges: 2 starch, 1 veg, 1½ med. fat meat

☼ Smart Choice

TOTAL FAT (g)	SATURATED FAT (g)	SODIUM (mg)	PROTEIN (g)	CARBOHYDRATE (g)	CARBOHYDRATE CHOICES	EXCHANGES
0	0	25	0	49	3	3 other carb
0	0	40	0	41	3	3 other carb
5	3	85	9	14	1	1 2% milk
0	0	90	0	48	3	3 other carb
0	0	20	2	34	2	2 fruit
12	5	890	18	30	2	2 starch, 2 med. fat meat
0	0	5	0	9	½	½ other carb
11	11	310	1	14	1	1 starch, 2 fat
12	3	980	13	59	4	4 starch, 2 fat
48	19	940	21	39	2½	2½ starch, 2 med. fat meat, 7 fat
21	8	1120	21	31	2	2 starch, 2 med. fat meat, 2 fat
36	7	1240	21	39	2½	2½ starch, 2 med. fat meat, 5 fat
36	15	1800	36	39	2½	2½ starch, 4½ med. fat meat, 2 fat

1 Carbohydrate Choice = 1 starch or 1 fruit or 1 milk exchange
* Grams of fiber subtracted from total carbohydrate

MENU ITEM	SERVING SIZE	CALORIES	CALORIES FROM FAT
KFC			
TENDER ROAST™ CHICKEN			
Breast (with skin)	1 (4.9 oz)	251	97
Breast (without skin)	1 (4.2 oz)	169	39
Drumstick (with skin)	1 (1.9 oz)	97	39
Drumstick (without skin)	1 (1.2 oz)	67	22
Thigh (with skin)	1 (3.2 oz)	207	126
Thigh (without skin)	1 (2.1 oz)	106	50
Wing (with skin)	1 (1.8 oz)	121	69
ORIGINAL RECIPE® CHICKEN			
Breast	1 (5.4 oz)	400	220
Drumstick	1 (2.2 oz)	140	80
Thigh	1 (3.2 oz)	250	160
Whole Wing	1 (1.6 oz)	140	90
EXTRA TASTY CRISPY™ CHICKEN			
Breast	1 (5.9 oz)	470	250
Drumstick	1 (2.4 oz)	190	100
Thigh	1 (4.2 oz)	370	220
Whole Wing	1 (1.9 oz)	200	100
HOT & SPICY CHICKEN			
Breast	1 (6.5 oz)	530	310
Drumstick	1 (2.3 oz)	190	100
Thigh	1 (3.8 oz)	370	240
Whole Wing	1 (1.9 oz)	210	130
OTHER ENTREES			
Chunky Chicken Pot Pie	1 (13 oz)	770	378

 Smart Choice

TOTAL FAT (g)	SATURATED FAT (g)	SODIUM (mg)	PROTEIN (g)	CARBOHYDRATE (g)	CARBOHYDRATE CHOICES	EXCHANGES
11	3	830	37	1	0	5 lean meat
4	1	797	32	1	0	4½ very lean meat
4	1	271	15	<1	0	2 lean meat
2	<1	259	11	<1	0	1½ very lean meat
12	4	504	18	<2	0	2½ med. fat meat
6	2	312	13	<1	0	2 lean meat
8	2	331	12	1	0	2 med. fat meat
24	6	1116	29	16	1	1 starch, 4 med. fat meat, 1 fat
9	2	422	13	4	0	2 med. fat meat
18	5	747	16	6	½	½ starch, 2 med. fat meat, 2 fat
10	3	414	9	5	0	1 med. fat meat, 1 fat
28	7	930	31	25	1½	1½ starch, 4 med. fat meat, 1½ fat
11	3	260	13	8	½	½ starch, 2 med. fat meat
25	6	540	19	18	1	1 starch, 2 med. fat meat, 3 fat
13	4	290	10	10	½	½ starch, 1 med. fat meat, 2 fat
35	8	1110	32	23	1½	1½ starch, 4 med. fat meat, 3 fat
11	3	300	13	10	½	½ starch, 2 med. fat meat
27	7	570	18	13	1	1 starch, 2 med. fat meat, 3 fat
15	4	340	10	9	½	½ starch, 1 med. fat meat, 2 fat
42	13	2160	29	64*	4	4 starch, 3 med. fat meat, 4 fat

1 Carbohydrate Choice = 1 starch or 1 fruit or 1 milk exchange
* Grams of fiber subtracted from total carbohydrate

MENU ITEM

MENU ITEM	SERVING SIZE	CALORIES	CALORIES FROM FAT
☼ Crispy Strips	3 (3.25 oz)	261	142
Hot Wings™, 6-piece	1 order (4.8 oz)	471	297
Kentucky Nuggets®, 6-piece	1 order (3.4 oz)	284	162
Original Recipe® Chicken Sandwich	1 (7.3 oz)	497	201
☼ Value BBQ Flavored Chicken Sandwich	1 (5.3 oz)	256	74

SIDE ORDERS

☼ BBQ Baked Beans	1 order (5.5 oz)	190	25
Cole Slaw	1 order (5 oz)	180	80
☼ Corn on the Cob	1 order (5 oz)	190	25
☼ Garden Rice	1 order (4.4 oz)	120	10
☼ Green Beans	1 order (4.7 oz)	45	15
☼ Macaroni & Cheese	1 order (5.4 oz)	180	70
☼ Mashed Potatoes with Gravy	1 order (4.8 oz)	120	50
☼ Mean Greens™	1 order (5.4 oz)	70	30
Potato Salad	1 order (5.6 oz)	230	130
Potato Wedges	1 order (4.8 oz)	280	120
☼ Red Beans & Rice	1 order (4.5 oz)	130	30

BREADS

Biscuit	1 (2 oz)	180	80
Cornbread	1 (2 oz)	228	117

SMART MEAL, KFC

Tender Roast™ Chicken Breast (without skin)
BBQ Baked Beans
Green Beans

Calories: 594
Fat: 12 grams
Carb Choices: 4½
Exchanges: 4 starch, 1 veg, 4½ very lean meat, 1 fat

☼ Smart Choice

TOTAL FAT (g)	SATURATED FAT (g)	SODIUM (mg)	PROTEIN (g)	CARBOHYDRATE (g)	CARBOHYDRATE CHOICES	EXCHANGES
16	4	658	20	10	½	½ starch, 3 med. fat meat
33	8	1230	27	18	1	1 starch, 3½ med. fat meat, 3 fat
18	4	865	16	15	1	1 starch, 2 med. fat meat, 1½ fat
22	5	1213	29	46	3	3 starch, 3 med. fat meat, 1fat
8	1	782	17	28	2	2 starch, 2 lean meat
3	1	760	6	27*	2	2 starch, ½ fat
9	2	280	2	21	1½	1½ starch, 2 fat
3	<1	20	5	34	2	2 starch, ½ fat
1	0	890	3	23	1½	1½ starch
2	<1	730	1	7	½	1 veg
8	3	860	7	21	1½	1½ starch, 1 fat
6	1	440	1	17	1	1 starch, 1 fat
3	1	650	4	11	1	1 starch
14	2	540	4	23	1½	1½ starch, 3 fat
13	4	750	5	28	2	2 starch, 2½ fat
3	1	360	5	21	1½	1½ starch
10	3	560	4	20	1	1 starch, 2 fat
13	2	194	3	25	1½	1½ starch, 2½ fat

1 Carbohydrate Choice = 1 starch or 1 fruit or 1 milk exchange
* Grams of fiber subtracted from total carbohydrate

MENU ITEM	SERVING SIZE	CALORIES	CALORIES FROM FAT
KOO KOO ROO			
TURKEY			
☀ Breast, light meat	1 (4.7 oz)	195	9
☀ Thigh, dark meat	1 (5 oz)	232	71
☀ Turkey Sandwich without mayonnaise	1 sandwich	375	72
CHICKEN			
☀ Chicken Breast (2)	1 order (6.25 oz)	289	70
SIDE ORDERS			
☀ Baby Carrots	1 order (4.25 oz)	54	54
☀ Baked Yam	½ large	93	0
☀ Bulgur Wheat	1 order (3.5 oz)	78	0
☀ Butternut Squash	1 order (5.5 oz)	61	9
☀ Coleslaw	1 order (4 oz)	58	9
☀ Confetti Rice	1 order (4.5 oz)	148	9
☀ Corn	1 order (4.25 oz)	96	9
☀ Corn on the Cob, 6"	½ ear	97	9
Creamed Spinach	1 order (4.5 oz)	139	99
☀ Garlic Roasted Potatoes	1 order (4 oz)	117	18
☀ Green Beans	1 order (3.5 oz)	49	27
☀ Hot Potatoes	1 order (4 oz)	156	63
☀ Italian Vegetables	1 order (4.25 oz)	34	18
☀ Mashed Potatoes	1 order (6.5 oz)	191	54
☀ Steamed Vegetables	1 order (3.75 oz)	33	0
Three Bean Salad	1 order (5 oz)	247	144
Turkey Gravy	1 order (5 oz)	161	108
☀ Turkey Stuffing	1 order (4 oz)	167	63

☀ Smart Choice

TOTAL FAT (g)	SATURATED FAT (g)	SODIUM (mg)	PROTEIN (g)	CARBOHYDRATE (g)	CARBOHYDRATE CHOICES	EXCHANGES
1	<1	97	NA	NA	0	6 very lean meat
8	2	124	NA	NA	0	6 lean meat
8	2	463	NA	NA	3	3 starch, 3 lean meat
8	1	775	NA	NA	0	8 very lean meat
0	0	365	NA	NA	1	1 starch or 3 veg
0	0	9	NA	NA	1½	1½ starch
0	0	587	NA	NA	1	1 starch or 3 veg
1	<1	2	NA	NA	1	1 starch
1	<1	299	NA	NA	1	1 starch or 3 veg
1	<1	401	NA	NA	2	2 starch
1	<1	278	NA	NA	1½	1½ starch
1	<1	15	NA	NA	1½	1½ starch
11	5	396	NA	NA	0	2 veg, 2 fat
2	1	128	NA	NA	1½	1½ starch
3	2	175	NA	NA	0	1 veg, ½ fat
7	3	455	NA	NA	2	2 starch, 1 fat
2	<1	123	NA	NA	0	1 veg
6	4	448	NA	NA	1½	1½ starch, 1 fat
0	0	39	NA	NA	0	1 veg
16	2	619	NA	NA	1½	1½ starch, 3 fat
12	4	240	NA	NA	1	1 starch, 2 fat
7	4	626	NA	NA	1½	1½ starch, 1 fat

1 Carbohydrate Choice = 1 starch or 1 fruit or 1 milk exchange
* Grams of fiber subtracted from total carbohydrate

MENU ITEM	SERVING SIZE	CALORIES	CALORIES FROM FAT
SOUPS			
Vegetable Soup	5 oz	36	0
SALADS			
BBQ Chicken Salad, with no-fat dressing	1 large	955	387
BBQ Chicken Salad, with low-fat dressing	1 large	1027	147
BBQ Chicken Salad, with regular dressing	1 large	1193	387
Caesar Salad, with no dressing	1 large	132	54
Caesar Salad, with low-fat dressing	1 large	338	198
Caesar Salad, with regular dressing	1 large	417	324
Chicken Caesar Salad, with no dressing	1 large	366	99
Chicken Caesar Salad, with low-fat dressing	1 large	572	81
Chicken Caesar Salad, with regular dressing	1 large	651	369
Chinese Chicken Salad, with no dressing	1 large	530	153
Chinese Chicken Salad, with no-oil dressing	1 large	603	153
Chinese Chicken Salad, with regular dressing	1 large	1148	729
Cucumber Salad	1 (4.5 oz)	36	0
House Salad, with no dressing	1 large	111	27
House Salad, with low-fat dressing	1 large	352	135
House Salad, with regular dressing	1 large	683	567
Lentil Salad	1 (4.5 oz)	158	27
Pesto Pasta Salad	1 (4 oz)	205	72

 Smart Choice

TOTAL FAT (g)	SATURATED FAT (g)	SODIUM (mg)	PROTEIN (g)	CARBOHYDRATE (g)	CARBOHYDRATE CHOICES	EXCHANGES
0	0	33	NA	NA	0	1 veg
43	8	2262	NA	NA	5	5 other carb, 8 lean meat, 3 fat
49	NA	2172	NA	NA	5	5 other carb, 8 lean meat, 4 fat
73	NA	2109	NA	NA	5	5 other carb, 8 lean meat, 8 fat
6	NA	371	NA	NA	1	1 starch, 1 fat
22	NA	1227	NA	NA	2½	1½ starch, 1 other carb, 4 fat
36	NA	1395	NA	NA	1½	1½ starch, 7 fat
11	8	569	NA	NA	1	1 starch, 4 lean meat, 1 fat
27	NA	1425	NA	NA	2½	1½ starch, 1 other carb, 4 lean meat, 4 fat
41	NA	1592	NA	NA	1½	1½ starch, 4 lean meat, 7 fat
17	8	492	NA	NA	2	2 other carb, 8 lean meat
17	NA	1968	NA	NA	2½	2½ other carb, 8 lean meat
81	NA	1533	NA	NA	2	2 other carb, 8 lean meat, 12 fat
0	0	205	NA	NA	0	1 veg
3	NA	148	NA	NA	1½	1½ starch
15	NA	958	NA	NA	3	2 starch, 1 other carb, 3 fat
63	NA	832	NA	NA	3	2 starch, 12 fat
3	<1	382	NA	NA	2	2 starch
8	2	274	NA	NA	2	2 starch, 1 fat

1 Carbohydrate Choice = 1 starch or 1 fruit or 1 milk exchange
* Grams of fiber subtracted from total carbohydrate

MENU ITEM	SERVING SIZE	CALORIES	CALORIES FROM FAT
☀ Potato Salad	1 (4 oz)	93	9
Santa Fe Pasta Salad	1 (5 oz)	262	108
☀ Tangy Tomato Salad	1 (5.5 oz)	66	36
☀ Tomato Basil Pasta Salad	1 (4 oz)	133	45
☀ Twelve Vegetable Salad, with no dressing	1 large	124	9
Twelve Vegetable Salad, with low-fat dressing	1 large	270	99
Twelve Vegetable Salad, with regular dressing	1 large	330	153

CONDIMENTS

☀ Salsa	2 oz	14	0

FRUIT

☀ Fruit Salad	1 (5.5 oz)	61	0
☀ Strawberries, fresh	7 whole	31	0
☀ Watermelon	5.5 oz	50	9

SMART MEAL, KOO KOO ROO

Turkey Breast, Light Meat
Garlic Roasted Potatoes
Steamed Vegetables
Tangy Tomato Salad
Watermelon

Calories: 461
Fat: 8 grams
Carb Choices: 3
Exchanges: 1½ starch, 1 fruit, 2 veg, 6 very lean meat, 1 fat

☀ Smart Choice

TOTAL FAT (g)	SATURATED FAT (g)	SODIUM (mg)	PROTEIN (g)	CARBOHYDRATE (g)	CARBOHYDRATE CHOICES	EXCHANGES
1	<1	347	NA	NA	1½	1½ starch
12	2	401	NA	NA	2½	2½ starch, 2 fat
4	<1	291	NA	NA	0	1 veg, 1 fat
5	1	223	NA	NA	1½	1½ starch, 1 fat
1	NA	115	NA	NA	2	2 starch
11	NA	1033	NA	NA	2½	2 starch, ½ other carb, 2 fat
17	NA	971	NA	NA	2½	2½ starch, 3 fat
0	0	134	NA	NA	0	free
0	0	13	NA	NA	1	1 fruit
0	0	1	NA	NA	½	½ fruit
1	0	3	NA	NA	1	1 fruit

SMART MEAL, KOO KOO ROO

Chicken Breasts (2)
Confetti Rice
Green Beans
Cucumber Salad
Whole Fresh Strawberries

Calories: 553
Fat: 12 grams
Carb Choices: 3
Exchanges: 2 starch, ½ fruit, 2 veg, 8 very lean meat, ½ fat

1 Carbohydrate Choice = 1 starch or 1 fruit or 1 milk exchange
* Grams of fiber subtracted from total carbohydrate

MENU ITEM	SERVING SIZE	CALORIES	CALORIES FROM FAT

KRYSTAL

SANDWICHES

Bacon Cheeseburger	1 (7.4 oz)	521	306
Big K	1 (8 oz)	540	315
Burger Plus	1 (6.5 oz)	415	234
Burger Plus with Cheese	1 (7.1 oz)	473	279
Cheese Krystal Burger	1 (2.5 oz)	187	90
Crispy Crunchy Chicken Sandwich	1 (5.75 oz)	467	216
Double Cheese Krystal Burger	1 (4.5 oz)	337	171
☀ Double Krystal Burger	1 (4 oz)	277	126
☀ Krystal Burger	1 (2.2 oz)	158	63

HOT DOGS

Chili Pup Hot Dog	1 (2.5 oz)	182	90
Chili Cheese Pup Hot Dog	1 (2.7 oz)	211	117
Corn Pup Hot Dog	1 (2.3 oz)	214	126
Plain Pup Hot Dog	1 (1.9 oz)	160	81

SIDE ORDERS

French Fries, small	1 order (3 oz)	262	117
French Fries, regular	1 order (4.1 oz)	358	162
French Fries, large	1 order (5.3 oz)	463	207

SHAKES

Chill Shake, regular	8 oz	218	72
Chill Shake, large	12 oz	327	108

TOTAL FAT (g)	SATURATED FAT (g)	SODIUM (mg)	PROTEIN (g)	CARBOHYDRATE (g)	CARBOHYDRATE CHOICES	EXCHANGES
34	14	1083	26	29	2	2 starch, 3 med. fat meat, 3 fat
35	14	1283	29	29	2	2 starch, 4 med. fat meat, 2 fat
26	10	614	20	28	2	2 starch, 2 med. fat meat, 3 fat
31	13	867	23	28	2	2 starch, 3 med. fat meat, 3 fat
10	4	453	11	16	1	1 starch, 1 med. fat meat, 1 fat
24	7	949	16	48	3	3 starch, 2 med. fat meat, 2 fat
19	8	815	21	25	1½	1½ starch, 2½ med. fat meat, 1 fat
14	4	547	18	24	1½	1½ starch, 2 med. fat meat
7	2	324	10	16	1	1 starch, 1 med. fat meat
10	6	597	7	13	1	1 starch, 1 high fat meat
13	7	642	9	14	1	1 starch, 1 high fat meat, 1 fat
14	6	710	6	17	1	1 starch, 1 high fat meat, 1 fat
9	5	470	6	12	1	1 starch, 1 high fat meat
13	5	115	3	33	2	2 starch, 2½ fat
18	6	157	4	45	3	3 starch, 3 fat
23	8	203	5	59	4	4 starch, 4 fat
8	3	855	11	27	2	2 other carb, 1½ fat
12	5	1283	16	41	3	3 other carb, 2 fat

1 Carbohydrate Choice = 1 starch or 1 fruit or 1 milk exchange
* Grams of fiber subtracted from total carbohydrate

MENU ITEM	SERVING SIZE	CALORIES	CALORIES FROM FAT
LITTLE CAESAR'S			
PIZZA!PIZZA!®			
Cheese Pizza, medium	1 slice	201	63
Pepperoni Pizza, medium	1 slice	220	78
PAN!PAN!® PIZZA			
Cheese Pizza, medium	1 slice	181	55
Pepperoni Pizza, medium	1 slice	199	69
Baby Pan!Pan!® Pizza	1 pizza	616	218
HOT OVEN-BAKED SANDWICHES			
Cheeser Sandwich	1 (12.1 oz)	822	355
Meatsa Sandwich	1 (15 oz)	1036	499
Pepperoni Sandwich	1 (11.2 oz)	899	425
Supreme Sandwich	1 (13.1 oz)	894	412
Veggie Sandwich	1 (13.7 oz)	669	215
COLD DELI-STYLE SANDWICHES			
Ham & Cheese Sandwich	1 (11.6 oz)	728	318
Italian Sandwich	1 (11.9 oz)	740	335
Veggie Sandwich	1 (11.9 oz)	647	261
SIDE ORDERS			
Crazy Bread®	1 piece (1.4 oz)	106	31
Crazy Sauce	1 pkt (6 oz)	74	4
SALADS			
Antipasto Salad	1 (8.4 oz)	176	106
Caesar Salad	1 (5 oz)	140	49
Greek Salad	1 (10.3 oz)	168	86
Tossed Salad	1 (8.5 oz)	116	27

 Smart Choice

TOTAL FAT (g)	SATURATED FAT (g)	SODIUM (mg)	PROTEIN (g)	CARBOHYDRATE (g)	CARBOHYDRATE CHOICES	EXCHANGES
7	4	281	11	24	1½	1½ starch, 1 high fat meat
9	4	358	12	24	1½	1½ starch, 1 med. fat meat, 1 fat
6	3	379	9	22	1½	1½ starch, 1 med. fat meat
8	4	452	11	22	1½	1½ starch, 1 med. fat meat
24	12	1466	33	67	4½	4½ starch, 3 med. fat meat, 1 fat
39	20	2244	40	70*	4½	4½ starch, 4 high fat meat, 4 fat
56	24	3302	55	70*	4½	4½ starch, 6 med. fat meat, 5 fat
47	23	2428	43	74*	5	5 starch, 4 med. fat meat, 4 fat
46	21	2367	41	72*	5	5 starch, 4 med. fat meat, 5 fat
24	14	1534	33	73*	5	5 starch, 3 med. fat meat, 1 fat
35	13	1602	30	71	4½	4½ starch, 3 med. fat meat, 4 fat
37	12	1831	29	71	4½	4½ starch, 3 med. fat meat, 4 fat
29	9	1195	22	74	5	5 starch, 2 med. fat meat, 3 fat
3	<1	114	3	16	1	1 starch, ½ fat
<1	0	381	5	14	1	1 other carb
12	2	542	12	7	½	2 veg, 1 med. fat meat, 1 fat
5	3	372	9	14	1	3 veg or 1 starch, 1 med. fat meat
10	<1	653	9	12	1	2 veg, 1 med. fat meat, 1 fat
3	<1	170	5	19	1	3 veg or 1 starch, ½ fat

1 Carbohydrate Choice = 1 starch or 1 fruit or 1 milk exchange
* Grams of fiber subtracted from total carbohydrate

MENU ITEM	SERVING SIZE	CALORIES	CALORIES FROM FAT
SALAD DRESSINGS			
Blue Cheese Salad Dressing	1 pkt (1.5 oz)	160	124
Caesar Salad Dressing	1 pkt (1.5 oz)	255	239
French Salad Dressing	1 pkt (1.5 oz)	166	141
Greek Salad Dressing	1 pkt (1.5 oz)	268	269
Italian Salad Dressing	1 pkt (1.5 oz)	200	187
☼ Italian Salad Dressing, Fat-Free	1 pkt (1.5 oz)	15	0
Ranch Salad Dressing	1 pkt (1.5 oz)	221	197
Thousand Island Salad Dressing	1 pkt (1.5 oz)	183	153

SMART MEAL, LITTLE CAESAR'S

Cheese Pan Pan® Pizza (2 slices)
Caesar Salad
Italian Salad Dressing, Fat Free (1.5 oz)

Calories: 517
Fat: 17 grams
Carb Choices: 4
Exchanges: 3 starch, 3 veg, 3 med. fat meat

LONG JOHN SILVER'S
SEAFOOD/CHICKEN ENTREES

MENU ITEM	SERVING SIZE	CALORIES	CALORIES FROM FAT
☼ Batter-Dipped Chicken	1 piece (2 oz)	120	50
Batter-Dipped Fish	1 piece (3 oz)	170	100
Batter-Dipped Shrimp	5 pieces (2 oz)	175	113
Clams	1 order (3 oz)	300	150
☼ Flavorbaked™ Chicken	1 piece (2.6 oz)	110	30
☼ Flavorbaked™ Fish	1 piece (2.3 oz)	90	25
Popcorn Chicken	1 order (3.3 oz)	250	120
Popcorn Fish	1 order (3.6 oz)	290	130
Popcorn Shrimp	1 order (3.3 oz)	280	130

☼ Smart Choice

TOTAL FAT (g)	SATURATED FAT (g)	SODIUM (mg)	PROTEIN (g)	CARBOHYDRATE (g)	CARBOHYDRATE CHOICES	EXCHANGES
14	2	600	NA	8	½	½ other carb, 3 fat
27	4	404	NA	3	0	5 fat
16	2	553	NA	6	0	3 fat
30	8	202	NA	0	0	6 fat
21	3	468	NA	3	0	4 fat
0	0	420	NA	3	0	free
22	3	340	NA	5	0	4 fat
17	3	542	NA	6	0	3 fat
6	2	400	8	11	1	1 starch, 1 med. fat meat
11	3	470	11	7*	½	½ starch, 1½ med. fat meat, ½ fat
13	3	285	5	10	½	½ starch, 1 med. fat meat, 1 fat
17	4	670	11	26*	2	2 starch, 1 med. fat meat, 2 fat
3	1	600	19	<1	0	2½ lean meat
3	1	320	14	1	0	2 lean meat
14	4	590	15	17	1	1 starch, 2 med. fat meat, 1 fat
14	4	1090	13	27	2	2 starch, 1 med. fat meat, 1½ fat
15	4	920	11	27	2	2 starch, 1 med. fat meat, 1½ fat

1 Carbohydrate Choice = 1 starch or 1 fruit or 1 milk exchange
* Grams of fiber subtracted from total carbohydrate

MENU ITEM	SERVING SIZE	CALORIES	CALORIES FROM FAT
SANDWICHES			
☀ Batter-Dipped Fish Sandwich, no sauce	1 (5.4 oz)	320	120
☀ Flavorbaked™ Chicken Sandwich	1 (5.8 oz)	290	90
☀ Flavorbaked™ Fish Sandwich	1 (6 oz)	320	120
Ultimate Fish™ Sandwich	1 (6.4 oz)	430	190
FISH WRAPS			
Caesar Fish Wrap, regular	1 (11.5 oz)	730	330
Caesar Fish Wrap, large	1 (23 oz)	1460	650
Cajun Fish Wrap, regular	1 (11.5 oz)	730	310
Cajun Fish Wrap, large	1 (23 oz)	1450	630
Classic Fish Wrap, regular	1 (11.5 oz)	730	320
Classic Fish Wrap, large	1 (23 oz)	1470	640
Ranch Fish Wrap, regular	1 (11.5 oz)	730	320
Ranch Fish Wrap, large	1 (23 oz)	1460	640
South of the Border Fish Wrap, regular	1 (11.5 oz)	690	290
South of the Border Fish Wrap, large	1 (23 oz)	1380	570
CHICKEN WRAPS			
Caesar Chicken Wrap, regular	1 (11 oz)	730	330
Caesar Chicken Wrap, large	1 (22 oz)	1450	660
Cajun Chicken Wrap, regular	1 (11 oz)	720	320
Cajun Chicken Wrap, large	1 (22 oz)	1440	630
Classic Chicken Wrap, regular	1 (11 oz)	730	320
Classic Chicken Wrap, large	1 (22 oz)	1450	650
Ranch Chicken Wrap, regular	1 (11 oz)	730	320
Ranch Chicken Wrap, large	1 (22 oz)	1450	650
South of the Border Chicken Wrap, regular	1 (11 oz)	690	290

☀ Smart Choice

TOTAL FAT (g)	SATURATED FAT (g)	SODIUM (mg)	PROTEIN (g)	CARBOHYDRATE (g)	CARBOHYDRATE CHOICES	EXCHANGES
13	4	800	17	34*	2	2 starch, 2 med. fat meat
10	2	970	24	27	2	2 starch, 2½ lean meat
14	7	930	23	28	2	2 starch, 2½ med. fat meat
21	7	1340	18	44	3	3 starch, 2 med. fat meat, 1½ fat
37	8	1810	18	83	5½	5½ starch, 1 med. fat meat, 5 fat
73	16	3610	36	167	11	11 starch, 2 med. fat meat, 10 fat
35	8	1820	18	85	5½	5½ starch, 1 med. fat meat, 5 fat
70	15	3630	36	170	11	11 starch, 2 med. fat meat, 10 fat
36	8	1730	18	85	5½	5½ starch, 1 med. fat meat, 5 fat
72	15	3460	35	170	11	11 starch, 2 med. fat meat, 10 fat
36	8	1760	18	85	5½	5½ starch, 1 med. fat meat, 5 fat
72	15	3520	35	170	11	11 starch, 2 med. fat meat, 10 fat
32	7	1640	18	84	5½	5½ starch, 1 med. fat meat, 4 fat
64	14	3280	35	167	11	11 starch, 2 med. fat meat, 8 fat
37	7	1860	18	81	5½	5½ starch, 1 med. fat meat, 5 fat
73	15	3710	37	162	11	11 starch, 2 med. fat meat, 10 fat
35	7	1860	18	83	5½	5½ starch, 1 med. fat meat, 5 fat
71	14	3730	37	165	11	11 starch, 2 med. fat meat, 10 fat
36	7	1780	18	83	5½	5½ starch, 1 med. fat meat, 5 fat
72	14	3560	36	165	11	11 starch, 2 med. fat meat, 10 fat
36	7	1810	18	82	5½	5½ starch, 1 med. fat meat, 5 fat
72	14	3620	36	165	11	11 starch, 2 med. fat meat, 10 fat
32	7	1690	18	81	5½	5½ starch, 1 med. fat meat, 4 fat

1 Carbohydrate Choice = 1 starch or 1 fruit or 1 milk exchange
* Grams of fiber subtracted from total carbohydrate

MENU ITEM	SERVING SIZE	CALORIES	CALORIES FROM FAT
South of the Border Chicken Wrap, large	1 (22 oz)	1370	570

POPCORN SHRIMP WRAPS

MENU ITEM	SERVING SIZE	CALORIES	CALORIES FROM FAT
Caesar Popcorn Shrimp Wrap, regular	1 (11 oz)	730	330
Caesar Popcorn Shrimp Wrap, large	1 (22 oz)	1460	660
Cajun Popcorn Shrimp Wrap, regular	1 (11 oz)	720	320
Cajun Popcorn Shrimp Wrap, large	1 (22 oz)	1450	630
Classic Popcorn Shrimp Wrap, regular	1 (11 oz)	730	320
Classic Popcorn Shrimp Wrap, large	1 (22 oz)	1460	650
Ranch Popcorn Shrimp Wrap, regular	1 (11 oz)	720	320
Ranch Popcorn Shrimp Wrap, large	1 (22 oz)	1460	650
South of the Border Popcorn Shrimp Wrap, regular	1 (11 oz)	690	290
South of the Border Popcorn Shrimp Wrap, large	1 (22 oz)	1380	580

SIDE ORDERS

MENU ITEM	SERVING SIZE	CALORIES	CALORIES FROM FAT
☀ Baked Potato	1 (8 oz)	210	0
Cheese Sticks	1 order (1.6 oz)	160	80
☀ Coleslaw	1 order (3.4 oz)	140	60
Corn Cobbette	1 order (3.3 oz)	140	70
☀ Corn Cobbette, without butter	1 order (35 oz)	80	5
French Fries	1 order (3 oz)	250	130
☀ Green Beans	1 order (3.5 oz)	30	0
☀ Hushpuppy	1 (0.8 oz)	60	20
☀ Rice Pilaf	1 order (3 oz)	140	25

☀ Smart Choice

Total Fat (g)	Saturated Fat (g)	Sodium (mg)	Protein (g)	Carbohydrate (g)	Carbohydrate Choices	Exchanges
64	13	3370	36	162	11	11 starch, 2 med. fat meat, 8 fat
37	9	1820	16	84	5½	5½ starch, 1 med. fat meat, 5 fat
73	19	3650	32	169	11	11 starch, 1½ med. fat meat, 11 fat
35	9	1830	16	86	6	6 starch, 1 med. fat meat, 4 fat
71	18	3660	32	172	11½	11½ starch, 1½ med. fat meat, 10 fat
36	9	1750	16	86	6	6 starch, 1 med. fat meat, 4 fat
72	18	3500	32	172	11½	11½ starch, 1½ med. fat meat, 10 fat
35	9	1830	16	86	6	6 starch, 1 med. fat meat, 4 fat
72	18	3560	32	171	11½	11½ starch, 1½ med. fat meat, 10 fat
32	9	1660	16	84	5½	5½ starch, 1 med. fat meat, 4 fat
64	17	3310	32	169	11	11 starch, 1½ med. fat meat, 9 fat
0	0	10	4	49	3	3 starch
9	4	360	6	12	1	1 starch, 1 high fat meat
6	NA	260	1	20	1	1 starch, 1 fat
8	2	0	3	19	1	1 starch, 1½ fat
1	0	0	3	19	1	1 starch
15	3	500	3	28	2	2 starch, 2 fat
1	0	310	2	5	0	1 veg
3	0	25	1	9	½	½ starch, ½ fat
3	1	210	3	26	2	2 starch

1 Carbohydrate Choice = 1 starch or 1 fruit or 1 milk exchange
* Grams of fiber subtracted from total carbohydrate

MENU ITEM	SERVING SIZE	CALORIES	CALORIES FROM FAT
SALADS			
Side Salad	1 (4.3 oz)	25	0
SALAD DRESSINGS			
French Salad Dressing, Fat-Free	1.5 oz	50	0
Italian Salad Dressing	1 oz	130	120
Ranch Salad Dressing	1 oz	170	160
Ranch Salad Dressing, Fat-Free	1.5 oz	50	0
Thousand Island Salad Dressing	1 oz	110	90
CONDIMENTS			
Honey Mustard Sauce	1 (0.42 oz)	20	0
Ketchup	1 (0.32 oz)	10	0
Malt Vinegar	1 (0.28 oz)	0	0
Margarine	1 (0.18 oz)	35	35
Shrimp Sauce	1 (0.42 oz)	15	0
Sour Cream	1 (1 oz)	60	50
Sweet 'N' Sour Sauce	1 (0.42 oz)	20	0
Tartar Sauce	1 (0.42 oz)	35	10

SMART MEAL, LONG JOHN SILVER'S

Flavorbaked™ Fish (3 pieces)
Tartar Sauce (.42 oz)
Rice Pilaf
Green Beans
Side Salad
French Salad Dressing, Fat-Free (1 pkt)

Calories: 550
Fat: 15 grams
Carb Choices: 3½
Exchanges: 2 starch, 1 other carb, 2 veg, 6 lean meat

Smart Choice

TOTAL FAT (g)	SATURATED FAT (g)	SODIUM (mg)	PROTEIN (g)	CARBOHYDRATE (g)	CARBOHYDRATE CHOICES	EXCHANGES
0	0	15	1	4	0	1 veg
0	0	360	0	14	1	1 other carb
14	2	280	0	2	0	3 fat
18	3	260	0	1	0	3½ fat
0	0	380	2	13	1	1 other carb
10	2	280	0	5	0	2 fat
0	0	60	0	5	0	free
0	0	110	0	2	0	free
0	0	15	0	0	0	free
4	<1	35	0	0	0	1 fat
0	0	180	0	3	0	free
6	4	15	<1	1	0	1 fat
0	0	45	0	5	0	free
2	NA	35	0	5	0	free

SMART MEAL, LONG JOHN SILVER'S

Flavorbaked™ Chicken (2 pieces)
Baked Potato
Sour Cream (1 oz)
Green Beans
Side Salad
Ranch Salad Dressing, Fat-Free (1 pkt)

Calories: 595
Fat: 13 grams
Carb Choices: 5
Exchanges: 3 starch, 1 other carb, 5 lean meat, 1 fat

1 Carbohydrate Choice = 1 starch or 1 fruit or 1 milk exchange
* Grams of fiber subtracted from total carbohydrate

MENU ITEM	SERVING SIZE	CALORIES	CALORIES FROM FAT
MCDONALD'S			
SANDWICHES			
Arch Deluxe™	1 (8.4 oz)	550	280
Arch Deluxe™ with Bacon	1 (8.7 oz)	590	310
Big Mac®	1 (7.6 oz)	560	280
Cheeseburger	1 (4.2 oz)	320	120
Crispy Chicken Biscuit	1 (5.5 oz)	430	190
Crispy Chicken Deluxe™	1 (7.8 oz)	500	220
Fish Filet Deluxe™	1 (8 oz)	560	250
Grilled Chicken Deluxe™	1 (7.8 oz)	440	180
☀ Grilled Chicken Deluxe™ (plain)	1 (7.25 oz)	300	45
☀ Hamburger	1 (3.7 oz)	260	80
McRib™	1 (7 oz)	490	220
☀ Quarter Pounder®	1 (6 oz)	420	190
Quarter Pounder® with Cheese	1 (7 oz)	530	270
CHICKEN MCNUGGETS®			
Chicken McNuggets®, 4-Piece	1 order (2.5 oz)	190	100
Chicken McNuggets®, 6-Piece	1 order (3.7 oz)	290	150
Chicken McNuggets®, 9-Piece	1 order (5.6 oz)	430	230
SIDE ORDERS			
French Fries, small	1 order (2.4 oz)	210	90
French Fries, large	1 order (5.1 oz)	450	200
French Fries, Super Size®	1 order (6.2 oz)	540	230
SALADS			
☀ Garden Salad	1 (6.2 oz)	35	0
☀ Grilled Chicken Deluxe Salad	1 (7.5 oz)	120	10

☀ Smart Choice

TOTAL FAT (g)	SATURATED FAT (g)	SODIUM (mg)	PROTEIN (g)	CARBOHYDRATE (g)	CARBOHYDRATE CHOICES	EXCHANGES
31	11	1010	28	39	3	2½ starch, 3 med. fat meat, 3 fat
34	12	1150	32	39	3	2½ starch, 4 med. fat meat, 3 fat
31	10	1070	26	45	3	3 starch, 3 med. fat meat, 3 fat
13	6	820	15	35	2	2 starch, 1½ med. fat meat, 1 fat
21	5	1340	20	40	2½	2½ starch, 2 med. fat meat, 2 fat
25	4	1100	26	43	3	3 starch, 3 med. fat meat, 2 fat
28	6	1060	23	54	4	3½ starch, 2½ med. fat meat, 3 fat
20	3	1040	27	38	3	2½ starch, 3 med. fat meat, 1 fat
5	1	930	27	38	2½	2½ starch, 3 very lean meat
9	4	580	13	34	2	2 starch, 1½ med. fat meat
25	9	970	24	42	2	2 starch, 2½ med. fat meat, 2 fat
21	8	820	23	37	2½	2½ starch, 3 med. fat meat
30	13	1290	28	38	2½	2½ starch, 3½ med. fat meat, 2 fat
11	3	340	12	10	1	1 starch, 1 med. fat meat, 1 fat
17	4	510	18	15	1	1 starch, 2 med. fat meat, 1 fat
26	5	770	27	23	1½	1½ starch, 3 med. fat meat, 2 fat
10	2	135	3	26	1½	1½ starch, 2 fat
22	4	290	6	52*	3½	3½ starch, 4 fat
26	5	350	8	62*	4	4 starch, 5 fat
0	0	20	2	7	½	1 veg
2	0	240	21	7	½	1 veg, 3 very lean meat

1 Carbohydrate Choice = 1 starch or 1 fruit or 1 milk exchange
* Grams of fiber subtracted from total carbohydrate

MENU ITEM	SERVING SIZE	CALORIES	CALORIES FROM FAT
SALAD DRESSINGS			
Caesar Salad Dressing	1 pkt (1.8 oz)	160	130
Herb Vinaigrette Salad Dressing, Fat Free	1 pkt (1.8 oz)	50	0
Ranch Salad Dressing	1 pkt (1.8 oz)	230	180
Red French Salad Dressing, Reduced Calorie	1 pkt (1.8 oz)	160	70
CONDIMENTS			
Barbeque Sauce	1 pkt (1 oz)	45	0
Croutons	1 pkt (0.4 oz)	50	10
Honey	1 pkt (0.5 oz)	45	0
Honey Mustard	1 pkt (0.5 oz)	50	40
Hot Mustard	1 pkt (0.5 oz)	60	30
Light Mayonnaise	1 pkt (0.4 oz)	40	35
Margarine	2 pats (0.4 oz)	90	90
Sweet 'N Sour Sauce	1 pkt (1 oz)	50	0
Syrup	1 pkt (2.1 oz)	180	0
DESSERTS			
Baked Apple Pie	1 (2.7 oz)	260	120
Chocolate Chip Cookie	1 (1.2 oz)	170	90
McDonaldland® Cookies	1 pkg (1.5 oz)	180	45
Nuts (for Sundaes)	1 (0.2 oz)	40	30
Hot Caramel Sundae	1 (6.4 oz)	360	90
Hot Fudge Sundae	1 (6.3 oz)	340	100
Strawberry Sundae	1 (6.2 oz)	290	70
Vanilla Ice Cream Cone, Reduced Fat	1 (3.2 oz)	150	40
SHAKES			
Chocolate Shake, small	12.4 oz	360	80

 Smart Choice

TOTAL FAT (g)	SATURATED FAT (g)	SODIUM (mg)	PROTEIN (g)	CARBOHYDRATE (g)	CARBOHYDRATE CHOICES	EXCHANGES
14	3	450	2	7	½	½ other carb, 3 fat
0	0	330	0	11	½	½ other carb
21	3	550	1	10	½	½ other carb, 4 fat
8	1	490	0	23	1½	1½ other carb, 1 fat
0	0	250	0	10	1	1 other carb
2	0	80	2	7	½	½ starch
0	0	0	0	12	1	1 other carb
5	<1	85	0	3	0	1 fat
4	0	240	1	7	½	½ other carb, ½ fat
4	<1	85	0	<1	0	1 fat
9	2	130	0	0	0	2 fat
0	0	140	0	11	1	1 other carb
0	0	20	0	47	3	3 other carb
13	4	200	3	34	2	2½ other carb, 3 fat
10	6	120	2	22	1½	1½ other carb, 2 fat
5	1	190	3	32	2	2 other carb, 1 fat
4	0	0	2	2	0	1 fat
10	6	180	7	61	4	4 other carb, 2 fat
12	9	170	8	52	3½	3½ other carb, 2 fat
7	5	95	7	50	3½	3½ other carb, 1 fat
5	3	75	4	23	1½	1½ other carb, 1 fat
9	6	250	11	60	4	4 other carb, 2 fat

1 Carbohydrate Choice = 1 starch or 1 fruit or 1 milk exchange
* Grams of fiber subtracted from total carbohydrate

MENU ITEM	SERVING SIZE	CALORIES	CALORIES FROM FAT
Strawberry Shake, small	12.4 oz	360	80
Vanilla Shake, small	12.4 oz	360	80

SOFT DRINKS

Coca-Cola Classic®, child	12 oz	110	0
Coca-Cola Classic®, small	16 oz	150	0
Coca-Cola Classic®, medium	21 oz	210	0
Coca-Cola Classic®, large	32 oz	310	0
Diet Coke®, child	12 oz	0	0
Diet Coke®, small	16 oz	0	0
Diet Coke®, medium	21 oz	0	0
Diet Coke®, large	32 oz	0	0
Hi-C® Orange Drink, child	12 oz	120	0
Hi-C® Orange Drink, small	16 oz	160	0
Hi-C® Orange Drink, medium	21 oz	240	0
Hi-C® Orange Drink, large	32 oz	350	0
Sprite®, child	12 oz	110	0
Sprite®, small	16 oz	150	0
Sprite®, medium	21 oz	210	0
Sprite®, large	32 oz	310	0

OTHER BEVERAGES

Milk, 1%	8 oz	100	20
Orange Juice	6 oz	80	0

BREAKFAST

Apple Danish	1 (3.7 oz)	360	140
Bacon, Egg & Cheese Biscuit	1 (5 oz)	440	230
Biscuit	1 (2.7 oz)	260	120
Breakfast Burrito	1 (4.1 oz)	320	180

 Smart Choice

TOTAL FAT (g)	SATURATED FAT (g)	SODIUM (mg)	PROTEIN (g)	CARBOHYDRATE (g)	CARBOHYDRATE CHOICES	EXCHANGES
9	6	180	11	60	4	4 other carb, 2 fat
9	6	250	11	59	4	4 other carb, 2 fat
0	0	10	0	29	2	2 other carb
0	0	15	0	40	2½	2½ other carb
0	0	20	0	58	4	4 other carb
0	0	30	0	86	6	6 other carb
0	0	20	0	0	0	free
0	0	30	0	0	0	free
0	0	40	0	0	0	free
0	0	60	0	0	0	free
0	0	20	0	32	2	2 other carb
0	0	30	0	44	2½	3 other carb
0	0	40	0	64	4	4 other carb
0	0	60	0	94	6	6 other carb
0	0	40	0	28	2	2 other carb
0	0	55	0	39	2½	2½ other carb
0	0	80	0	56	4	4 other carb
0	0	115	0	83	6	6 other carb
3	2	115	8	13	1	1 1% milk
0	0	20	1	20	1	1 fruit
16	5	290	5	51	3	3 starch, 3 fat
26	8	1310	17	33	2	2 starch, 2 med. fat meat, 3 fat
13	3	840	4	32	2	2 starch, 2 fat
20	7	600	13	23	1½	1½ starch, 1½ med. fat meat, 2 fat

1 Carbohydrate Choice = 1 starch or 1 fruit or 1 milk exchange
* Grams of fiber subtracted from total carbohydrate

MENU ITEM	SERVING SIZE	CALORIES	CALORIES FROM FAT
Cheese Danish	1 (3.7 oz)	410	200
Cinnamon Roll	1 (3.3 oz)	400	180
☀ Egg McMuffin®	1 (4.8 oz)	290	110
☀ English Muffin	1 (1.9 oz)	140	20
☀ Hash Browns	1 order (1.9 oz)	130	70
☀ Hotcakes (plain)	1 order (5.3 oz)	310	60
☀ Hotcakes (with syrup)	1 order (7.4 oz)	490	60
Hotcakes (with syrup and 2 pats margarine)	1 order (7.8 oz)	580	150
☀ Lowfat Apple Bran Muffin	1 (4 oz)	300	30
Sausage	1 order (1.5 oz)	170	150
Sausage Biscuit	1 (4.2 oz)	430	260
Sausage Biscuit with Egg	1 (6 oz)	510	310
Sausage McMuffin®	1 (3.9 oz)	360	210
Sausage McMuffin® with Egg	1 (5.7 oz)	440	250
☀ Scrambled Eggs (2)	1 order (3.6 oz)	160	100

SMART MEAL, MCDONALD'S

Grilled Chicken Deluxe™ (plain)
Garden Salad
Herb Vinaigrette Salad Dressing,
   Fat Free (1 pkt)
Diet Soft Drink

Calories: 385
Fat: 5 grams
Carb Choices: 3½
Exchanges: 2½ starch, ½ other carb, 1 veg, 3 very lean meat

Egg McMuffin®
Orange Juice (6 oz)

Calories: 370
Fat: 12 grams
Carb Choices: 3
Exchanges: 2 starch, 1 fruit, 2 med. fat meat

☀ Smart Choice

TOTAL FAT (g)	SATURATED FAT (g)	SODIUM (mg)	PROTEIN (g)	CARBOHYDRATE (g)	CARBOHYDRATE CHOICES	EXCHANGES
22	8	340	7	47	3	3 starch, 4 fat
20	5	340	7	47	3	3 starch, 4 fat
12	5	710	17	27	2	2 starch, 2 med. fat meat
2	0	210	4	25	2	2 starch
8	2	330	1	14	1	1 starch, 1 fat
7	2	610	9	53	3½	3½ starch, 1 fat
7	2	630	9	100	6	3 starch, 3 other carb, 1 fat
16	3	760	9	100	6.5	3½ starch, 3 other carb, 3 fat
3	<1	380	6	61	4	4 starch
16	5	290	6	0	0	1 high fat meat, 1½ fat
29	9	1130	10	32	2	2 starch, 1 med. fat meat, 4½ fat
35	10	1210	16	33	2	2 starch, 2 med. fat meat, 5 fat
23	8	740	13	26	2	2 starch, 1 med. fat meat, 3 fat
28	10	810	19	27	2	2 starch, 2 med. fat meat, 3 fat
11	4	170	13	1	0	2 med. fat meat

SMART MEAL, MCDONALD'S

Hamburger
Garden Salad
Herb Vinaigrette Salad Dressing,
   Fat Free (1 pkt)
Milk, 1% (8 oz)
Vanilla Ice Cream Cone, Reduced Fat

Calories: 595
Fat: 17 grams
Carb Choices: 6
Exchanges: 2 starch, 1 1% milk,
2 other carb, 1 veg,
1½ med. fat meat,
1 fat

Hotcakes (plain)
Honey (1 pkt)
Orange Juice (6 oz)

Calories: 435
Fat: 7 grams
Carb Choices: 5½
Exchanges: 3½ starch,
1 other
carb, 1 fruit, 1 fat

1 Carbohydrate Choice = 1 starch or 1 fruit or 1 milk exchange
* Grams of fiber subtracted from total carbohydrate

MENU ITEM	SERVING SIZE	CALORIES	CALORIES FROM FAT

1 POTATO 2

BAKED POTATOES

Bacon & Cheese Baked Potato	1	657	424
Bacon Double Cheeseburger Baked Potato	1	766	489
BBQ Chicken, Cheddar & Bacon Baked Potato	1	684	383
Broccoli & Cheese Baked Potato	1	545	324
Butter Baked Potato	1	327	167
Chicken, Broccoli & Cheddar Baked Potato	1	591	335
Chicken Santa Fe Baked Potato	1	647	372
Crab, Broccoli & Cheese Baked Potato	1	593	315
Margarine Baked Potato	1	366	205
Mexican Baked Potato	1	669	413
Philly Steak & Cheese Baked Potato	1	676	359
Steak Santa Fe Baked Potato	1	689	398
Three Cheese Baked Potato	1	582	351

ULTRA-LITE BAKED POTATOES

💡 Caribbean Chicken Lite Baked Potato	1	292	15
💡 Chicken Fajita Lite Baked Potato	1	272	14
💡 Chicken Stir-fry Lite Baked Potato	1	330	26
💡 Chicken, Mushroom & Roasted Peppers Lite Baked Potato	1	242	17
💡 Crab & Broccoli DeLite Baked Potato	1	335	20
💡 Spinach Souffle Lite Baked Potato	1	310	85
💡 Vegie & Herb Cheese Lite Baked Potato	1	237	14

💡 Smart Choice

TOTAL FAT (g)	SATURATED FAT (g)	SODIUM (mg)	PROTEIN (g)	CARBOHYDRATE (g)	CARBOHYDRATE CHOICES	EXCHANGES
47	18	921	20	39	2½	2½ starch, 2 med. fat meat, 7 fat
54	21	1290	30	40	2½	2½ starch, 3 med. fat meat, 8 fat
43	17	1766	32	44	3	3 starch, 3 med. fat meat, 5 fat
36	14	575	16	42	3	3 starch, 1½ med. fat meat, 5 fat
19	12	131	4	38	2½	2½ starch, 3 fat
37	15	816	23	43	3	3 starch, 2 med. fat meat, 5 fat
41	17	929	27	44	3	3 starch, 3 med. fat meat, 4 fat
35	14	1229	25	46	3	3 starch, 3 med. fat meat, 3 fat
23	6	313	4	38	2½	2½ starch, 4 fat
46	17	1071	18	48	3	3 starch, 2 med. fat meat, 7 fat
40	15	1409	34	46	3	3 starch, 3 med. fat meat, 4 fat
44	18	965	31	43	3	3 starch, 3½ med. fat meat, 4 fat
39	16	753	20	40	2½	2½ starch, 2 med. fat meat, 6 fat
2	<1	655	16	54	3½	3½ starch, 1 very lean meat
2	<1	556	16	50	3	3 starch, 1 very lean meat
3	<1	1289	16	62	4	4 starch, 1 lean meat
2	<1	716	13	45	3	3 starch, 1 very lean meat
2	1	738	19	55	3½	3½ starch, 1½ very lean meat
9	4	569	13	44	3	3 starch, 1 med. fat meat
2	<1	423	13	44	3	3 starch, 1 very lean meat

1 Carbohydrate Choice = 1 starch or 1 fruit or 1 milk exchange
* Grams of fiber subtracted from total carbohydrate

MENU ITEM	SERVING SIZE	CALORIES	CALORIES FROM FAT
COUNTRY SKILLET COMBOS			
Bacon, Ranch & Cheddar Combo	1	1090	669
BBQ Chicken, Cheddar & Bacon Combo	1	890	141
Idaho "Nachos" Combo	1	1009	547
SIDE ORDERS			
Fresh Cut Fries, small	1 order	612	351
Fresh Cut Fries, medium	1 order	765	438
Fresh Cut Fries, large	1 order	1224	701
Fresh Fries 'n Chicken Tenders	1 order	917	447
Nacho Cheese Fries	1 order	838	489
Potato Skins, Bacon 'n Cheddar with Sour Cream	1 order	972	476
Potato Skins, Southwestern with Sour Cream	1 order	907	412
SOUPS			
Baked Potato Soup	1 order	640	231
Broccoli & Cheese Potato Soup	1 order	736	315

TOTAL FAT (g)	SATURATED FAT (g)	SODIUM (mg)	PROTEIN (g)	CARBOHYDRATE (g)	CARBOHYDRATE CHOICES	EXCHANGES
74	20	937	22	87	5½	5½ starch, 1½ med. fat meat, 10 fat
57	16	759	24	74	5	5 starch, 2 med. fat meat, 8 fat
61	20	838	30	89	6	6 starch, 2½ med. fat meat, 8 fat
39	7	321	5	63	4	4 starch, 7 fat
49	8	401	7	79	5	5 starch, 8 fat
78	13	642	11	126	8½	8½ starch, 12 fat
50	9	893	26	93	6	6 starch, 2 med. fat meat, 7 fat
54	11	622	10	81	5½	5½ starch, 9 fat
53	25	1337	27	100	6½	6½ starch, 2 med. fat meat, 7 fat
46	22	1423	23	105	7	7 starch, 1 med. fat meat, 6 fat
26	11	1630	20	81	5½	5½ starch, 1 med. fat meat, 3 fat
35	17	1549	25	80	5	5½ starch, 2 med. fat meat, 4 fat

1 Carbohydrate Choice = 1 starch or 1 fruit or 1 milk exchange
* Grams of fiber subtracted from total carbohydrate

MENU ITEM	SERVING SIZE	CALORIES	CALORIES FROM FAT
PAPA JOHN'S			
CHEESE PIZZA			
Original Crust Pizza, medium	1 slice	286	80
Thin Crust Pizza, medium	1 slice	220	98
GARDEN PIZZA			
Original Crust Pizza, medium	1 slice	298	100
Thin Crust Pizza, medium	1 slice	238	110
MEATS PIZZA			
Original Crust Pizza, medium	1 slice	410	160
Thin Crust Pizza, medium	1 slice	330	178
PEPPERONI PIZZA			
Original Crust Pizza, medium	1 slice	310	110
Thin Crust Pizza, medium	1 slice	266	135
SAUSAGE PIZZA			
Original Crust Pizza, medium	1 slice	340	120
Thin Crust Pizza, medium	1 slice	270	130
WORKS PIZZA			
Original Crust Pizza, medium	1 slice	369	149
Thin Crust Pizza, medium	1 slice	319	166
SIDE ORDERS			
Bread Sticks	1 piece (⅛ order)	170	27
Cheese Sticks	1 piece (⅛ order)	160	50
SAUCES			
Garlic Sauce	2 Tbsp	150	140
Nacho Cheese Sauce	2 Tbsp	60	36
Pizza Sauce	2 Tbsp	20	0

Smart Choice

TOTAL FAT (g)	SATURATED FAT (g)	SODIUM (mg)	PROTEIN (g)	CARBOHYDRATE (g)	CARBOHYDRATE CHOICES	EXCHANGES
9	3	540	14	37	2½	2½ starch, 1 med. fat meat
11	5	480	9	22	1½	1½ starch, 1 med. fat meat, 1 fat
11	4	570	14	36	2½	2½ starch, 1 med. fat meat, 1 fat
12	6	540	9	23	1½	1½ starch, 1 med. fat meat, 1 fat
18	7	1040	21	42	3	3 starch, 2 med. fat meat, 1 fat
20	9	919	15	23	1½	1½ starch, 2 med. fat meat, 2 fat
13	5	760	15	35	2	2 starch, 2 med. fat meat
15	7	580	11	22	1½	1½ starch, 1 med. fat meat, 2 fat
13	6	910	15	40	2½	2½ starch, 1½ med. fat meat, 1 fat
15	7	730	12	22	1½	1½ starch, 1 med. fat meat, 2 fat
17	6	840	18	37	2½	2½ starch, 2 med. fat meat, 1 fat
19	8	760	14	24	1½	1½ starch, 1½ med. fat meat, 2 fat
3	0	270	6	27	2	2 starch, ½ fat
6	2	290	7	21	1½	1½ starch, 1 fat
16	4	230	0	4	0	3 fat
4	4	226	2	0	0	1 fat
<1	0	120	0	2	0	free

1 Carbohydrate Choice = 1 starch or 1 fruit or 1 milk exchange
* Grams of fiber subtracted from total carbohydrate

MENU ITEM	SERVING SIZE	CALORIES	CALORIES FROM FAT

PIZZA HUT

BEEF PIZZA

Thin 'N Crispy® Pizza, medium	1 slice	229	99
Hand Tossed Pizza, medium	1 slice	260	81
Pan Pizza, medium	1 slice	286	117

CHEESE PIZZA

Thin 'N Crispy® Pizza, medium	1 slice	205	72
Hand Tossed Pizza, medium	1 slice	235	63
Pan Pizza, medium	1 slice	261	99

HAM PIZZA

☀ Thin 'N Crispy® Pizza, medium	1 slice	184	63
☀ Hand Tossed Pizza, medium	1 slice	213	45
Pan Pizza, medium	1 slice	239	81

ITALIAN SAUSAGE PIZZA

Thin 'N Crispy® Pizza, medium	1 slice	236	108
Hand Tossed Pizza, medium	1 slice	267	99
Pan Pizza, medium	1 slice	293	135

MEAT LOVER'S® PIZZA

Thin 'N Crispy® Pizza, medium	1 slice	288	117
☀ Hand Tossed Pizza, medium	1 slice	314	99
Pan Pizza	1 slice	340	162

PEPPERONI PIZZA

Thin 'N Crispy® Pizza, medium	1 slice	215	90
Hand Tossed Pizza, medium	1 slice	238	72
Pan Pizza, medium	1 slice	265	108

☀ Smart Choice

Total Fat (g)	Saturated Fat (g)	Sodium (mg)	Protein (g)	Carbohydrate (g)	Carbohydrate Choices	Exchanges
11	5	709	13	21	1½	1½ starch, 1 med. fat meat, 1 fat
9	4	797	15	29	2	2 starch, 1 med. fat meat, 1 fat
13	5	677	14	28	2	2 starch, 1 med. fat meat, 1½ fat
8	4	534	11	21	1½	1½ starch, 1 high fat meat
7	4	621	13	29	2	2 starch, 1 high fat meat
11	5	501	12	28	2	2 starch, 1 high fat meat, ½ fat
7	3	591	10	21	1½	1½ starch, 1 med. fat meat
5	3	657	12	29	2	2 starch, 1 med. fat meat
9	3	537	11	28	2	2 starch, 1 med. fat meat, ½ fat
12	5	650	11	21	1½	1½ starch, 1 high fat meat, ½ fat
11	5	737	13	29	2	2 starch, 1 high fat meat, ½ fat
15	5	617	12	27	2	2 starch, 1 high fat meat, 1 fat
13	6	892	15	21	1½	1½ starch, 2 med. fat meat, ½ fat
11	6	958	17	29	2	2 starch, 2 med. fat meat
18	7	838	16	28	2	2 starch, 2 med. fat meat, 1 fat
10	4	627	11	21	1½	1½ starch, 1 high fat meat
8	4	689	12	29	2	2 starch, 1 high fat meat
12	4	569	11	28	2	2 starch, 1 high fat meat, ½ fat

1 Carbohydrate Choice = 1 starch or 1 fruit or 1 milk exchange
* Grams of fiber subtracted from total carbohydrate

MENU ITEM	SERVING SIZE	CALORIES	CALORIES FROM FAT
PEPPERONI LOVER'S® PIZZA			
☀ Thin 'N Crispy® Pizza, medium	1 slice	289	144
☀ Hand Tossed Pizza, medium	1 slice	306	126
Pan Pizza, medium	1 slice	332	153
PORK TOPPING PIZZA			
Thin 'N Crispy Pizza, medium	1 slice	237	108
Hand Tossed Pizza, medium	1 slice	268	90
Pan Pizza, medium	1 slice	294	126
SUPER SUPREME PIZZA			
Thin 'N Crispy® Pizza, medium	1 slice	270	126
Hand Tossed Pizza, medium	1 slice	296	117
Pan Pizza, medium	1 slice	323	153
SUPREME PIZZA			
Thin 'N Crispy® Pizza, medium	1 slice	257	117
Hand Tossed Pizza, medium	1 slice	284	108
Pan Pizza, medium	1 slice	311	135
VEGGIE LOVER'S® PIZZA			
☀ Thin 'N Crispy® Pizza, medium	1 slice	186	63
☀ Hand Tossed Pizza, medium	1 slice	216	54
Pan Pizza, medium	1 slice	243	90
BIGFOOT™ PIZZA PIZZA			
☀ Cheese Bigfoot™ Pizza, medium	1 slice (2.7 oz)	186	54
☀ Pepperoni Bigfoot™ Pizza, medium	1 slice (2.8 oz)	205	63
Pepperoni, Mushroom, & Italian Sausage Bigfoot™ Pizza, medium	1 slice (3 oz)	214	72

☀ Smart Choice

TOTAL FAT (g)	SATURATED FAT (g)	SODIUM (mg)	PROTEIN (g)	CARBOHYDRATE (g)	CARBOHYDRATE CHOICES	EXCHANGES
16	7	862	15	22	1½	1½ starch, 2 med. fat meat
14	6	897	16	30	2	2 starch, 2 med. fat meat
17	7	777	15	28	2	2 starch, 2 med. fat meat, 1 fat
12	5	709	12	21	1½	1½ starch, 1 med. fat meat, 1 fat
10	5	797	14	29	2	2 starch, 1 med. fat meat, 1 fat
14	5	677	13	28	2	2 starch, 1 med. fat meat, 1½ fat
14	6	880	14	22	1½	1½ starch, 1½ med. fat meat, 1 fat
13	5	946	16	30	2	2 starch, 1½ med. fat meat, 1 fat
17	6	826	15	28	2	2 starch, 1½ med. fat meat, 1½ fat
13	5	795	14	21	1½	1½ starch, 1½ med. fat meat, 1 fat
12	5	884	16	30	2	2 starch, 1½ med. fat meat, ½ fat
15	6	764	15	28	2	2 starch, 1½ med. fat meat, 1 fat
7	3	545	9	22	1½	1½ starch, 1 med. fat meat
6	3	632	11	30	2	2 starch, 1 med. fat meat
10	3	512	10	29	2	2 starch, 1 med. fat meat, ½ fat
6	3	525	10	25	1½	1½ starch, 1 med. fat meat
7	3	589	10	25	1½	1½ starch, 1 med. fat meat
8	4	665	11	25	1½	1½ starch, 1 high fat meat

1 Carbohydrate Choice = 1 starch or 1 fruit or 1 milk exchange
* Grams of fiber subtracted from total carbohydrate

MENU ITEM	SERVING SIZE	CALORIES	CALORIES FROM FAT
PERSONAL PAN PIZZA®			
Pepperoni Personal Pan Pizza®	1 pizza (9 oz)	637	252
Supreme Personal Pan Pizza®	1 pizza (11.5 oz)	722	306

POPEYE'S CHICKEN & BISCUITS
CHICKEN

MENU ITEM	SERVING SIZE	CALORIES	CALORIES FROM FAT
☀ Breast, Mild	1 (3.7 oz)	270	143
☀ Breast, Spicy	1 (3.7 oz)	270	143
☀ Leg, Mild	1 (1.7 oz)	120	66
☀ Leg, Spicy	1 (1.7 oz)	120	66
☀ Mild Tender (chicken strip)	1 strip (1.2 oz)	110	63
☀ Spicy Tender (chicken strip)	1 strip (1.2 oz)	110	63
Thigh, Mild	1 (3.1 oz)	300	204
Thigh, Spicy	1 (3.1 oz)	300	204
Wing, Mild	1 (1.6 oz)	160	96
Wing, Spicy	1 (1.6 oz)	160	96

SHRIMP

Shrimp	1 order (2.8 oz)	250	148

SIDE ORDERS

Biscuit	1 (2.3 oz)	250	134
☀ Cajun Rice	1 order (3.9 oz)	150	49
Coleslaw	1 order (4 oz)	149	101
☀ Corn on the Cob	1 order (5.2 oz)	127	26
French Fries	1 order (3 oz)	240	110
Onion Rings	1 order (3.1 oz)	310	174
☀ Potatoes & Gravy	1 order (3.8 oz	100	54
Red Beans & Rice	1 order (5.9 oz)	270	152

☀ Smart Choice

TOTAL FAT (g)	SATURATED FAT (g)	SODIUM (mg)	PROTEIN (g)	CARBOHYDRATE (g)	CARBOHYDRATE CHOICES	EXCHANGES
28	10	1340	27	64*	4	4½ starch, 3 med. fat meat, 1½ fat
34	12	1760	33	64*	4	4½ starch, 4 med. fat meat, 2 fat
16	NA	660	23	9	½	½ starch, 3 med. fat meat
16	NA	590	23	9	½	½ starch, 3 med. fat meat
7	NA	240	10	4	0	1½ med. fat meat
7	NA	240	10	4	0	1½ med. fat meat
7	NA	160	6	6	½	½ starch, 1 med. fat meat
7	NA	215	6	6	½	½ starch, 1 med. fat meat
23	NA	620	15	9	½	½ starch, 2 med. fat meat, 2½ fat
23	NA	450	15	9	½	½ starch, 2 med. fat meat, 2½ fat
11	NA	290	9	7	½	½ starch, 1 med. fat meat, 1 fat
11	NA	290	9	7	½	½ starch, 1 med. fat meat, 1 fat
17	NA	650	16	13	1	1 starch, 2 med. fat meat, 1 fat
15	NA	430	4	26	2	2 starch, 3 fat
5	NA	1260	10	17	1	1 starch, 1 med. fat meat
11	NA	271	1	14	1	3 veg or 1 starch, 2 fat
3	NA	20	4	12*	1	1 starch, 1 fat
12	NA	610	4	31	2	2 starch, 2 fat
19	NA	210	5	31	2	2 starch, 3½ fat
6	NA	460	5	11	1	1 starch, 1 fat
17	NA	680	8	23*	1½	1½ starch, 1 med. fat meat, 2 fat

1 Carbohydrate Choice = 1 starch or 1 fruit or 1 milk exchange
* Grams of fiber subtracted from total carbohydrate

MENU ITEM	SERVING SIZE	CALORIES	CALORIES FROM FAT
DESSERTS			
Apple Pie	1 slice (3.1 oz)	290	142

SMART MEAL, POPEYE'S CHICKEN & BISCUITS

Chicken Breast (Mild or Spicy)	**Calories:**	547
Cajun Rice	**Fat:**	24 grams
Corn on the Cob	**Carb Choices:**	2½
	Exchanges:	2½ starch, 4 med. fat meat, 1 fat

RALLY'S

SANDWICHES

MENU ITEM	SERVING SIZE	CALORIES	CALORIES FROM FAT
Big Bufford Burger	1	743	414
☀ Chicken Fillet Sandwich	1	399	135
Rallyburger	1	433	198
Rallyburger with Cheese	1	488	243
Super Barbecue Bacon Sandwich	1	593	279
Super Double Cheeseburger	1	762	432

CHILI

MENU ITEM	SERVING SIZE	CALORIES	CALORIES FROM FAT
☀ Chili with Cheese and Onion, small	1 (7 oz)	360	198
Chili with Cheese and Onion, large	1 (13 oz)	669	369

SIDE ORDERS

MENU ITEM	SERVING SIZE	CALORIES	CALORIES FROM FAT
French Fries, regular	1 order (4 oz)	211	99
French Fries, large	1 order (6 oz)	317	144
French Fries, extra-large	1 order (8 oz)	423	189

BEVERAGES

MENU ITEM	SERVING SIZE	CALORIES	CALORIES FROM FAT
Coca-Cola Classic®	16 oz	132	0
Coca-Cola Classic®	20 oz	177	0
Coca-Cola Classic®	32 oz	264	0

☀ Smart Choice

TOTAL FAT (g)	SATURATED FAT (g)	SODIUM (mg)	PROTEIN (g)	CARBOHYDRATE (g)	CARBOHYDRATE CHOICES	EXCHANGES
16	NA	820	3	37	2½	2½ other carb, 3 fat
46	NA	1860	41	35	2	2 starch, 5½ med. fat meat, 4 fat
15	NA	790	21	43	3	3 starch, 2½ med. fat meat
22	NA	1176	20	35	2	2 starch, 2½ med. fat meat, 2 fat
27	NA	1376	23	35	2	2 starch, 3 med. fat meat, 2 fat
31	NA	1709	29	49	3	3 starch, 3 med. fat meat, 3 fat
48	NA	1734	41	37	2½	2½ starch, 5 med. fat meat, 4 fat
22	NA	1144	23	20	1	1 starch, 3 med. fat meat, 1 fat
41	NA	2125	43	37	2½	2½ starch, 5 med. fat meat, 2 fat
11	NA	293	3	26	1½	1½ starch, 2 fat
16	NA	439	5	39	2½	2½ starch, 3 fat
21	NA	585	7	52	3½	3½ starch, 4 fat
0	NA	13	0	35	2	2 other carb
0	NA	17	0	47	3	3 other carb
0	NA	26	0	70	4½	4½ other carb

1 Carbohydrate Choice = 1 starch *or* 1 fruit *or* 1 milk exchange
* Grams of fiber subtracted from total carbohydrate

MENU ITEM	SERVING SIZE	CALORIES	CALORIES FROM FAT
Coca-Cola Classic®	42 oz	372	0
Diet Coke®	16 oz	1	0
Diet Coke®	20 oz	1	0
Diet Coke®	32 oz	1	0
Diet Coke®	42 oz	2	0
Fanta Orange	16 oz	150	0
Fanta Orange	20 oz	202	0
Fanta Orange	32 oz	301	0
Fanta Orange	42 oz	424	0
Mr. Pibb®	16 oz	113	0
Mr. Pibb®	20 oz	159	0
Mr. Pibb®	32 oz	237	0
Mr. Pibb®	42 oz	334	0
Root Beer	16 oz	146	0
Root Beer	20 oz	197	0
Root Beer	32 oz	294	0
Root Beer	42 oz	414	0
Sprite®	16 oz	132	0
Sprite®	20 oz	161	0
Sprite®	32 oz	264	0
Sprite®	42 oz	338	0

TOTAL FAT (g)	SATURATED FAT (g)	SODIUM (mg)	PROTEIN (g)	CARBOHYDRATE (g)	CARBOHYDRATE CHOICES	EXCHANGES
0	NA	38	0	99	6½	6½ other carb
0	NA	13	0	0	0	free
0	NA	18	0	0	0	free
0	NA	27	0	0	0	free
0	NA	38	0	0	0	free
0	NA	11	0	38	2½	2½ other carb
0	NA	15	0	52	3½	3½ other carb
0	NA	22	0	77	5	5 other carb
0	NA	32	0	109	7	7 other carb
0	NA	16	0	29	2	2 other carb
0	NA	22	0	40	2½	2½ other carb
0	NA	33	0	60	4	4 other carb
0	NA	46	0	84	5½	5½ other carb
0	NA	16	0	38	2½	2½ other carb
0	NA	22	0	52	3½	3½ other carb
0	NA	33	0	77	5	5 other carb
0	NA	46	0	109	7	7 other carb
0	NA	29	0	33	2	2 other carb
0	NA	36	0	40	2½	2½ other carb
0	NA	59	0	66	4½	4½ other carb
0	NA	76	0	84	5½	5½ other carb

1 Carbohydrate Choice = 1 starch or 1 fruit or 1 milk exchange
* Grams of fiber subtracted from total carbohydrate

MENU ITEM	SERVING SIZE	CALORIES	CALORIES FROM FAT

ROUND TABLE PIZZA
ALFREDO CONTEMPO PIZZA
| Thin Crust Pizza, large | 1/16 pie (2.5 oz) | 170 | 59 |
| Pan Pizza, large | 1/12 pie (3.3 oz) | 220 | 67 |

BACON SUPER DELI PIZZA
| Thin Crust Pizza, large | 1/16 pie (2.5 oz) | 200 | 114 |
| Pan Pizza, large | 1/12 pie (3.3 oz) | 260 | 122 |

CHEESE PIZZA
| ☀ Thin Crust Pizza, large | 1/16 pie (2.2 oz) | 160 | 56 |
| ☀ Pan Pizza, large | 1/12 pie (3 oz) | 210 | 65 |

CHICKEN & GARLIC GOURMET PIZZA
| Thin Crust Pizza, large | 1/16 pie (2.6 oz) | 170 | 65 |
| Pan Pizza, large | 1/12 pie (3.6 oz) | 230 | 73 |

CLASSIC PESTO PIZZA
| Thin Crust Pizza, large | 1/16 pie (2.6 oz) | 170 | 71 |
| Pan Pizza, large | 1/12 pie (3.5 oz) | 230 | 79 |

GARDEN PESTO PIZZA
| Thin Crust Pizza, large | 1/16 pie (2.5 oz) | 170 | 69 |
| Pan Pizza, large | 1/12 pie (3.2 oz) | 230 | 77 |

GOURMET VEGGIE PIZZA
| ☀ Thin Crust Pizza, large | 1/16 pie (2.8 oz) | 160 | 59 |
| ☀ Pan Pizza, large | 1/12 pie (3.7 oz) | 220 | 67 |

GUINEVERE'S GARDEN DELIGHT PIZZA
| ☀ Thin Crust Pizza, large | 1/16 pie (2.8 oz) | 150 | 50 |
| ☀ Pan Pizza, large | 1/12 pie (3.5 oz) | 200 | 56 |

☀ Smart Choice

TOTAL FAT (g)	SATURATED FAT (g)	SODIUM (mg)	PROTEIN (g)	CARBOHYDRATE (g)	CARBOHYDRATE CHOICES	EXCHANGES
7	4	210	9	17	1	1 starch, 1 high fat meat
7	4	240	12	27	2	2 starch, 1 high fat meat
13	5	360	9	16	1	1 starch, 1 med. fat meat, 1 fat
14	5	380	12	26	2	2 starch, 1 med. fat meat, 1 fat
6	4	240	7	16	1	1 starch, 1 med. fat meat
7	5	250	10	26	2	2 starch, 1 med. fat meat
8	4	280	9	17	1	1 starch, 1 high fat meat
8	4	310	11	27	2	2 starch, 1 high fat meat
8	4	210	7	18	1	1 starch, 1 high fat meat
9	4	240	9	27	2	2 starch, 1 high fat meat
8	4	200	7	18	1	1 starch, 1 high fat meat
9	4	230	9	28	2	2 starch, 1 high fat meat
7	3	200	7	18	1	1 starch, 1 med. fat meat
7	4	230	9	28	2	2 starch, 1 med. fat meat
6	3	250	7	18	1	1 starch, 1 med. fat meat
6	4	250	9	27	2	2 starch, 1 med. fat meat

1 Carbohydrate Choice = 1 starch or 1 fruit or 1 milk exchange
* Grams of fiber subtracted from total carbohydrate

MENU ITEM	SERVING SIZE	CALORIES	CALORIES FROM FAT
ITALIAN GARLIC SUPREME PIZZA			
Thin Crust Pizza, large	¹⁄₁₆ pie (2.5 oz)	200	94
Pan Pizza, large	¹⁄₁₂ pie (3.3 oz)	250	95
KING ARTHUR'S SUPREME PIZZA			
Thin Crust Pizza, large	¹⁄₁₆ pie (3 oz)	200	91
Pan Pizza, large	¹⁄₁₂ pie (3.5 oz)	240	88
PEPPERONI PIZZA			
Thin Crust Pizza, large	¹⁄₁₆ pie. (2.1 oz)	170	72
Pan Pizza, large	¹⁄₁₂ pie (2.9 oz)	220	73
SALUTE CASHEW CHICKEN PIZZA			
☀ Thin Crust Pizza, large	¹⁄₁₆ pie (2.6 oz)	150	37
☀ Pan Pizza, large	¹⁄₁₂ pie (3.4 oz)	200	41
SALUTE CHICKEN & GARLIC PIZZA			
☀ Thin Crust Pizza, large	¹⁄₁₆ pie (3 oz)	150	49
☀ Pan Pizza, large	¹⁄₁₂ pie (3.7 oz)	200	53
SALUTE VEGGIE PIZZA			
☀ Thin Crust Pizza, large	¹⁄₁₆ pie (2.8 oz)	140	42
☀ Pan Pizza, large	¹⁄₁₂ pie (3.6 oz)	190	46
WESTERN BBQ CHICKEN SUPREME PIZZA			
☀ Thin Crust Pizza, large	¹⁄₁₆ pie (2.8 oz)	170	51
☀ Pan Pizza, large	¹⁄₁₂ pie (3.7 oz)	220	59
ZESTY SANTA FE CHICKEN PIZZA			
Thin Crust Pizza, large	¹⁄₁₆ pie (2.7 oz)	180	70
Pan Pizza, large	¹⁄₁₂ pie (3.5 oz)	240	83

☀ Smart Choice

TOTAL FAT (g)	SATURATED FAT (g)	SODIUM (mg)	PROTEIN (g)	CARBOHYDRATE (g)	CARBOHYDRATE CHOICES	EXCHANGES
10	4	220	8	17	1	1 starch, 1 med. fat meat, 1 fat
11	4	240	10	27	2	2 starch, 1 med. fat meat, 1 fat
10	4	340	9	18	1	1 starch, 1 med. fat meat, 1 fat
10	4	320	10	27	2	2 starch, 1 high fat meat
8	3	240	8	17	1	1 starch, 1 high fat meat
8	4	240	9	26	2	2 starch, 1 high fat meat
4	2	240	7	21	1½	1½ starch, 1 med. fat meat
5	2	260	9	31	2	2 starch, 1 med. fat meat
5	3	250	8	18	1	1 starch, 1 med. fat meat
6	3	270	9	28	2	2 starch, 1 med. fat meat
5	2	170	6	19	1	1 starch, 1 med. fat meat
5	3	190	8	28	2	2 starch, 1 med. fat meat
6	4	330	8	17	1	1 starch, 1 med. fat meat
7	4	360	11	27	2	2 starch, 1 med. fat meat
8	4	310	9	17	1	1 starch, 1 high fat meat
9	5	360	11	27	2	2 starch, 1 high fat meat

1 Carbohydrate Choice = 1 starch or 1 fruit or 1 milk exchange
* Grams of fiber subtracted from total carbohydrate

MENU ITEM	SERVING SIZE	CALORIES	CALORIES FROM FAT
ROY ROGERS			
SANDWICHES			
Bacon Cheeseburger	1 (5.5 oz)	520	297
Cheeseburger	1 (4.9 oz)	393	198
Cheesesteak Sandwich	1 (7.6 oz)	580	324
Fish Sandwich	1 (6.5 oz)	490	189
Gold Rush Chicken Sandwich	1 (6.6 oz)	558	270
☀ Grilled Chicken Sandwich	1 (7.5 oz)	294	72
Hamburger	1 (4.4 oz)	343	162
Quarter Pound Cheeseburger	1 (5.2 oz)	480	261
Quarter Pound Hamburger	1 (4.7 oz)	412	225
☀ Roast Beef Sandwich	1 (6.7 oz)	329	90
CHICKEN			
Chicken Nuggets, 6-piece	1 order (4 oz)	290	162
☀ Fried Chicken Breast	1 (5.2 oz)	370	135
☀ Fried Chicken Leg	1 (2.4 oz)	170	63
Fried Chicken Thigh	1 (4.2 oz)	330	135
Fried Chicken Wing	1 (2.3 oz)	200	72
Roy's Roaster™ (dark meat), ¼ chicken	1 (5 oz)	490	306
☀ Roy's Roaster™ (dark meat, without skin), ¼ chicken	1 (3.9 oz)	190	90
Roy's Roaster™ (white meat), ¼ chicken	1 (6.1 oz)	500	261
☀ Roy's Roaster™ (white meat, without skin), ¼ chicken	1 (4.7 oz)	190	54
SIDE ORDERS			
☀ Baked Beans	1 order (5 oz)	160	18
☀ Baked Potato	1 (3.9 oz)	130	9

 Smart Choice

TOTAL FAT (g)	SATURATED FAT (g)	SODIUM (mg)	PROTEIN (g)	CARBOHYDRATE (g)	CARBOHYDRATE CHOICES	EXCHANGES
33	13	1620	24	32	2	2 starch, 3 med. fat meat, 3 fat
22	12	1405	19	32	2	2 starch, 2 med. fat meat, 2 fat
36	14	860	26	37	2½	2½ starch, 3 med. fat meat, 4 fat
21	5	1048	21	56	4	4 starch, 2 med. fat meat, 2 fat
30	9	1326	22	51	3½	3½ starch, 2½ med. fat meat, 2 fat
8	3	864	26	29	2	2 starch, 3 lean meat
18	9	1168	15	32	2	2 starch, 2 med. fat meat, 1 fat
29	17	1509	23	32	2	2 starch, 3 med. fat meat, 2½ fat
25	14	1264	20	32	2	2 starch, 2½ med. fat meat, 2 fat
10	3	975	31	29	2	2 starch, 4 lean meat
18	4	610	12	20	1	1 starch, 1½ med. fat meat, 2 fat
15	4	1190	29	29	2	2 starch, 3 med. fat meat
7	2	570	13	15	1	1 starch, 1½ med. fat meat
15	4	1000	19	30	2	2 starch, 2 med. fat meat, 1 fat
8	3	740	10	23	1½	1½ starch, 1 high fat meat
34	10	1120	43	2	0	6 med. fat meat, 1 fat
10	3	400	24	1	0	3½ lean meat
29	9	1450	56	3	0	8 lean meat, 1 fat
6	2	700	32	2	0	4½ very lean meat
2	1	560	6	30	2	2 starch
1	0	65	3	27	2	2 starch

1 Carbohydrate Choice = 1 starch or 1 fruit or 1 milk exchange
* Grams of fiber subtracted from total carbohydrate

MENU ITEM

MENU ITEM	SERVING SIZE	CALORIES	CALORIES FROM FAT
Baked Potato with Margarine	1 (4.3 oz)	240	117
Cole Slaw	1 order (5 oz)	295	225
French Fries, regular	1 order (5 oz)	350	135
French Fries, large	1 order (6.1 oz)	430	162
☀ Gravy	1 (1.5 oz)	20	0
☀ Mashed Potatoes	1 order (5 oz)	92	0

SOUPS

☀ Chicken Soup	10.6 oz	225	63
☀ Chili	10.1 oz	295	135

SALADS

☀ Garden Salad	1 (9.7 oz)	110	45
☀ Grilled Chicken Salad	1 (13.2 oz)	221	81
☀ Side Salad	1 (4.9 oz)	20	0

DESSERTS

Hot Fudge Sundae	1 (5.9 oz)	320	80
Strawberry Shortcake	1 (6 oz)	440	171
Strawberry Sundae	1 (5.5 oz)	260	54
☀ Vanilla Frozen Yogurt Cone	1 (4.1oz)	190	36

BREAKFAST

Bacon & Egg Biscuit	1 (4.2 oz)	470	234
Bacon Biscuit	1 (3.1 oz)	420	207
Big Breakfast Platter™ with Ham	1 (9.3 oz)	710	351
Big Country Breakfast Platter™ with Bacon	1 (7.6 oz)	740	387
Big Country Breakfast Platter™ with Sausage	1 (9.6 oz)	920	540
Biscuit	1 (2.9 oz)	390	189

☀ Smart Choice

TOTAL FAT (g)	SATURATED FAT (g)	SODIUM (mg)	PROTEIN (g)	CARBOHYDRATE (g)	CARBOHYDRATE CHOICES	EXCHANGES
13	2	220	3	27	2	2 starch, 2 fat
25	4	430	2	16	1	3 veg or 1 starch, 5 fat
15	4	150	5	49	3	3 starch, 3 fat
18	5	190	6	59	4	4 starch, 3 fat
<1	<1	260	<1	3	0	free
<1	<1	320	2	20	1	1 starch
7	2	1580	16	24	1½	1½ starch, 2 lean meat
15	7	1607	15	30	2	2 starch, 2 med. fat meat
5	3	348	8	10	½	2 veg or ½ starch, 1 med. fat meat
9	4	851	29	10	½	2 veg or ½ starch, 4 lean meat
<1	<1	20	1	3	0	free
10	3	260	8	50	3	3 other carb, 2 fat
19	5	620	8	39	2½	2½ other carb, 4 fat
6	3	95	6	44	3	3 other carb, 1 fat
4	3	80	6	29	2	2 other carb, 1 fat
26	8	1190	14	44	3	3 starch, 1½ med. fat meat, 3 fat
23	7	1140	9	44	3	3 starch, 1 high fat meat, 2 fat
39	11	2210	24	67	4½	4½ starch, 2 med. fat meat, 5 fat
43	13	1800	35	61	4	4 starch, 4 med. fat meat, 3 fat
60	19	2230	33	61	4	4 starch, 4 med. fat meat, 7 fat
21	6	1000	6	44	3	3 starch, 4 fat

1 Carbohydrate Choice = 1 starch or 1 fruit or 1 milk exchange
* Grams of fiber subtracted from total carbohydrate

MENU ITEM	SERVING SIZE	CALORIES	CALORIES FROM FAT
Biscuits 'N' Gravy™	1 (7.7 oz)	510	252
Cinnamon 'N' Raisin™ Biscuit	1 (2.8 oz)	370	162
Ham & Cheese Biscuit	1 (4.4 oz)	450	216
Ham, Egg & Cheese Biscuit	1 (5.6 oz)	500	243
☼ Orange Juice	10.2 oz	140	0
Sausage & Egg Biscuit	1 (5.2 oz)	560	315
Sausage Biscuit	1 (4.1 oz)	510	279
Sourdough Ham, Egg & Cheese Biscuit	1 (6.8 oz)	480	216
☼ Pancakes (3)	1 (4.8 oz)	280	18
Pancakes (3) with Sausage (1 piece)	1 (6.2 oz)	430	144
Pancakes (3) with Bacon (2 pieces)	1 (5.3 oz)	350	81

SMART MEAL, ROY ROGERS

Roast Beef Sandwich
Baked Beans
Side Salad

Calories: 509
Fat: 12 grams
Carb Choices: 4
Exchanges: 4 starch,
4 lean meat

 Smart Choice

TOTAL FAT (g)	SATURATED FAT (g)	SODIUM (mg)	PROTEIN (g)	CARBOHYDRATE (g)	CARBOHYDRATE CHOICES	EXCHANGES
28	9	1500	10	55	3½	3½ starch, 5½ fat
18	5	450	3	48	3	3 starch, 3 fat
24	8	1570	11	48	3	3 starch, 1 med. fat meat, 3 fat
27	10	1620	16	48	3	3 starch, 2 med. fat meat, 3 fat
<1	<1	0	2	35	2	2 fruit
35	11	1400	18	44	3	3 starch, 2 med. fat meat, 4 fat
31	10	1360	14	44	3	3 starch, 1 high fat meat, 4 fat
24	9	1440	20	45	3	3 starch, 2 med. fat meat, 2 fat
2	1	890	8	56	4	4 starch
16	6	1290	16	56	4	4 starch, 1 high fat meat, 1 fat
9	3	1130	13	56	4	4 starch, 1 high fat meat

SMART MEAL, ROY ROGERS

¼ Roy Rogers Roaster™
(white meat, without skin)
Baked Potato
Margarine (1 pat)
Side Salad
Low-calorie Dressing

Calories: 415
Fat: 14 grams
Carb Choices: 2
Exchanges: 2 starch, 4½ very lean meat, 1 fat

1 Carbohydrate Choice = 1 starch or 1 fruit or 1 milk exchange
* Grams of fiber subtracted from total carbohydrate

MENU ITEM	SERVING SIZE	CALORIES	CALORIES FROM FAT

SUBWAY
COLD SUBS

B.L.T. Sub, 6-inch	1	327	90
Classic Italian B.M.T.® Sub, 6-inch	1	460	198
Cold Cut Trio Sub, 6-inch	1	378	117
Ham Sub, 6-inch	1	302	45
Roast Beef Sub, 6-inch	1	303	45
Subway Club® Sub, 6-inch	1	312	45
Subway Seafood & Crab® Sub, 6-inch	1	430	171
Subway Seafood & Crab® with Light Mayonnaise Sub, 6-inch	1	347	90
Tuna Sub, 6-inch	1	542	288
Tuna with Light Mayonnaise Sub, 6-inch	1	391	135
Turkey Breast Sub, 6-inch	1	289	36
Turkey Breast & Ham Sub, 6-inch	1	295	45
Veggie Delite™ Sub, 6-inch	1	237	27

HOT SUBS

Chicken Taco Sub, 6-inch	1	436	144
Meatball Sub, 6-inch	1	419	144
Pizza Sub	1	464	198
Roasted Chicken Breast Sub, 6-inch	1	348	54
Steak & Cheese Sub, 6-inch	1	398	90
Subway Melt™ Sub, 6-inch	1	382	108

DELI STYLE SANDWICHES

Bologna Sandwich, 6-inch	1	292	108
Ham Sandwich, 6-inch	1	234	36

Smart Choice

TOTAL FAT (g)	SATURATED FAT (g)	SODIUM (mg)	PROTEIN (g)	CARBOHYDRATE (g)	CARBOHYDRATE CHOICES	EXCHANGES
10	N/A	957	14	44	3	3 starch, 1 high fat meat
22	N/A	1664	21	45	3	3 starch, 2 med. fat meat, 2 fat
13	N/A	1412	20	46	3	3 starch, 2 med. fat meat
5	N/A	1319	19	45	3	3 starch, 2 very lean meat
5	N/A	939	20	45	3	3 starch, 2 very lean meat
5	N/A	1352	21	46	3	3 starch, 2 very lean meat
19	N/A	860	20	44	3	3 starch, 2 med. fat meat, 1 fat
10	N/A	884	20	45	3	3 starch, 2 lean meat
32	N/A	886	19	44	3	3 starch, 2 med. fat meat, 4 fat
15	N/A	940	19	46	3	3 starch, 2 med. fat meat
4	N/A	1403	18	46	3	3 starch, 2 very lean meat
5	N/A	1361	18	46	3	3 starch, 2 very lean meat
3	N/A	593	9	44	3	3 starch
16	N/A	1275	25	49	3	3 starch, 2 med. fat meat, 1 fat
16	N/A	1046	19	51	3½	3½ starch, 2 med. fat meat
22	N/A	1621	19	48	3	3 starch, 2 med. fat meat, 2 fat
6	N/A	978	27	47	3	3 starch, 3 very lean meat
10	N/A	1117	30	47	3	3 starch, 3 lean meat
12	N/A	1746	23	46	3	3 starch, 2 med. fat meat
12	N/A	744	10	38	2½	2½ starch, 1 med. fat meat, 1 fat
4	N/A	733	11	37	2½	2½ starch, 1 lean meat

1 Carbohydrate Choice = 1 starch or 1 fruit or 1 milk exchange
* Grams of fiber subtracted from total carbohydrate

MENU ITEM	SERVING SIZE	CALORIES	CALORIES FROM FAT
☼ Roast Beef Sandwich, 6-inch	1	245	36
Tuna Sandwich, 6-inch	1	354	162
Tuna with Light Mayonnaise Sandwich, 6-inch	1	279	81
☼ Turkey Breast Sandwich, 6-inch	1	235	36

SALADS

MENU ITEM	SERVING SIZE	CALORIES	CALORIES FROM FAT
B.L.T. Salad	1	140	72
☼ Bread Bowl	1	330	36
Chicken Taco Salad	1	250	126
Classic Italian B.M.T.® Salad	1	274	180
Cold Cut Trio Salad	1	191	99
☼ Ham Salad	1	116	27
Meatball Salad	1	233	126
Pizza Salad	1	277	180
☼ Roast Beef Salad	1	117	27
☼ Roasted Chicken Breast Salad	1	162	36
☼ Steak & Cheese Salad	1	212	72
☼ Subway Club Salad	1	126	27
☼ Subway Melt™ Salad	1	195	90
Subway Seafood & Crab® Salad	1	244	153
Subway Seafood & Crab with Light Mayonnaise Salad	1	161	72
Tuna Salad	1	356	270
Tuna with Light Mayonnaise Salad	1	205	117
☼ Turkey Breast Salad	1	102	18

☼ Smart Choice

TOTAL FAT (g)	SATURATED FAT (g)	SODIUM (mg)	PROTEIN (g)	CARBOHYDRATE (g)	CARBOHYDRATE CHOICES	EXCHANGES
4	N/A	638	13	38	2½	2½ starch, 1 lean meat
18	N/A	557	11	37	2½	2½ starch, 1 med. fat meat, 2 fat
9	N/A	583	11	38	2½	2½ starch, 1 lean meat, 1 fat
4	N/A	944	12	38	2½	2½ starch, 1 lean meat
8	N/A	672	7	10	½	2 veg, 2 fat
4	N/A	760	12	63	4	4 starch
14	N/A	990	18	15	1	3 veg or 1 starch, 2 med. fat meat, 1 fat
20	N/A	1379	14	11	1	2 veg, 2 med. fat meat, 2 fat
11	N/A	1127	13	11	1	2 veg, 1 med. fat meat, 1 fat
3	N/A	1034	12	11	1	2 veg, 1 lean meat
14	N/A	761	12	16	1	3 veg or 1 starch, 1 med. fat meat, 2 fat
20	N/A	1336	12	13	1	3 veg or 1 starch, 1 med. fat meat, 3 fat
3	N/A	654	12	11	1	2 veg, 1 lean meat
4	N/A	693	20	13	1	3 veg or 1 starch, 2 lean meat
8	N/A	832	22	13	1	3 veg or 1 starch, 2 med. fat meat
3	N/A	1067	14	12	1	2 veg, 2 very lean meat
10	N/A	1461	16	12	1	2 veg, 2 med. fat meat
17	N/A	575	13	10	½	2 veg, 2 med. fat meat, 1 fat
8	N/A	599	13	11	1	2 veg, 1 med. fat meat, 1 fat
30	N/A	601	12	10	½	2 veg, 1 med. fat meat, 5 fat
13	N/A	654	12	11	1	2 veg, 1 med. fat meat, 2 fat
2	N/A	1117	11	12	1	2 veg, 1 lean meat

1 Carbohydrate Choice = 1 starch or 1 fruit or 1 milk exchange
* Grams of fiber subtracted from total carbohydrate

MENU ITEM	SERVING SIZE	CALORIES	CALORIES FROM FAT
☀ Turkey Breast & Ham Salad	1	109	27
☀ Veggie Delite™ Salad	1	51	9

SALAD DRESSINGS

☀ Creamy Italian Salad Dressing	1 Tbsp	65	54
☀ French Salad Dressing	1 Tbsp	65	45
☀ French Salad Dressing, Fat Free	1 Tbsp	15	0
☀ Italian Salad Dressing, Fat Free	1 Tbsp	5	0
Ranch Salad Dressing	1 Tbsp	87	81
☀ Ranch Salad Dressing, Fat Free	1 Tbsp	12	0
☀ Thousand Island Salad Dressing	1 Tbsp	65	54

CONDIMENTS

Bacon	2 pieces	45	36
Cheese	2 triangles	41	27
Mayonnaise	1 tsp	37	36
☀ Mayonnaise, Light	1 tsp	18	18
☀ Mustard	2 tsp	8	0
Olive Oil Blend	1 tsp	45	45
☀ Vinegar	1 tsp	1	0

COOKIES

Chocolate Chip Cookie	1	210	90
Chocolate Chip M&M® Cookie	1	210	90
Chocolate Chunk Cookie	1	210	90
Double Chocolate Brazil Nut Cookie	1	230	108
☀ Oatmeal Raisin Cookie	1	200	72
Peanut Butter Cookie	1	220	108
Sugar Cookie	1	230	108

☀ Smart Choice

TOTAL FAT (g)	SATURATED FAT (g)	SODIUM (mg)	PROTEIN (g)	CARBOHYDRATE (g)	CARBOHYDRATE CHOICES	EXCHANGES
3	N/A	1076	11	11	1	2 veg, 1 lean meat
1	N/A	308	2	10	½	½ starch or 2 veg
6	N/A	132	0	2	0	1 fat
5	N/A	100	0	5	0	1 fat
0	N/A	85	0	4	0	free
0	N/A	152	0	1	0	free
9	N/A	117	0	1	0	2 fat
0	N/A	177	0	3	0	free
6	N/A	107	0	2	0	1 fat
4	N/A	182	2	0	0	1 fat
3	N/A	204	2	0	0	1 fat
4	N/A	27	0	0	0	1 fat
2	N/A	33	0	0	0	free
0	N/A	0	1	1	0	free
5	N/A	0	0	0	0	1 fat
0	N/A	0	0	0	0	free
10	N/A	140	2	29	2	2 other carb, 1½ fat
10	N/A	140	2	29	2	2 other carb, 1½ fat
10	N/A	140	2	29	2	2 other carb, 1½ fat
12	N/A	115	3	27	2	2 other carb, 2 fat
8	N/A	160	3	29	2	2 other carb, 1 fat
12	N/A	180	3	26	2	2 other carb, 2 fat
12	N/A	180	2	28	2	2 other carb, 2 fat

1 Carbohydrate Choice = 1 starch or 1 fruit or 1 milk exchange
* Grams of fiber subtracted from total carbohydrate

MENU ITEM	SERVING SIZE	CALORIES	CALORIES FROM FAT
White Chocolate Macadamia Nut Cookie	1	230	108

SMART MEAL, SUBWAY

Subway Club® Sub, 6-inch	**Calories:**	375
Veggie Delite™ Salad	**Fat:**	6 grams
Ranch Salad Dressing, Fat Free	**Carb Choices:**	4
	Exchanges:	3 starch, 2 veg, 2 very lean meat

SWISS CHALET

CHICKEN

MENU ITEM	SERVING SIZE	CALORIES	CALORIES FROM FAT
☼ Breaded Chicken Strips, 7-piece	1 order (4.5 oz)	319	99
☼ Chicken (without skin)	½ chicken (8.5 oz)	457	162
☼ Chicken (with skin)	½ chicken (10.5 oz)	694	351
☼ Chicken, Dark Meat (without skin)	¼ chicken (4 oz)	232	90
☼ Chicken, Dark Meat (with skin)	¼ chicken (4.9 oz)	313	153
☼ Chicken, White Meat (without skin)	¼ chicken (4.4 oz)	225	72
☼ Chicken, White Meat (with skin)	¼ chicken (5.6 oz)	381	198
Chicken Pot Pie	1 (11.2 oz)	494	216
☼ Chicken Sandwich on a Bun	1 (7.7 oz)	434	81
☼ Grilled Chicken Breast & Rice	1 (16.1 oz)	627	83
Hot Chicken Sandwich with French Fries, Vegetables, Gravy	1 (21.3 oz)	1007	369
☼ Wings with Sauce, 10-piece	1 order (7.3 oz)	658	293

RIBS

MENU ITEM	SERVING SIZE	CALORIES	CALORIES FROM FAT
Full Back Rib	1 order (11.3 oz)	810	468
Full Side Rib	1 order (5.8 oz)	516	306
Half Back Rib	1 order (5.6 oz)	405	234
☼ Half Side Rib	1 order (2.9 oz)	258	153

☼ Smart Choice

TOTAL FAT (g)	SATURATED FAT (g)	SODIUM (mg)	PROTEIN (g)	CARBOHYDRATE (g)	CARBOHYDRATE CHOICES	EXCHANGES
12	N/A	140	2	28	2	2 other carb, 2 fat

SMART MEAL, SUBWAY

Roast Beef Salad in a Bread Bowl
Italian Salad Dressing, Fat Free (4 Tbsp)

Calories: 467
Fat: 7 grams
Carb Choices: 5
Exchanges: 4 starch, 2 veg, 1 lean meat

TOTAL FAT (g)	SATURATED FAT (g)	SODIUM (mg)	PROTEIN (g)	CARBOHYDRATE (g)	CARBOHYDRATE CHOICES	EXCHANGES
11	2	721	22	34	2	2 starch, 3 lean meat
18	5	1980	75	0	0	11 very lean meat
39	9	375	87	0	0	12 lean meat
10	3	130	35	0	0	5 lean meat
17	5	200	40	0	0	5½ lean meat
8	2	84	40	0	0	5½ very lean meat
22	4	175	47	0	0	6½ lean meat
24	5	951	17	53	3½	3½ starch, 1½ med. fat meat, 3 fat
9	3	410	50	37	2½	2½ starch, 6 very lean meat
9	3	2420	45	91	6	6 starch, 5 very lean meat
41	10	1320	58	102	7	6 starch, 2 veg, 6 med. fat meat, 1 fat
33	8	843	51	40	2½	2½ starch, 6½ med. fat meat
52	18	608	74	12	1	1 other carb, 10 med. fat meat
34	12	360	48	6	½	½ other carb, 6½ med. fat meat
26	9	304	37	6	½	½ other carb, 5 med. fat meat
17	6	180	24	3	0	3½ med. fat meat

1 Carbohydrate Choice = 1 starch or 1 fruit or 1 milk exchange
* Grams of fiber subtracted from total carbohydrate

MENU ITEM	SERVING SIZE	CALORIES	CALORIES FROM FAT
HAMBURGERS			
Charbroiled Beef Burger	1 (8.6 oz)	548	243
Charbroiled Cheese Burger	1 (9.4 oz)	605	276
SIDE ORDERS			
Baked Potato	1 (8.8 oz)	272	trace
Bun	1 (1.8 oz)	116	9
Coleslaw	1 order (5.3 oz)	210	126
Corn	1 order (3.5 oz)	95	19
French Fries	1 order (5.3 oz)	446	198
French Roll	1 (1 oz)	91	4
Mashed Potatoes	1 order (7.3 oz)	180	41
Mixed Vegetables	1 order (3.5 oz)	42	14
Rice	1 order (3.5 oz)	149	4
SOUPS			
Chicken Soup	8.1 oz	97	18
SALADS			
Caesar Salad	1 (4.1 oz)	345	171
Chicken Salad Amandine	1 (17 oz)	868	540
Garden Salad	1 (5.7 oz)	33	0
Grilled Chicken Breast & Caesar Salad	1 (13.7 oz)	832	477
Rotisserie Chicken Salad Entree	1 (18.4 oz)	444	189
SALAD DRESSINGS			
House Dressing	1 oz	128	99
Italian Salad Dressing, Low Calorie	1 oz	11	9
CONDIMENTS			
Barbecue Dipping Sauce	1.2 oz	54	0

 Smart Choice

TOTAL FAT (g)	SATURATED FAT (g)	SODIUM (mg)	PROTEIN (g)	CARBOHYDRATE (g)	CARBOHYDRATE CHOICES	EXCHANGES
27	11	980	31	45	3	3 starch, 3½ med. fat meat, 1 fat
31	15	1275	35	45	3	3 starch, 4 med. fat meat, 2 fat
trace	trace	19	6	62	4	4 starch
1	trace	194	3	24	1½	1½ starch
14	1	540	2	18	1	1 starch, 3 fat
2	1	19	3	16	1	1 starch
22	5	180	8	53	3½	3½ starch, 4 fat
<1	,1	178	4	18	1	1 starch
5	2	580	4	31	2	2 starch, 1 fat
2	<1	26	2	5	0	1 veg
0	<1	500	4	32	2	2 starch
2	trace	820	9	11	1	1 starch
19	2	350	2	12	1	1 starch, 4 fat
60	10	2220	40	42	3	3 starch, 5 med. fat meat, 6 fat
0	0	26	3	7	½	1 veg
53	10	214	49	41	3	3 starch, 6 med. fat mat, 4 fat
21	4	470	30	33	2	2 starch, 4 med. fat meat
11	3	386	0	6	0	2 fat
1	trace	395	0	1	0	free
0	0	454	0	13	1	1 other carb

1 Carbohydrate Choice = 1 starch or 1 fruit or 1 milk exchange
* Grams of fiber subtracted from total carbohydrate

MENU ITEM	SERVING SIZE	CALORIES	CALORIES FROM FAT
☀ BBQ Rib Sauce	1 oz	38	0
Butter	2 pats (0.5 oz)	100	99
☀ Chalet Sauce	3.5 oz	24	5
☀ Gravy	3.5 oz	38	8
☀ Honey Mustard Dipping Sauce	1.2 oz	75	9
☀ Plum Dipping Sauce	1.2 oz	66	0
Sour Cream	1 oz	49	36
☀ Sweet & Sour Dipping Sauce	1.2 oz	49	0
DESSERTS			
Apple Pie	6.3 oz	427	153
Carrot Cake	4.3 oz	533	279
Cheesecake	4.2 oz	378	252
Chocolate Cake	5 oz	488	252
Coconut Cream Pie	4.4 oz	410	243
Lemon Meringue Pie	5.3 oz	410	144
Pecan Pie	4 oz	412	216
☀ Raspberry Frozen Yogurt	5.3 oz	246	45
Sugar Pie (Quebec only)	4 oz	394	189
Vanilla Ice Cream	5.3 oz	333	126

SMART MEAL, SWISS CHALET

¼ Chicken (white meat, without skin)
Chalet Sauce (3.5 oz)
Mashed Potatoes
Gravy (3.5 oz)
Corn
Garden Salad
Italian Salad Dressing,
  Low Calorie (1 oz)

Calories: 606
Fat: 18 grams
Carb Choices: 4
Exchanges: 3 starch, ½ other carb, 1 veg, 5½ very lean meat, 1 fat

☀ Smart Choice

TOTAL FAT (g)	SATURATED FAT (g)	SODIUM (mg)	PROTEIN (g)	CARBOHYDRATE (g)	CARBOHYDRATE CHOICES	EXCHANGES
0	0	304	0	10	½	½ other carb
11	7	116	0	0	0	2 fat
1	<1	570	0	4	0	free
1	<1	26	2	6	½	½ other carb
1	trace	154	0	19	1	1 other carb
0	0	334	0	17	1	1 other carb
4	3	15	1	2	0	1 fat
0	0	66	0	13	1	1 other carb
17	3	340	4	66	4½	4½ other carb, 3 fat
31	10	236	5	61	4	4 other carb, 6 fat
28	16	241	9	24	1½	1½ other carb, 5 fat
28	8	354	4	61	4	4 other carb, 5 fat
27	22	252	2	41	3	3 other carb, 5 fat
16	8	201	3	66	4½	4½ other carb, 3 fat
24	5	422	7	53	3½	3½ other carb, 4 fat
5	1	99	6	39	2½	2½ other carb, 1 fat
21	7	193	3	52	3½	3½ other carb, 4 fat
14	9	111	6	30	2	2 other carb, 3 fat

1 Carbohydrate Choice = 1 starch or 1 fruit or 1 milk exchange
* Grams of fiber subtracted from total carbohydrate

MENU ITEM	SERVING SIZE	CALORIES	CALORIES FROM FAT

TACO BELL

TACOS

BLT Soft Taco	1 (4.25 oz)	340	210
Double Decker™ Taco	1 (5.5 oz)	340	130
Double Decker™ Taco Supreme®	1 (6.75 oz)	390	170
Kid's Soft Taco Roll-Up	1 (3.75 oz)	290	140
Soft Taco	1 (3.5 oz)	210	90
Soft Taco Supreme®	1 (4.75 oz)	260	120
Steak Soft Taco	1 (5 oz)	200	60
Taco	1 (2.75 oz)	170	90
Taco Supreme®	1 (4 oz)	220	120

BURRITOS

Bacon Cheeseburger Burrito	1 (8.25)	560	270
Bean Burrito	1 (7 oz)	380	110
Big Beef Burrito Supreme®	1 (10.25 oz)	520	210
Burrito Supreme®	1 (8.75 oz)	440	170
Chicken Club Burrito	1 (7.75 oz)	540	280
Chili Cheese Burrito	1 (5 oz)	330	120
Seven-Layer Burrito	1 (10 oz)	540	210

SPECIALTIES

Big Beef MexiMelt®	1 (4.5 oz)	300	150
Cheese Quesadilla	1 (4.25 oz)	370	180
Chicken Quesadilla	1 (5.75 oz)	420	190
Mexican Pizza	1 (7.75 oz)	570	330
Taco Salad with Salsa	1 (19 oz)	840	470
Taco Salad with Salsa (without shell)	1 (16 oz)	420	190

 Smart Choice

TOTAL FAT (g)	SATURATED FAT (g)	SODIUM (mg)	PROTEIN (g)	CARBOHYDRATE (g)	CARBOHYDRATE CHOICES	EXCHANGES
23	8	610	11	22	1½	1½ starch, 1 med. fat meat, 3½ fat
15	5	700	16	29*	2	2 starch, 2 med. fat meat, 2 fat
18	8	710	16	31*	2	2 starch, 2 med. fat meat, 1 fat
16	8	790	16	20	1	1 starch, 2 med. fat meat, 1 fat
10	5	530	12	20	1	1 starch, 1 med. fat meat, 1 fat
14	7	540	13	22	1½	1½ starch, 1 med. fat meat, 2 fat
7	3	500	14	18	1	1 starch, 2 lean meat
10	4	280	10	11	1	1 starch, 1 med. fat meat, 1 fat
13	6	290	11	13	1	1 starch, 1 med. fat meat, 1½ fat
30	12	1360	29	43	3	3 starch, 3 med. fat meat, 2½ fat
12	4	1140	13	43*	3	3 starch, 1 med. fat meat, 1 fat
23	10	1450	26	43*	3	3 starch, 3 med. fat meat, 1½ fat
18	8	1220	19	42*	3	3 starch, 2 med. fat meat, 1½ fat
31	10	1290	22	43	3	3 starch, 2 med. fat meat, 4 fat
13	6	880	14	37	2½	2½ starch, 1 med. fat meat, 1½ fat
24	9	1310	16	51*	3½	3½ starch, 1½ med. fat meat, 3 fat
16	8	860	16	21	1½	1½ starch, 2 med. fat meat, 1 fat
20	12	730	16	32	2	2 starch, 1½ med. fat meat, 2 fat
22	12	1020	24	33	2	2 starch, 3 med. fat meat, 1 fat
36	11	1050	21	35*	2	2 starch, 2½ med. fat meat, 5 fat
52	15	1670	32	49*	3½	3½ starch, 3 med. fat meat, 7 fat
21	11	1420	26	16*	1	1 starch, 2 med. fat meat, 1 fat

1 Carbohydrate Choice = 1 starch or 1 fruit or 1 milk exchange
* Grams of fiber subtracted from total carbohydrate

MENU ITEM	SERVING SIZE	CALORIES	CALORIES FROM FAT
Tostada	1 (6.25 oz)	300	130
BORDER WRAPS™			
Chicken Fajita Wrap™	1 (7.75 oz)	460	190
Chicken Fajita Wrap™ Supreme	1 (9 oz)	500	230
Steak Fajita Wrap™	1 (7.75 oz)	460	190
Steak Fajita Wrap™ Supreme	1 (9 oz)	510	230
Veggie Fajita Wrap™	1 (7.75 oz)	420	170
Veggie Fajita Wrap™ Supreme	1 (9 oz)	460	210
BORDER LIGHTS™			
☀ Light Chicken Burrito	1 (6.25 oz)	310	70
Light Chicken Burrito Supreme®	1 (8.75 oz)	430	120
☀ Light Chicken Soft Taco	1 (4.25 oz)	180	45
☀ Light Kid's Chicken Soft Taco	1 (3.5 oz)	180	45
SIDE ORDERS			
Big Beef Nachos Supreme	1 order (6.75 oz)	430	210
☀ Cinnamon Twists	1 order (1 oz)	140	50
Mexican Rice	1 order (4.75 oz)	190	90
Nachos	1 order (3.5 oz)	310	160
Nachos BellGrande®	1 order (10.75 oz)	740	350
☀ Pintos 'n Cheese	1 order 4.5 oz	190	80
CONDIMENTS			
☀ Cheddar Cheese	.25 oz	30	20
☀ Cheddar Cheese, Fat Free	.25 oz	10	0
☀ Green Sauce	1 oz	5	0
Guacamole	1.5 oz	70	50
☀ Hot Taco Sauce	.33 oz	0	0

☀ Smart Choice

TOTAL FAT (g)	SATURATED FAT (g)	SODIUM (mg)	PROTEIN (g)	CARBOHYDRATE (g)	CARBOHYDRATE CHOICES	EXCHANGES
14	5	700	11	20*	1½	1½ starch, 1 med. fat meat, 2 fat
21	6	1220	18	49	3	3 starch, 2 med. fat meat, 2 fat
25	8	1230	19	51	3½	3½ starch, 2 med. fat meat, 2 fat
21	6	1130	20	48	3	3 starch, 2 med. fat meat, 2 fat
25	8	1140	21	50	3	3 starch, 2 med. fat meat, 3 fat
19	5	920	11	51	3½	3 starch, 1 veg, 3 fat
23	8	930	11	53	3½	3 starch, 1 veg, 2½ fat
8	2	980	18	41	3	3 starch, 2 lean meat
13	3	1410	25	52	3½	3½ starch, 2 lean meat, 1 fat
5	2	660	13	21	1½	1½ starch, 1½ lean meat
5	2	590	13	20	1½	1½ starch, 1½ lean meat
24	7	720	12	34*	2	2 starch, 1 med. fat meat, 4 fat
6	0	190	1	19	1	1 starch, 1 fat
10	4	510	6	20	1	1 starch, 2 fat
18	4	540	2	34	2	2 starch, 3½ fat
39	10	1200	16	66*	4½	4½ starch, 1 med. fat meat, 7 fat
8	4	690	9	8*	½	½ starch, 1 med. fat meat, 1 fat
2	2	45	2	0	0	free
0	0	50	2	0	0	free
0	0	150	0	1	0	free
6	<1	280	0	4	0	1 fat
0	0	85	0	0	0	free

1 Carbohydrate Choice = 1 starch or 1 fruit or 1 milk exchange
* Grams of fiber subtracted from total carbohydrate

MENU ITEM	SERVING SIZE	CALORIES	CALORIES FROM FAT
☀ Mild Taco Sauce	.33 oz	0	0
Nacho Cheese Sauce	2 oz	120	90
☀ Pepper Jack Cheese	.25 oz	30	25
☀ Picante Sauce	.33 oz	0	0
☀ Pico de Gallo	.75 oz	5	0
☀ Red Sauce	1 oz	10	0
☀ Salsa	3 oz	25	0
Sour Cream	.75 oz	40	35
☀ Sour Cream, Non-Fat	.75 oz	20	0
SOFT DRINKS			
Diet Pepsi®	16 oz	0	0
Dr. Pepper®	16 oz	208	0
Mountain Dew®	16 oz	227	0
Pepsi Cola®	16 oz	200	0
Slice®	16 oz	200	0
OTHER BEVERAGES			
Coffee, black	12 oz	5	0
Lipton® Brisk Iced Tea (sweetened)	16 oz	140	0
Lipton® Brisk Iced Tea (unsweetened)	16 oz	0	0
☀ Milk, 2%	8 oz	110	40
☀ Orange Juice	6 oz	80	0
BREAKFAST			
Breakfast Cheese Quesadilla	1 (5.5 oz)	390	200
Breakfast Quesadilla with Bacon	1 (6 oz)	460	250
Breakfast Quesadilla with Sausage	1 (6 oz)	440	240
Country Breakfast Burrito	1 (4 oz)	270	130
Double Bacon & Egg Burrito	1 (6.25 oz)	480	250

☀ Smart Choice

TOTAL FAT (g)	SATURATED FAT (g)	SODIUM (mg)	PROTEIN (g)	CARBOHYDRATE (g)	CARBOHYDRATE CHOICES	EXCHANGES
0	0	75	0	0	0	free
10	3	470	2	5	0	2 fat
2	1	105	1	0	0	free
0	0	110	0	1	0	free
0	0	65	0	1	0	free
0	0	260	0	2	0	free
0	0	490	1	5	0	free
4	3	10	1	1	0	1 fat
0	0	55	1	2	0	free
0	0	47	0	0	0	free
0	0	9	0	52	3½	3½ other carb
0	0	93	0	61	4	4 other carb
0	0	47	0	51	3½	3½ other carb
0	0	73	0	53	3½	3½ other carb
0	0	5	0	1	0	free
0	0	60	0	40	2½	2½ other carb
0	0	60	0	0	0	free
5	3	115	8	11	1	1 2% milk
0	0	0	1	18	1	1 fruit
22	10	940	15	32	2	2 starch, 2 med. fat meat, 2 fat
28	12	1130	20	33	2	2 starch, 2½ med. fat meat, 3 fat
26	12	1010	17	33	2	2 starch, 2 med. fat meat, 3 fat
14	5	690	8	26	2	2 starch, 1 med. fat meat, 1 fat
27	9	1240	18	39	2½	2½ starch, 2 med. fat meat, 3 fat

1 Carbohydrate Choice = 1 starch or 1 fruit or 1 milk exchange
* Grams of fiber subtracted from total carbohydrate

MENU ITEM	SERVING SIZE	CALORIES	CALORIES FROM FAT
Fiesta Breakfast Burrito	1 (3.5 oz)	280	140
Grande Breakfast Burrito	1 (6.25 oz)	420	200

SMART MEAL, TACO BELL

Light Chicken Burrito
Salsa (3 oz)
Pintos 'n Cheese
Orange Juice (6 oz)

Calories:	605
Fat:	16 grams
Carb Choices:	5
Exchanges:	3½ starch, 1 fruit, 3 med. fat meat

TACO JOHN'S
TACOS

MENU ITEM	SERVING SIZE	CALORIES	CALORIES FROM FAT
Crispy Taco	1 (3.25 oz)	182	98
☼ Softshell Taco	1 (4.25 oz)	230	93
Taco Bravo®	1 (6.25 oz)	346	130
☼ Taco Burger	1 (5 oz)	280	108

BURRITOS

MENU ITEM	SERVING SIZE	CALORIES	CALORIES FROM FAT
Bean Burrito	1 (6.5 oz)	387	100
Beef Burrito	1 (6.5 oz)	449	180
Combination Burrito	1 (6.5 oz)	418	140
Meat & Potato Burrito	1 (7.5 oz)	503	221
Ranch Burrito	1 (7 oz)	447	204
Super Burrito	1 (8.5 oz)	465	175

FAJITAS

MENU ITEM	SERVING SIZE	CALORIES	CALORIES FROM FAT
☼ Chicken Fajita Burrito	1 (6.25 oz)	370	106
Chicken Fajita Salad (with bowl, no dressing)	1 (12.25 oz)	557	299
☼ Chicken Fajita Softshell	1 (4.5 oz)	200	62

☼ Smart Choice

TOTAL FAT (g)	SATURATED FAT (g)	SODIUM (mg)	PROTEIN (g)	CARBOHYDRATE (g)	CARBOHYDRATE CHOICES	EXCHANGES
16	6	590	9	25	1½	1½ starch, 1 med. fat meat, 2 fat
22	7	1050	13	43	3	3 starch, 1 med. fat meat, 3 fat
11	4	272	9	12	1	1 starch, 1 med. fat meat, 1 fat
10	4	520	14	23	1½	1½ starch, 1½ med. fat meat
14	5	677	15	39	2½	2½ starch, 1½ med. fat meat, 1 fat
12	5	576	15	28	2	2 starch, 2 med. fat meat
11	5	866	15	57	3.5	3½ starch, 1 med. fat meat, 1 fat
20	9	863	23	44	3	3 starch, 2½ med. fat meat, 1 fat
16	7	865	19	50	3	3 starch, 2 med. fat meat, 1 fat
24	7	1341	17	53	3½	3½ starch, 1½ med. fat meat, 3 fat
23	8	804	18	44	3	3 starch, 2 med. fat meat, 2 fat
19	9	922	20	53	3½	3½ starch, 2 med. fat meat, 1 fat
12	5	1536	21	45	3	3 starch, 2 med. fat meat
33	9	1541	22	44	3	3 starch, 2 med. fat meat, 4 fat
7	3	903	13	21	1½	1½ starch, 1½ med. fat meat

1 Carbohydrate Choice = 1 starch or 1 fruit or 1 milk exchange
* Grams of fiber subtracted from total carbohydrate

MENU ITEM	SERVING SIZE	CALORIES	CALORIES FROM FAT
PLATTERS			
Chimichanga Platter	1 (18 oz)	979	338
Double Enchilada Platter	1 (18.25 oz)	967	381
Sampler Platter	1 (25.5 oz)	1406	545
Smothered Burrito Platter	1 (19.5 oz)	1031	360
KID'S MEALS			
Kid's Meal with Crispy Taco	1 (8 oz)	579	305
Kid's Meal with Softshell Taco	1 (8.5 oz)	617	294
SPECIALTIES			
Mexi Rolls® with Nacho Cheese	1 order (9.75 oz)	863	435
Potato Oles Bravo®	1 order (8.88 oz)	579	339
Sierra Chicken Fillet Sandwich	1 (8.5 oz)	534	260
Super Nachos	1 order (13 oz)	919	508
Taco Salad (with bowl, no dressing)	1 (12.4 oz)	584	340
SIDE ORDERS			
Chili	9.25 oz	350	190
Mexican® Ice	1 order (8 oz)	367	159
Nachos	1 order (3.5 oz)	333	185
Potato Oles®, regular	1 order (4.63 oz)	363	203
Potato Oles®, large	1 order (6.12 oz)	484	271
Potato Oles® with Nacho Cheese	1 order (6.63 oz)	483	293
Refried Beans	1 order (9.5 oz)	357	77
CONDIMENTS			
Nacho Cheese	1 pkt (2 oz)	125	90
Sour Cream	1 pkt (1 oz)	60	45

TOTAL FAT (g)	SATURATED FAT (g)	SODIUM (mg)	PROTEIN (g)	CARBOHYDRATE (g)	CARBOHYDRATE CHOICES	EXCHANGES
38	15	2341	33	127	8½	8½ starch, 2 med. fat meat, 4 fat
42	16	1921	42	106	7	7 starch, 4 med. fat meat, 2 fat
61	24	2875	61	156	10	10 starch, 6 med. fat meat, 4 fat
40	16	2351	39	132	8½	8½ starch, 3 med. fat meat, 3 fat
34	10	789	13	54	3½	3½ starch, 1 med. fat meat, 5 fat
33	10	1037	15	64	4	4 starch, 1 med. fat meat, 5 fat
48	11	1392	30	72	5	5 starch, 3 med. fat meat, 6 fat
38	7	1550	11	47	3	3 starch, 1 med. fat meat, 6 fat
29	8	1406	30	40	2½	2½ starch, 3½ med. fat meat, 2 fat
56	13	1484	26	72	5	5 starch, 2 med. fat meat, 9 fat
38	11	766	20	43	3	3 starch, 2 med. fat meat, 5 fat
21	10	865	20	19	1	1 starch, 2½ med. fat meat, 2 fat
18	5	1293	8	40	2½	2½ starch, 3 fat
21	2	611	7	27	2	2 starch, 4 fat
23	5	964	3	38	2½	2½ starch, 4 fat
30	7	1285	4	50	3	3 starch, 6 fat
33	5	1564	8	38	2½	2½ starch, 1 med. fat meat, 5 fat
9	2	1032	18	53	3½	3½ starch, 1½ med. fat meat
10	0	600	5	0	0	1 high fat meat
5	0	15	1	1	0	1 fat

1 Carbohydrate Choice = 1 starch or 1 fruit or 1 milk exchange
* Grams of fiber subtracted from total carbohydrate

MENU ITEM	SERVING SIZE	CALORIES	CALORIES FROM FAT
DESSERTS			
☀ Apple Flauta	1 (2 oz)	84	10
☀ Cherry Flauta	1 (2 oz)	143	32
Churro	1 (1.5 oz)	147	70
☀ Cream Cheese Flauta	1 (2 oz)	181	71
Choco Taco	1 (3.5 oz)	320	153
☀ Italian Ice	1 (4 oz)	80	0

SMART MEAL, TACO JOHN'S

2 Softshell Tacos	**Calories:**	544
Apple Flauta	**Fat:**	21 grams
	Carb Choices:	4
	Exchanges:	3 starch,
		1 other carb,
		3 med. fat meat

"TCBY"

MENU ITEM	SERVING SIZE	CALORIES	CALORIES FROM FAT
☀ Soft-Serve Frozen Yogurt, No Sugar Added & Nonfat	½ cup	80	0
☀ Soft-Serve Frozen Yogurt, Nonfat	½ cup	110	0
☀ Soft-Serve Frozen Yogurt, Regular	½ cup	130	30
☀ Sorbet	½ cup	100	0

☀ Smart Choice

TOTAL FAT (g)	SATURATED FAT (g)	SODIUM (mg)	PROTEIN (g)	CARBOHYDRATE (g)	CARBOHYDRATE CHOICES	EXCHANGES
1	<1	72	1	19	1	1 other carb
4	<1	110	2	27	2	2 other carb
8	2	160	2	17	1	1 other carb, 1½ fat
8	3	135	2	27	2	2 other carb, 1 fat
17	11	100	3	38	2½	2½ other carb, 3 fat
0	0	5	0	19	1	1 other carb

SMART MEAL, TACO JOHN'S

Chicken Fajita Softshell
Refried Beans

Calories: 557
Fat: 16 grams
Carb Choices: 5
Exchanges: 5 starch, 3 med. fat meat

TOTAL FAT (g)	SATURATED FAT (g)	SODIUM (mg)	PROTEIN (g)	CARBOHYDRATE (g)	CARBOHYDRATE CHOICES	EXCHANGES
0	0	35	4	20	1	1 other carb
0	0	60	4	23	1½	1½ other carb
3	2	60	4	23	1½	1½ other carb, ½ fat
0	0	30	0	24	1½	1½ other carb

1 Carbohydrate Choice = 1 starch or 1 fruit or 1 milk exchange
* Grams of fiber subtracted from total carbohydrate

MENU ITEM	SERVING SIZE	CALORIES	CALORIES FROM FAT
WENDY'S			
SANDWICHES			
Big Bacon Classic Sandwich	1 (10 oz)	570	260
☀ Breaded Chicken Sandwich	1 (7.3 oz)	440	160
Cheeseburger, Kid's Meal	1 (4.3 oz)	320	120
Chicken Club Sandwich	1 (7.6 oz)	470	180
☀ Grilled Chicken Sandwich	1 (6.6 oz)	310	70
☀ Hamburger, Kid's Meal	1 (4 oz)	270	90
Jr. Bacon Cheeseburger	1 (6 oz)	380	170
Jr. Cheeseburger	1 (4.5 oz)	320	120
Jr. Cheeseburger Deluxe	1 (6.3 oz)	360	150
☀ Jr. Hamburger	1 (4 oz)	270	90
☀ Single Hamburger, plain	1 (4.7 oz)	360	140
Single Hamburger, with everything	1 (7.7 oz)	420	180
☀ Spicy Chicken Sandwich	1 (7.5 oz)	410	130
SANDWICH INGREDIENTS			
American Cheese	1 slice (0.6 oz)	70	50
American Cheese, Jr.	1 slice (0.4 oz)	45	30
Bacon	1 piece (14 oz)	20	10
Breaded Chicken Fillet	1 (3.5 oz)	230	100
☀ Grilled Chicken Fillet	1 (3 oz)	110	25
☀ Hamburger Patty	1 (¼ lb)	200	120
☀ Hamburger Patty	1 (2 oz)	100	`60
☀ Honey Mustard, Reduced Calorie	1 tsp	25	15
☀ Kaiser Bun	1 (2.4 oz)	190	30
☀ Ketchup	1 tsp	10	0

☀ Smart Choice

TOTAL FAT (g)	SATURATED FAT (g)	SODIUM (mg)	PROTEIN (g)	CARBOHYDRATE (g)	CARBOHYDRATE CHOICES	EXCHANGES
29	12	1320	34	46	3	3 starch, 4 med. fat meat, 1 fat
18	3	840	28	44	3	3 starch, 3 med. fat meat
13	6	770	17	33	2	2 starch, 1½ med. fat meat, 1 fat
20	4	980	31	44	3	3 starch, 3 med. fat meat, 1 fat
8	2	780	27	35	2	2 starch, 3 lean meat
10	3	560	15	33	2	2 starch, 1½ med. fat meat
19	7	790	21	34	2	2 starch, 2½ med. fat meat, 1 fat
13	6	770	17	34	2	2 starch, 2 med. fat meat, ½ fat
16	6	840	18	36	2½	2½ starch, 2 med. fat meat, 1 fat
10	3	560	15	34	2	2 starch, 1 med. fat meat
16	6	460	25	31	2	2 starch, 3 med. fat meat
20	7	810	26	37	2	2 starch, 1 veg, 3 med. fat meat, 1 fat
15	3	1280	28	43	3	3 starch, 3 med. fat meat
5	3	320	3	1	0	½ med. fat meat, 1 fat
4	3	220	2	0	0	1 fat
1	0	65	1	0	0	free
12	2	490	22	10	½	½ starch, 3 med. fat meat
3	1	450	22	0	0	3 very lean meat
13	6	170	20	0	0	3 med. fat meat
7	3	85	10	0	0	1 med. fat meat
2	0	35	0	2	0	free
3	<1	340	6	36	2½	2½ starch
0	0	80	0	2	0	free

1 Carbohydrate Choice = 1 starch or 1 fruit or 1 milk exchange
* Grams of fiber subtracted from total carbohydrate

MENU ITEM	SERVING SIZE	CALORIES	CALORIES FROM FAT
☀ Lettuce	1 leaf	0	0
Mayonnaise	1½ tsp	30	30
☀ Mustard	½ tsp	0	0
☀ Onion	4 rings (0.5 oz)	0	0
☀ Pickles	4 slices (0.4 oz)	0	0
☀ Sandwich Bun	1 (2 oz)	160	25
☀ Spicy Chicken Fillet	1 (3.7 oz)	210	80
☀ Tomatoes	1 slice (1 oz)	5	0

STUFFED PITAS™

Chicken Caesar Pita	1 (8.5 oz)	490	160
Classic Greek Pita	1 (8.25 oz)	430	170
☀ Garden Ranch Chicken Pita	1 (10 oz)	480	160
Garden Veggie Pita	1 (9 oz)	390	140

CHICKEN NUGGETS

Chicken Nuggets, 5-piece	1 order (2.6 oz)	210	130

BAKED POTATOES

Bacon & Cheese Potato	1 (13.4 oz)	540	160
Broccoli & Cheese Potato	1 (14.5 oz)	470	120
Cheese Potato	1 (13.4 oz)	570	210
Chili & Cheese Potato	1 (15.5 oz)	620	220
☀ Plain Potato	1 (10 oz)	310	0
☀ Sour Cream & Chives Potato	1 (11 oz)	380	60

SIDE ORDERS

French Fries, small	1 order (3.2 oz)	260	120
French Fries, medium	1 order (4.6 oz)	380	170
French Fries, Biggie	1 order (5.6 oz)	460	200

☀ Smart Choice

TOTAL FAT (g)	SATURATED FAT (g)	SODIUM (mg)	PROTEIN (g)	CARBOHYDRATE (g)	CARBOHYDRATE CHOICES	EXCHANGES
0	0	0	0	0	0	free
3	0	60	0	1	0	½ fat
0	0	55	0	0	0	free
0	0	0	0	1	0	free
0	0	140	0	0	0	free
3	<1	280	5	29	2	2 starch
9	2	920	22	10	½	½ starch, 3 med. fat meat
0	0	0	0	1	0	free
17	5	1300	36	46	3	3 starch, 4 lean meat, 1 fat
19	7	1070	17	49	3	3 starch, 2 med. fat meat, 1 fat
17	4	1170	32	44*	3	3 starch, 4 lean meat
15	3	780	13	45*	3	3 starch, 1 med. fat meat, 2 fat
14	3	460	14	7	½	½ other carb, 2 med. fat meat, 1 fat
18	4	1430	17	71*	5	5 starch, 3 fat
14	3	470	9	71*	5	5 starch, 2 fat
23	9	640	14	71*	5	5 starch, 5 fat
24	9	780	20	74*	5	5 starch, 1½ med. fat meat, 3 fat
0	0	25	7	64*	4	4 starch
6	4	40	8	66*	4½	4½ starch, 1 fat
13	3	85	3	33	2	2 starch, 2 fat
19	4	120	5	42*	3	3 starch, 3 fat
23	5	150	6	52*	4	4 starch, 4 fat

1 Carbohydrate Choice = 1 starch or 1 fruit or 1 milk exchange
* Grams of fiber subtracted from total carbohydrate

MENU ITEM	SERVING SIZE	CALORIES	CALORIES FROM FAT
CHILI			
💡 Chili, small	8 oz	210	60
💡 Chile, large	12 oz	310	90
SALADS			
💡 Caesar Side Salad	1 (3 oz)	110	40
Deluxe Garden Salad	1 (10 oz)	110	50
💡 Grilled Chicken Caesar Salad	1 (9 oz)	260	90
💡 Grilled Chicken Salad	1 (12 oz)	200	70
💡 Side Salad	1 (5.5 oz)	60	25
Taco Salad	1 (7.4 oz)	590	270
SALAD DRESSINGS			
Blue Cheese Salad Dressing	2 Tbsp	170	170
French Salad Dressing	2 Tbsp	120	90
💡 French Salad Dressing, Fat Free	2 Tbsp	30	0
French Salad Dressing, Sweet Red	2 Tbsp	130	90
Hidden Valley® Ranch Salad Dressing	2 Tbsp	90	90
💡 Hidden Valley® Ranch Salad Dressing, Reduced Fat, Reduced Calorie	2 Tbsp	60	50
Italian Caesar	2 Tbsp	150	140
💡 Italian Salad Dressing, Reduced Fat, Reduced Calorie	2 Tbsp	40	30
Salad Oil	1 Tbsp	130	130
Thousand Island Salad Dressing	2 Tbsp	130	110
💡 Wine Vinegar Salad Dressing	1 Tbsp	0	0
GARDEN SPOT SALAD BAR			
💡 Applesauce	2 Tbsp	30	0
Bacon Bits	2 Tbsp	45	20

💡 Smart Choice

TOTAL FAT (g)	SATURATED FAT (g)	SODIUM (mg)	PROTEIN (g)	CARBOHYDRATE (g)	CARBOHYDRATE CHOICES	EXCHANGES
7	3	800	15	16*	1	1 starch, 2 med. fat meat
10	4	1190	23	25*	2	2 starch, 3 med. fat meat
5	2	660	8	8	½	1 veg, 1 med. fat meat
6	1	320	7	10	½	2 veg, 1 fat
10	3	1210	28	17	1	3 veg, 3 lean meat
8	2	690	25	10	½	2 veg, 3 lean meat
3	<1	160	4	5	0	1 veg
30	11	1230	29	43*	3	3 starch, 3 med. fat meat, 3 fat
19	3	190	1	0	0	4 fat
10	2	330	0	6	0	2 fat
0	0	150	0	8	½	½ starch
10	2	230	0	9	½	½ starch, 2 fat
10	2	240	0	1	0	2 fat
5	1	240	0	2	0	1 fat
16	3	250	1	1	0	3 fat
3	0	340	0	2	0	½ fat
14	2	0	0	0	0	3 fat
13	2	170	0	3	0	3 fat
0	0	0	0	0	0	free
0	0	0	0	7	½	½ fruit
3	1	570	6	0	0	1 med. fat meat

1 Carbohydrate Choice = 1 starch or 1 fruit or 1 milk exchange
* Grams of fiber subtracted from total carbohydrate

MENU ITEM	SERVING SIZE	CALORIES	CALORIES FROM FAT
☀ Bananas & Strawberry Glaze	¼ cup	30	0
☀ Broccoli	¼ cup	0	0
☀ Cantaloupe	1 slice	15	0
☀ Carrots	¼ cup	5	0
☀ Cauliflower	¼ cup	0	0
Cheese, shredded (imitation)	2 Tbsp	50	40
Chicken Salad	2 Tbsp	70	45
☀ Chow Mein Noodles	¼ cup	35	20
Cole Slaw	2 Tbsp	45	25
☀ Cottage Cheese	2 Tbsp	30	15
☀ Croutons	2 Tbsp	30	10
☀ Cucumbers	2 slices	0	0
Eggs, hard cooked	2 Tbsp	40	25
☀ Green Peas	2 Tbsp	15	0
☀ Green Peppers	2 pieces	0	0
☀ Honeydew Melon	1 slice	20	0
☀ Lettuce (Iceberg/Romaine)	1 cup	10	0
☀ Lettuce (Iceberg/Romaine)	3 cups	30	0
☀ Mushrooms	¼ cup	0	0
☀ Orange	2 slices	15	0
Parmesan Blend	2 Tbsp	70	35
☀ Pasta Salad	2 Tbsp	25	0
☀ Peaches	1 slice	15	0
Pepperoni	6 slices	30	25
☀ Pineapple	4 chunks	20	0
Potato Salad	2 Tbsp	80	60
Pudding, Chocolate	¼ cup	70	30

☀ Smart Choice

Total Fat (g)	Saturated Fat (g)	Sodium (mg)	Protein (g)	Carbohydrate (g)	Carbohydrate Choices	Exchanges
0	0	0	0	8	½	½ fruit
0	0	0	0	1	0	free
0	0	0	0	4	0	free
0	0	5	0	2	0	free
0	0	0	0	1	0	free
4	1	230	3	1	0	1 fat
5	1	135	4	2	0	1 med. fat meat
2	0	30	0	4	0	free
3	0	65	0	5	0	1 veg, 1 fat
2	1	125	4	1	0	½ lean meat
1	0	75	0	4	0	free
0	0	0	0	0	0	free
3	1	30	3	0	0	½ med. fat meat
0	0	25	1	3	0	free
0	0	0	0	1	0	free
0	0	5	0	5	0	free
0	0	5	0	2	0	free
0	0	15	0	4	0	1 veg
0	0	0	0	1	0	free
0	0	0	0	4	0	free
4	2	290	4	5	0	1 med. fat meat
0	0	75	1	3	0	free
0	0	0	0	4	0	free
3	1	70	1	0	0	½ fat
0	0	0	0	5	0	free
7	3	180	0	5	0	1 veg, 1 fat
3	<1	60	0	10	½	½ other carb, ½ fat

1 Carbohydrate Choice = 1 starch or 1 fruit or 1 milk exchange
* Grams of fiber subtracted from total carbohydrate

MENU ITEM	SERVING SIZE	CALORIES	CALORIES FROM FAT
Pudding, Vanilla	¼ cup	70	30
Red Onions	3 rings	0	0
Seafood Salad	¼ cup	70	40
Sesame Breadstick	1 (0.1 oz)	15	0
Strawberries	1 (1 oz)	10	0
Sunflower Seeds & Raisins	2 Tbsp	80	45
Tomato	1 wedge (1 oz)	5	0
Turkey Ham, diced	2 Tbsp	50	35
Watermelon	1 wedge (2 oz)	20	0

CONDIMENTS

Barbecue Sauce	1 pkt (1 oz)	50	0
Cheddar Cheese, shredded	2 Tbsp	70	50
Honey Mustard Sauce	1 pkt (1 oz)	130	110
Margarine, whipped	1 pkt (0.5 oz)	60	60
Saltine Crackers	2 crackers (0.2 oz)	25	5
Soft Breadstick	1 (1.5 oz)	130	30
Sour Cream	1 pkt (1 oz)	60	50
Spicy Buffalo Wing Sauce	1 pkt (1 oz)	25	10
Sweet & Sour Sauce	1 pkt (1 oz)	50	0

DESSERTS

Chocolate Chip Cookie	1 (2 oz)	270	100
Frosty™ Dairy Dessert, small	1 (12 oz)	340	90
Frosty™ Dairy Dessert, medium	1 (16 oz)	460	120
Frosty™ Dairy Dessert, large	1 (20 oz)	570	150

SOFT DRINKS

Cola Soft Drink, small	8 oz	90	0
Diet Cola Soft Drink, small	8 oz	0	0

 Smart Choice

TOTAL FAT (g)	SATURATED FAT (g)	SODIUM (mg)	PROTEIN (g)	CARBOHYDRATE (g)	CARBOHYDRATE CHOICES	EXCHANGES
3	<1	60	0	10	½	½ other carb, ½ fat
0	0	0	0	1	0	free
4	<1	300	3	5	0	½ med. fat meat
0	0	20	0	2	0	free
0	0	0	0	2	0	free
5	<1	0	0	5	0	1 fat
0	0	0	0	1	0	free
4	1	280	3	0	0	1 fat
0	0	0	0	4	0	free
0	0	100	1	11	½	½ other carb
6	3	110	4	1	0	1 med. fat meat
12	2	220	0	6	½	½ other carb, 2 fat
7	1	110	0	0	0	1 fat
1	0	80	0	4	0	free
3	<1	250	4	24	1½	1½ starch
6	4	15	1	1	0	1 fat
1	0	210	0	4	0	free
0	0	120	0	12	0	1 other carb
11	8	150	4	38	2½	2½ other carb, 2 fat
10	5	200	9	57	4	4 other carb, 2 fat
13	7	260	12	76	5	5 other carb, 3 fat
17	9	330	15	90*	6	6 other carb, 4 fat
0	0	10	0	24	1½	1½ other carb
0	0	20	0	0	0	free

1 Carbohydrate Choice = 1 starch or 1 fruit or 1 milk exchange
* Grams of fiber subtracted from total carbohydrate

MENU ITEM	SERVING SIZE	CALORIES	CALORIES FROM FAT
Lemon-Lime Soft Drink, small	8 oz	90	0
OTHER BEVERAGES			
Coffee, black	6 oz	0	0
Decaffeinated Coffee, black	6 oz	0	0
Hot Chocolate	6 oz	80	25
Lemonade, small	8 oz	90	0
Milk, 2%	8 oz	110	40
Tea, Hot	6 oz	0	0
Tea, Iced	6 oz	0	0

SMART MEAL, WENDY'S

Single Hamburger with lettuce, tomato, and onions
Side Salad
French Salad Dressing, Fat Free (2 Tbsp)
Lemonade, small

Calories: 545
Fat: 19 grams
Carb Choices: 4½ carb
Exchanges: 2½ starch,
1½ other carb,
3 med. fat meat

 Smart Choice

TOTAL FAT (g)	SATURATED FAT (g)	SODIUM (mg)	PROTEIN (g)	CARBOHYDRATE (g)	CARBOHYDRATE CHOICES	EXCHANGES
0	0	25	0	24	1½	1½ other carb
0	0	0	0	1	0	free
0	0	0	0	1	0	free
3	0	135	1	15	1	1 other carb
0	0	5	0	24	1½	1½ other carb
4	3	115	8	11	1	1 2% milk
0	0	0	0	0	0	free
0	0	0	0	0	0	free

SMART MEAL, WENDY'S

Chili, large	**Calories:** 550
Caesar Side Salad	**Fat:** 18 grams
Wine Vinegar Salad Dressing	**Carb Choices:** 4
Soft Breadstick	**Exchanges:** 3½ starch, 1 veg,
Diet Soft Drink	4 med. fat meat

1 Carbohydrate Choice = 1 starch *or* 1 fruit *or* 1 milk exchange
* Grams of fiber subtracted from total carbohydrate

MENU ITEM	SERVING SIZE	CALORIES	CALORIES FROM FAT

WHATABURGER

SANDWICHES

Grilled Chicken Sandwich	1	442	128
Grilled Chicken Sandwich (without salad dressing)	1	385	77
Justaburger®	1	276	102
Whataburger®	1	598	234
Whataburger® Double Meat	1	823	378
Whataburger JR.®	1	300	104
Whatacatch® Sandwich	1	467	225
Whatachick'n® Sandwich	1	501	207

CHICKEN STRIPS

Chicken Strips	2 pieces	120	49

FAJITAS

Beef Fajita	1	326	107
Chicken Fajita	1	272	60

TAQUITOS

Bacon Taquito	1	335	145
Potato Taquito	1	446	196
Sausage Taquito	1	443	233

SIDE ORDERS

Baked Potato, plain	1	310	0
Baked Potato with broccoli & cheese	1	453	90
Baked Potato with cheese	1	510	144
French Fries, junior	1 order	221	109
French Fries, regular	1 order	332	218

 Smart Choice

TOTAL FAT (g)	SATURATED FAT (g)	SODIUM (mg)	PROTEIN (g)	CARBOHYDRATE (g)	CARBOHYDRATE CHOICES	EXCHANGES
14	NA	1103	34	48	3	3 starch, 4 lean meat
9	NA	989	34	46	3	3 starch, 4 very lean meat
11	NA	578	13	30	2	2 starch, 1 med. fat meat, 1 fat
26	NA	1096	30	61	4	4 starch, 3 med. fat meat, 2 fat
42	NA	1298	49	62	4	4 starch, 6 med. fat meat, 2 fat
12	NA	583	14	35	2	2 starch, 1½ med. fat meat, 1 fat
25	NA	636	18	43	3	3 starch, 2 med. fat meat, 2 fat
23	NA	1122	27	51	3½	3½ starch, 3 med. fat meat, 1 fat
5	NA	420	7	10	½	½ starch, 1 med. fat meat
12	NA	670	22	34	2	2 starch, 2 med. fat meat
7	NA	691	18	35	2	2 starch, 2 lean meat
16	NA	761	15	32	2	2 starch, 1 med. fat meat, 2 fat
22	NA	883	14	48	3	3 starch, 1 med. fat meat, 3 fat
26	NA	790	20	32	2	2 starch, 2 med. fat meat, 3 fat
0	NA	23	6	72	4½	4½ starch
10	NA	636	13	79	5	5 starch, 2 fat
16	NA	863	15	80	5	5 starch, 3 fat
12	NA	139	4	25	1½	1½ starch, 2 fat
18	NA	208	5	37	2½	2½ starch, 3 fat

1 Carbohydrate Choice = 1 starch or 1 fruit or 1 milk exchange
* Grams of fiber subtracted from total carbohydrate

MENU ITEM	SERVING SIZE	CALORIES	CALORIES FROM FAT
French Fries, large	1 order	442	208
Onion Rings, regular	1 order	329	172
Onion Rings, large	1 order	493	258
☀ Texas Toast	1 slice	147	41
SALADS			
☀ Garden Salad	1	56	5
☀ Grilled Chicken Salad	1	150	11
SALAD DRESSINGS			
French Salad Dressing	1 pkt	260	189
Ranch Salad Dressing	1 pkt	320	297
Thousand Island Salad Dressing	1 pkt	160	108
☀ Vinaigrette Salad Dressing, Lite	1 pkt	37	16
CONDIMENTS			
Bacon	2 pieces	76	60
Butter	1 pkt	36	37
Cheese Slice, small	1	46	35
Cheese Slice, large	1	89	67
Chicken Gravy	3 oz	75	41
☀ Club Crackers	2 pkts	62	24
☀ Croutons	1 pkt	29	8
☀ Grape Jelly	1 pkt	45	0
☀ Honey	1 pkt	25	0
☀ Jalapeno Pepper	1	3	0
☀ Ketchup	1 pkt	30	0
Margarine	1 pkt	25	27
☀ Pancake Syrup	1 pkt	180	0
☀ Picante Sauce	1 pkt	5	0

☀ Smart Choice

TOTAL FAT (g)	SATURATED FAT (g)	SODIUM (mg)	PROTEIN (g)	CARBOHYDRATE (g)	CARBOHYDRATE CHOICES	EXCHANGES
24	NA	277	7	49	3	3 starch, 5 fat
19	NA	596	5	34	2	2 starch, 4 fat
29	NA	893	8	51	3½	3½ starch, 5 fat
5	NA	250	4	22	1½	1½ starch, 1 fat
1	NA	32	3	11	½	2 veg
1	NA	434	23	14	1	1 starch, 2 very lean meat
21	NA	560	0	18	1	1 other carb, 4 fat
33	NA	750	0	4	0	7 fat
12	NA	470	0	12	1	1 other carb, 2 fat
2	NA	896	0	6	½	½ other carb
6	NA	212	4	0	0	1 fat
4	NA	42	0	0	0	1 fat
4	NA	176	3	4	0	½ high fat meat
7	NA	338	5	0	0	1 high fat meat
5	NA	375	0	8	½	½ starch, 1 fat
2	NA	144	2	8	½	½ starch
1	NA	88	1	5	0	free
0	0	15	0	10	½	½ other carb
0	0	0	0	7	½	½ other carb
0	NA	190	0	1	0	free
0	NA	344	0	7	½	free
3	NA	40	0	0	0	1 fat
0	0	50	0	42	3	3 other carb
0	0	130	0	1	0	free

1 Carbohydrate Choice = 1 starch or 1 fruit or 1 milk exchange
* Grams of fiber subtracted from total carbohydrate

MENU ITEM	SERVING SIZE	CALORIES	CALORIES FROM FAT
Strawberry Jam	1 pkt	40	0

DESSERTS

Apple Turnover	1	215	97
Chocolate Chunk Cookie	1	247	144
Macadamia Nut Cookie	1	269	144
Oatmeal Raisin Cookie	1	222	63
Peanut Butter Cookie	1	257	121

SHAKES

Chocolate Shake	12 oz	364	84
Strawberry Shake	12 oz	352	80
Vanilla Shake	12 oz	325	86

SOFT DRINKS

Cherry Coke®	24 oz	227	0
Coca-Cola Classic®	24 oz	211	0
Diet Coke®	24 oz	2	0
Dr. Pepper®	24 oz	207	5
Root Beer	24 oz	237	0
Sprite®	24 oz	211	0

OTHER BEVERAGES

Iced Tea	24 oz	5	0
Milk, 2%	8 oz	113	39
Orange Juice	6 oz	77	0

BREAKFAST

Biscuit, plain	1	280	121
Biscuit with Bacon	1	359	182
Biscuit with Egg and Cheese	1	434	237

 Smart Choice

TOTAL FAT (g)	SATURATED FAT (g)	SODIUM (mg)	PROTEIN (g)	CARBOHYDRATE (g)	CARBOHYDRATE CHOICES	EXCHANGES
0	0	15	0	9	½	½ other carb
11	NA	241	2	27	2	2 other carb, 2 fat
16	NA	75	4	28	2	2 other carb, 3 fat
16	NA	80	3	31	2	2 other carb, 3 fat
7	NA	70	4	37	2½	2½ other carb, 1 fat
13	NA	36	5	30	2	2 other carb, 2 fat
9	NA	172	9	61	4	4 other carb, 2 fat
9	NA	168	9	60	4	4 other carb, 2 fat
10	NA	172	9	51	3½	3½ other carb, 2 fat
0	NA	11	0	60	4	4 other carb
0	NA	19	0	56	4	4 other carb
0	NA	26	0	1	0	free
1	NA	51	0	52	3½	3½ other carb
0	NA	25	0	63	4	4 other carb
0	NA	45	0	48	3	3 other carb
0	NA	15	0	2	0	free
4	NA	113	8	11	1	1 2% milk
0	NA	2	1	18	1	1 fruit
13	NA	509	5	37	2½	2½ starch, 2 fat
20	NA	730	10	37	2½	2½ starch, 4 fat
26	NA	797	14	38	2½	2½ starch, 1 med. fat meat, 4 fat

1 Carbohydrate Choice = 1 starch *or* 1 fruit *or* 1 milk exchange
* Grams of fiber subtracted from total carbohydrate

MENU ITEM	SERVING SIZE	CALORIES	CALORIES FROM FAT
Biscuit with Egg, Cheese and Bacon	1	511	296
Biscuit with Egg, Cheese and Sausage	1	601	374
Biscuit with Gravy	1	479	247
Biscuit with Sausage	1	446	258
☀ Blueberry Muffin	1	239	71
Breakfast On a Bun™ Sandwich	1	455	253
Breakfast On a Bun™ with Bacon Sandwich	1	365	175
Breakfast Platter with Bacon Biscuit	1	695	396
Breakfast Platter with Sausage Biscuit	1	785	474
Egg Omelette Sandwich	1	288	115
Hash Brown	1 order	150	81
☀ Pancakes (3)	1 order	259	52
Pancakes (3) with sausage	1 order	426	190
☀ Scrambled Eggs (2)	1 order	189	135

SMART MEAL, WHATABURGER

Beef Fajita	**Calories:**	424
Garden Salad	**Fat:**	15 grams
Vinaigrette Salad Dressing, Lite (1 pkt)	**Carb Choices:**	3½
Iced Tea (unsweetened)	**Exchanges:**	2 starch, ½ other carb, 2 veg, 2 med. fat meat

Pancakes (3)	**Calories:**	516
Pancake Syrup (1 pkt)	**Fat:**	6 grams
Orange Juice (6 oz)	**Carb Choices:**	6½
	Exchanges:	2½ starch, 1 fruit, 3 other carb, 1 fat

☀ Smart Choice

TOTAL FAT (g)	SATURATED FAT (g)	SODIUM (mg)	PROTEIN (g)	CARBOHYDRATE (g)	CARBOHYDRATE CHOICES	EXCHANGES
33	NA	1010	18	38	2½	2½ starch, 2 med. fat meat, 4 fat
42	NA	1081	21	38	2½	2½ starch, 2 med. fat meat, 6 fat
27	NA	1253	9	48	3	3 starch, 5½ fat
29	NA	794	12	37	2½	2½ starch, 1 med fat meat, 4 fat
8	NA	538	6	36	2½	2½ starch, 1 fat
28	NA	886	20	30	2	2 starch, 2½ med. fat meat, 3 fat
19	NA	815	18	29	2	2 starch, 2 med. fat meat, 1½ fat
44	NA	1162	22	54	3½	3½ starch, 2 med. fat meat, 6 fat
53	NA	1234	25	54	3½	3½ starch, 2½ med. fat meat, 8 fat
13	NA	602	13	29	2	2 starch, 1½ med. fat meat, 1 fat
9	NA	228	1	16	1	1 starch, 2 fat
6	NA	842	11	40	2½	2½ starch, 1 fat
21	NA	1127	18	40	2½	2½ starch, 2 med. fat meat, 2 fat
15	NA	211	11	2	0	2 med. fat meat

SMART MEAL, WHATABURGER

Grilled Chicken Salad
Vinaigrette Salad Dressing, Lite (1 pkt)
Oatmeal Raisin Cookie
Milk, 2% (8 oz)

Calories: 522
Fat: 14 grams
Carb Choices: 4½
Exchanges: 1 starch,
1 2% milk,
3 other carb,
2 very lean meat,
1 fat

1 Carbohydrate Choice = 1 starch or 1 fruit or 1 milk exchange
* Grams of fiber subtracted from total carbohydrate

MENU ITEM	SERVING SIZE	CALORIES	CALORIES FROM FAT
WHITE CASTLE			
SANDWICHES			
Bacon Cheeseburger	1	200	115
Cheeseburger	1	160	85
Chicken Sandwich	1	190	70
Double Cheeseburger	1	285	165
Double Hamburger	1	235	125
Fish Sandwich	1	160	60
Hamburger	1	135	65
SIDE ORDERS			
Chicken Rings	6 rings	310	190
French Fries, small	1 order	115	50
Onion Rings	8 rings	540	234
SHAKES			
Chocolate Shake	20 oz	310	90
SOFT DRINKS			
Coca-Cola Classic®	20 oz	170	0
Diet Coke®	20 oz	1	0
OTHER BEVERAGES			
Coffee, black	1 small	6	0
Iced Tea	14 oz	45	0

SMART MEAL, WHITE CASTLE

Hamburgers (2)
French Fries, small
(Add fresh vegetables or fruit)

Calories: 385
Fat: 20 grams
Carb Choices: 2½
Exchanges: 3 starch, 2 med. fat meat, 1 fat

Smart Choice

TOTAL FAT (g)	SATURATED FAT (g)	SODIUM (mg)	PROTEIN (g)	CARBOHYDRATE (g)	CARBOHYDRATE CHOICES	EXCHANGES
13	6	400	10	12	1	1 starch, 1 med. fat meat, 1½ fat
9	4	250	7	11	1	1 starch, 1 med. fat meat, 1 fat
8	2	360	8	21	1½	1½ starch, 1 med. fat meat
18	8	430	14	11*	1	1 starch, 1½ med. fat meat, 2 fat
14	6	200	11	16	1	1 starch, 1½ med. fat meat, 1 fat
6	1	220	8	18	1	1 starch, 1 med. fat meat
7	3	135	6	11	1	1 starch, 1 med. fat meat
21	4	620	16	14	1	1 starch, 2 med. fat meat, 2 fat
6	1	15	NA	15	1	1 starch, 1 fat
26	NA	1300	8	69	4½	4½ starch, 4 fat
10	1	200	11	46	3	3 other carb, 2 fat
0	0	15	0	46	3	3 other carb
0	0	20	0	0	0	free
0	0	5	0	1	0	free
0	0	15	0	12	1	1 other carb

1 Carbohydrate Choice = 1 starch or 1 fruit or 1 milk exchange
* Grams of fiber subtracted from total carbohydrate

Books of Related Interest from
IDC Publishing

Convenience Food Facts
A Quick Guide for Choosing Healthy Brand-Name Foods in Every Aisle of the Supermarket
Fourth Edition

Arlene Monk, RD, LD, CDE, and Nancy Cooper, RD, LD, CDE

Completely revised and expanded, Convenience Food Facts has everything you need to plan quick, healthy meals using prepared foods. This edition highlights low-fat choices among more than 4,500 popular brand-name products. Also includes carbohydrate choices and exchange values. Ideal for anyone using a meal-planning method to lose weight or to manage a health problem such as diabetes.

$12.95; ISBN 1-885115-36-9

Exchanges for All Occasions
Your Guide to Choosing Healthy Foods Anytime Anywhere
Fourth Edition

Marion J. Franz, MS, RD, LD, CDE

Exchanges for All Occasions is still the best resource there is for applying good nutrition to everyday life. Updated to reflect the new exchange lists and carbohydrate counting, this best-selling book is essential for anyone following a meal plan for weight control, diabetes, or another health condition. Includes nutrition information on over 2,500 foods, including ethnic foods, fast foods, and more.

$13.95; ISBN 1-885115-35-0

These books are available at your local bookstore.

Visit our website at www.idcpublishing.com